SACRED HEALING STORIES

SACRED HEALING STORIES

Glimpses Into the Biblical Psyche

Jack Graham

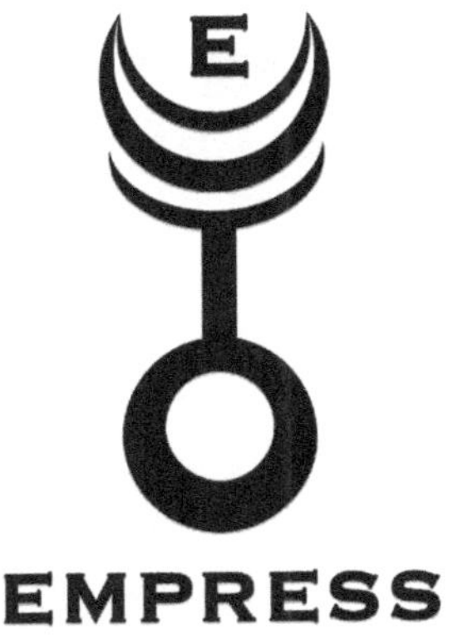

EMPRESS
PUBLICATIONS
WWW.EMPRESSPUBLICATIONS.COM

Dedicated to
Helen Graham
my beloved
who loved The Ancient One
and searched for Her
divine feminine expressions

TABLE OF CONTENTS

LIST OF FIGURES

CHAPTER 1

HEALING AND LOSING ONE'S MIND

One of the main functions of organized religion is to protect people against a direct experience of God.[1]

— *Carl Jung*

A Five-Year-Old Girl Topples the House of Cards

Dali is a village of four thousand people not far from the center of the island of Cyprus. The roads run flat and straight until they approach Dali. Here they begin to arduously twist and climb the foothills to the country's tallest mountains to the southwest. Twentieth-century "civilization" has only superficially grazed this village, whereas it has maimed others only thirty miles away. Electricity made its debut a decade before, its triumph more evident in the presence of television than in interior lighting. Most of the village still went to bed and arose with the chickens.

And that was the major problem. As far as most folks were concerned, it was the old ways versus the new ways. The elders (all men) were deeply divided over what to do about the animals in the village, for most houses dedicated their ground floors to donkeys, cows, pigs, ducks, rabbits, and chickens. It was a live-in grocery store, and the children made friends with "supper" all too frequently, bemoaning the loss

---

[1] https://medium.com/illumination/religion-is-a-defence-against-the-experience-of-god-writes-carl-jung-ed8f5b6bbc9d.

of favorite pets. Morning was unmistakable, even for the hardiest sleeper, for a cacophony of donkeys braying, pigs squealing, roosters boasting, and cows pleading prevented any sleep past dawn's early light.

It wasn't difficult to know where folks stood on the issue of animals remaining in the village. The old timers saw little advantage to the single light bulbs hanging in the center of the downstairs rooms. Men, dressed in knee-length stockings and long skirts, said life was better in the old days. The progressives, who wore Western suits and shaved, and talked about urban planning and sanitation, were troubling to the old-timers. Younger folk talked of watching "Dallas" on TV rather than joining in the ever-present games of backgammon on the outside edge of the village shops.

What drew me to Dali was the opportunity to serve as an excavation supervisor on the archaeological staff exploring the site of Idalion, located on the southern fringes of the village. One can see the modern name of Dali embedded in its ancient Greek name. Idalion was one of the five major kingdom cities of ancient Cyprus during the splendor of the first millennium B.C.E. Its prominence in antiquity was far greater than any modern dweller in Dali would ever guess.

The Idalion Project was developed out of a vision by my mentor, Paul W. Lapp, to integrate the archaeological research of all the various national departments of antiquities (Israel, Jordan, Iraq, Turkey, Greece, Cyprus, Egypt, Tunisia, Libya, Lebanon, and Syria, for starters) into a regional Mediterranean research effort. Paul Lapp was not oblivious to the impact such cooperative efforts could make on political peace in the region. The fact that each country has its own research agendas and perceptions of history, often to support nationalistic political and economic interests, the fact that each country has its own historical chronologies, and the fact that each has its own excavation standards have resulted in a fragmented and distorted picture of history. The ancient empires did not respect modern national boundaries and interests, and it has been difficult for scholars to relate the findings, for example, in Syria with the findings in Greece. Paul Lapp was interested in establishing standardized chronologies and methods, universal use of state-of-the-art technologies, international accountability and quality control, and shared resources. With two Harvard Ph. D.s, having served for a decade as the Director of the American Schools of Oriental Research in Jerusalem, having directed five major excavation projects, having a solid international reputation, and having established effective working relationships with the government antiquities officials in most of these countries, Paul was in an unusual position to initiate such an unprecedented international project. Tragically, a week before the start of the Idalion dig, Paul, who was an expert swimmer, mysteriously drowned along the north coast of Cyprus. This affected me personally, for I was a godparent to his five children, including twins a year and a half old. With him died an intellectual vision for pan-Mediterranean studies.

To save the Project on a much smaller scale, the skeleton staff that assembled in the aftermath of Paul's death shifted its objective to conducting an archaeological survey of the region around Dali. The staff included a Colonel in the U.S. Marines, who had played a key role in negotiating the ceasefire between Egypt and Israel in 1967; he was an engineer by training and was our surveyor. Joining the team were two British archaeologists who were also excavating the earliest known Greek ship, found on the north coast of Cyprus. In subsequent seasons, the scientific staff would be expanded to include a geologist, a metallurgist, a potter who was a specialist in ancient ceramics, paleobotanists, an agronomist, museum conservationists, artists, and photographers.

I had come to Dali from Jerusalem, where I had been researching the origins of the Philistines, their ties to the Sea Peoples, and the breakup six centuries earlier of the great Aegean civilization to the west. I have long been fascinated with the fact that, as long as we remember, there has been conflict between East and West.

Idalion was a site nearly unexcavated, with remains dating from the Late Bronze Age (1300 B.C.E.) through the Byzantine Period, as late as 1000 C.E. Today, the ancient city is covered by small fields and pastures framed by crumbling limestone walls. Our survey turned up various concentrations of potsherds that have worked their way to the surface, and serve as indicators of remains and their dates under the surface. These findings were integrated into photographs taken in aerial infrared moisture studies, and served to determine where we would begin our excavations.

More exciting that summer was the discovery of a Middle Bronze fortress city perched on a bluff about two miles to the north of Dali. While it was unknown in the modern literature, maps from antiquity suggested we had found the village that from ancient records we identified as Kafkallia, flourishing between 1300-1100 BCE. At the edge of the cliff that protected the southern side of Kafkallia, we found a cemetery with many tombs having multiple chambers cut into the soft limestone scarp. In one of these, we found a remarkably preserved bronze belt and dagger along with a trove of pots and jars. These pots had a delicate beige slip and geometric designs similar to the exquisite Mycenaean ware, suggesting that the people who lived here at Kafkallia were related to the breakup of the Mycenaean culture and the migrations of these Aegean Sea Peoples toward Egypt and the eastern Mediterranean. We spent the first month mapping and developing architectural drawings of the nine-meter-thick fortress walls, the streets, and domestic buildings of this once busy town.

During this particular summer, I and three others were living in the house of the village priest in Dali. It was a two-story house with a thatched roof, packed earthen floors, no plumbing, and mud brick walls a meter thick laminated in plaster. The priest and his wife had moved into a single room and rented the remaining three rooms to the Idalion Project. Some of the elders in the village saw the educational and political advantages to developing the archeological site and the economic possibilities of opening their town to tourism; the priest was quick to see the entrepreneurial advantages. In subsequent seasons, the Project rented the village school to avoid playing into the hands of competing factions among the Dali townspeople.

In the cool of the evenings, we sat outside the house of the kindly village priest, whom we called "Pappos." We enjoyed visiting with the friendly old man and his shy wife, pantomiming stories until our Greek improved. Using drama and fumbling about in Greek dictionaries, we responded to our host's questions about our families, our homes, and our work back in the United States. Eventually our facility with language improved to the point where conversation was much more normal.

We, in turn, were relentless in learning about customs, holidays, food, dances, and family stories. In the backyard where these nightly rituals took place, there was a shed with large rolls of paper weighing a thousand pounds apiece. We learned that the priest was storing these rolls for his son, who worked for a toilet paper manufacturer based in Upsala, Sweden. I laughed when I learned that the name of the company was Krappe, although this made more sense when I learned that the inventor of the toilet was a man named Krappe.

Outside the house, we were more on the wife's turf, for this was where her family oven was located, cooling off from a day's labor. It was made of packed mudbrick shaped like a dome beehive six feet high. A fire would be built inside, reduced to warm ashes, and then bread would be baked on long paddles. Such bread was hearty, chewy, and flavorful compared to our typical, insubstantial American fare.

Everywhere we walked, there would be a line of curious children trailing along, chirping the only American word they knew: "Hello! Hello!" It is strange to claim "hello" as an American word, for it is the Hebrew name of God, *el*, more recognizable in the other name for God, *Allah*. What would the world be like if we looked at one another and first recognized the presence of God in them, "ella', ella'?" I always enjoyed the children and made friends with them, particularly the granddaughter of Pappos, a cute, shy little girl, five years old, named Georgina Papakarageorgis.

As I listened and learned from these people with whom I lived, I began to catch on to a worldview different from mine. It was a worldview where native dances beat the earth every night, and women did needlework that told of the unique mythology of that area; where gestures and body language held entirely different meanings from Western body talk; where men talk only with men, and women only with women. Here friendship was not necessarily part of a marriage. I observed that so much of the world sees friendship forming along same-sex lines; I had been used to opposite-sex friendship.

Here in Dali passions were alive. Soccer matches and politics were inseparable and heated; the outcomes of both were settled in one forum or the other. Eventually I heard talk of blood feuds and centuries-old resentments that were revived in the energetic rivalries of local soccer teams. But I also heard people laugh with abandonment. I watched them express wonderment over the morning sun that confirmed a sense of mystery about both the past and the future. In Dali, the present felt utterly important.

Gradually, I began to awaken to a different way of feeling inside. I began to feel a freedom from the panic of schedules and the performance demands of Pittsburgh, my home town and the location of my graduate school. Most people here in Dali ignored wrist watches. There were no clock or bell towers to punctuate the time. No trolleys to catch, or for that matter, no deadlines to meet.

One of the people with little appreciation for time was the hired cook for our dig. He operated a restaurant with two tables and eight chairs in the center of town where the two main roads crossed, but as far as I could tell, few if any locals ever ate out. Frequently he would bring in a live sheep, show it off, admire it, and then slaughter it on the spot in front of us. His stove was a small charcoal grill. We waited hungrily, sometimes for hours, until it was ready. Living took on a different kind of importance with different priorities. The process was just as important as the result. Here in this village lost to time, I thought I could almost hear the light step of Zorba's dance and the enchantment of a world vital and unburdened, a world full of imagination and laughter, where experience and being alive was what mattered. Dali was alive with stories.

The past was alive too. I have always felt a kind of powerful energy in places where a major event once happened, perhaps at Monticello, the Acropolis, Stonehenge, Jerusalem, Wounded Knee, Machu Picchu. In places such as these, one can sense the residual spirit of that event or of the person who belongs to that place. One has a sense that "even the stones would shout!" That's how I began to feel about Idalion.

The ancient capital city had two acropoli. The east one was tall and steep, the west acropolis more rounded and sloping. Cradled between these acropolises was a wheat field that flowed gently to the south. At the edge, where the field met the west acropolis, there was a small, present-day, ramshackle slaughterhouse. The local people called this field "Paradisio." In folklore, it was the place where the goddess Aphrodite and the god Adonis first met.

Sometimes, as the sun was low, I loved to sit on top of the west acropolis, with a blanket of earth covering the sleeping palaces of royalty and the temples of forgotten gods and goddesses. There I would look out over Paradisio. I thought I could see the ancient drama of Aphrodite and Adonis, and the mythic awakening of love and passion on the planet. I wondered where the lovely and beguiling Aphrodite awaited, she who stole away the wits of the wise. This island was sacred for her and sometimes she was known more properly as Cyprian.

How was it that Adonis entered this Eden? In my imagination, the slaughterhouse became a garden house. Like Persephone, Adonis was shared with the underworld, and hence, the secrets of the unconscious. Anyone who was familiar with the underworld was a figure of great interest to me, as I have always been interested in the great Mysteries. Perhaps not far from this very place, Aphrodite wept and cradled Adonis in her bosom when he had been mortally gored by the bull. As he died, according to legend, she cried to her lover, "Kiss me yet once again, the last long kiss, until I draw your soul within my lips, and drink down all your love."[2]

For me, in the fading light, Paradisio came alive with such energies and voices. One could feel the power and presence of the gods here. The memory of the people is powerful, because it's in the land. The land talks. The actual *facts* of history are irrelevant.

There was yet another experience I had of the sacred. In the center of the village is a large Greek Orthodox church. It is made of great limestone blocks, weathered to a golden brown, scarred and pitted by forgotten battles. Although gothic in style, the sixty-foot vaulted ceilings were far from beautiful and majestic. There was only the large sanctuary room. No educational buildings, no fellowship halls, no nurseries. No pews.

Prior to the fifteenth century, there were no church pews. Johann Gutenberg, with his invention of movable type, opened the door to the publishing industry and public literacy. Books brought linear, sequential thinking, row after row. It is interesting that, in the aftermath of Gutenberg, the churches organized themselves accordingly, word after word, line after line, pew after pew. This experience in Dali was beginning to challenge my linear logic and insistence on rationality. More than ever before, I reflected about how Gutenberg played a significant role in reorganizing the structure of our thinking, and our religion as well. This Greek Orthodox Church, however, was not a place of linear thinking.

One Sunday, I ventured into a Greek Orthodox service. It changed my life. Inside, as the service progressed, the people simply milled around. Perched in pulpits on opposite walls, two priests alternately

---

[2] Edith Hamilton, *Mythology* (New York: Black Dog & Leventhal, 2017), Ch. 9.

canted beautiful, ancient songs, answering one another like birds. Now and then, they came down amongst the people, swinging pungent censers, puffing smoke. "Taste the Lord, smell the Lord, and know the Lord is good!" they chanted. Full of graduate school, and the endless questions of my busy intellect in my quest for truth, I repeatedly turned to those around me, speaking to them in faltering Greek. "What is happening? Why are they doing that? What does this mean?" My questions drew blank stares. Their responses seemed to go beyond "I don't know" or "I've never thought about it." I sensed a certain bewilderment from them toward me, as if to say, "Why are you asking questions? *Just experience the experience.*" They seemed to not ask questions about religion. Why not, I wondered?

It was then that I recognized the foolishness of my rational, Cartesian mind, the mind of the Presbyterian Church, the mind of Western scholasticism. In 1619, René Descartes, the French philosopher and mathematician, awakened us from our repose around tribal fireplaces where meaning was played out in stories and dance. Sensing the new world-spirit, Descartes invited us to *think*, and to think differently. He invited us to step away from our experiencing ways. *"I think, therefore I am,"* he said. He started us on a path where we could *live entirely without stories.* If only we could master nature, objectify knowledge, tame the unconscious, rationalize and conquer experience, then stories would be unnecessary. As a result, we in the West have been willing to settle for the Reader's Digest version of the stories; that is, the lesson, the moral of the story, the bottom line. I, too, had abandoned stories.

In religion, doctrines began to take the place of stories. Ideas replaced experience. To this day, we have continued to press for the theological understanding and the truth behind the story. Therein, we have lost the story, and we have lost the experience. Our tendency has been to forget the story; it embellishes, it illustrates, it has multiple meanings, and it confuses. For us, the key thing is the point of the story, and in that, we miss the elements of the story that heal, engage the soul, and deepen experience. Accordingly, religious experience has taken a back seat to academic, empirical, rational, factual learning as a way to understand the world and where we are going.

I saw the one-sidedness of my Quest for a decade in the halls of graduate classrooms. Here in this unpretentious sanctuary in Dali, these uneducated folk were not in any way dismissing the importance of intellectualism. We would expect to find such a critique in American fundamentalism, but not here in Dali. These people were not conscious and analytical about what they were doing. Rather, they stepped into the experience and let the experience become alive in them. It became clear to me that this was not rote religion, full of empty phrases.

I was aware of how Jungian typology characterizes culture itself, not just the mind. For millennia, people lived with the "Sensate Mind," ruled by the physical senses, meaning a life driven by physical needs, health, having enough food, and having enough wood to survive the cold. Descartes shifted the world to the "Thinking Mind," a mind ruled by logic, intellect, science, and empirical proof. I was becoming aware that at the present the world was experiencing yet another shift, the shift to the "Intuitive Mind," that seeing things as separate is an illusion, that the mind that sees everything being affected by everything, and that things need to be seen as an interacting field.

I had lived with these people, worked with them, and been present at their weddings. Oh, the celebrations! The elderly, as well as the children, all generations, would clap and dance at these events. In this village and in this sanctuary, there was a spiritual presence that was real, very mysterious, and ancient.

What was emerging within me was outside my experience. I was experiencing the Christian faith untainted by the Protestant Reformation. It was closer to the experience of the early church than anything I had known. This Orthodox tradition precedes the schisms, councils, and confessions. The religious experience of these people was earthy, simple, symbolic, direct, unreflective, and full of laughter. It embraced sweat, chants, and tears.

I will never forget the ritual of communion that morning. My little friend, five-year-old Georgina Papakarageorgis, came up to me near the end of the service. She handed me a big chunk of bread. "Here, for you," she said in faltering English. "It is Jesu. Eat him. And take him home." In Dali, it is a custom to eat part of the sacramental bread and take the remainder home. There, the first act of the next family meal is to continue the sacrament by eating the remainder of the body of Christ.

I left the church in a daze. I realize that for years I had been building an intellectual House of Cards that had suddenly collapsed. The House of Cards had to do with the search for facts, gaining credibility and support from recognized scholars, securing opportunities to publish articles, and delivering professional papers. Little Georgina awakened me to the illusion of self-importance and the illusory seriousness of my path.

As I received the bread and her words, another kind of knowing came over me, a kind of knowing that I unfold in this book. It was an awareness of an older and deeper way of knowing and understanding faith. A realization came upon me that this faith is transmitted through a structure entirely apart from content, apart from theology in our sense of the discipline. I was awakened to a faith that comes through ancient practice, through ritual, through *story*... not analyzed, but acted out and lived. Stories are openings or clearings where gods come to play and where angels speak. It is in these openings that we discover that our imaginative words and our yearnings have the power to alter the world. All this was a gift from this little girl.

I had grown up in a world that seemed determined to separate fantasy from fact at all costs. I had been taught that fact was truth and fantasy was falsehood. At first, it seemed as though these village folk didn't care about religious meaning, for they showed little interest in searching out the history that birthed their rituals. Yet their faith was alive and vital. In a deeper sense, they were saying that all of life and experience is fiction and fantasy in that *we create our world* and the meanings we find helpful for our living. The folk from Dali saw little need for church school, or catechism classes, or the distinctions that place a different church denomination on every city block. By opening to the experience of living without the secular-sacred distinctions, they were free to immerse themselves in images, much as we would in a dream. They allowed themselves to be touched directly by music, ritual, and images, carrying them into those areas of themselves that needed attention, expression, and healing.

This perspective does not say that our preoccupation with ideas, analysis, and theology in the West is a waste of time. We want to be intellectually responsible and use all of our faculties. We don't want to lose the "Thinking Mind." However, mainstream religious experience in America and Europe, on its calorie-less diet of doctrines and beliefs separated from daily experience and exercise, has starved itself. We are spiritual anorexics.

Alexander Schmemann, a remarkable Greek Orthodox theologian, commented that in the Orthodox tradition, the gap between religion and life is damaging to the soul. He says the "original" sin is *not* that we have primarily disobeyed God, but that we have ceased to be hungry for God and thirsty for communion. The sin is that we have been taught to think of God in conceptual terms, thereby separating God from life. We beheld the world as something material instead of transforming it into life-in-God, filled with meaning and spirit.[3]

This is not easy for the West to stomach. We have preferred head religion to body religion. The primary organ of spirituality in ancient times used to be the ear. "*Hear*, O Israel, the Lord your God is One." It was a religion of singing songs and chants, and telling stories. People heard, and they remembered.

This elaboration of visual experience, with Latin pageantry, frescoes, statuary, and stained glass windows, seemed profane to the Reformers. While they changed the language of the mass to the common vernacular, they also turned away from images and stories toward ideas and that which cannot be seen and experienced by the senses. The Protestant Reformation saw a shift in emphasis to the *word* of God. Written words, authoritative words, the Bible, doctrines, concepts, beliefs—these became the instruments of faith and the communal features binding or dividing people. It was a shift from seeing to knowing. The brain became the organ of faith.

Perhaps a new organ of faith is emerging in our own time as the vehicle for spiritual experience, the organ of touch and connectedness. Touch requires a very different kind of spiritual process, a whole-body process. It is a process that knows passion and fire in the belly, hunger and savory filling, feeling the rhythms of dancing before the Lord. Touch is not a new spiritual sense. Feminist theologians and biblical scholars are awakening us to an experience of religion that comes from the womb and the belly. These peasants of Dali knew it well.

---

[3] Alexander Schmemann, *For the Life of the World* (Yonkers, NY: St. Vladimir's Seminary Press: 1973), p. 18. This was published also under the title *Sacraments and Orthodoxy* by Herder and Herder in 1965.

But what *is* new for us in the West is becoming conscious about the function of images, energies, and imagination in the realm of touch. Once again, contemporary spirituality has to do with learning to experience deeply and to trust images that impact us with such directness and power.

So it was that I took Jesus home in the form of leftover bread. To this day I remember the words of little Georgina, "It's Jesu. Eat him. Take him home." Such simple words, such a lovely image that cuts through all the pretentiousness of graduate school and a lifetime of questing for meaning. For me, this little child opened the door to deeper understanding and higher spirituality in a way that listens to the language of the heart.

An Epilogue: Beyond The Mind

Do not conform to the pattern of this world, but keep letting yourselves be transformed by the renewing of your mind.
— Romans 12:2

The ultimate point of the "Story of Stories" (the Bible) is that the way to God asks us each one to lose our minds and fall into experience.

To suggest that there is soul-healing in losing one's mind seems contradictory in a culture where the intellect and mindfulness is an ideal. Losing one's mind sounds crazy. Or, on the other hand, to try to make sense of the chaotic world we live in may be another form of insanity. There is no cause for worry or alarm in the transformation of mind called for in spiritual renewal; this is the way to freedom or liberation.

The core issue is this. The human mind is finite. The mind is limited in perception, and perception is conditioned by culture and language. Cognitive anthropologists now say that we make up everything we see. We see the world with complete subjectivity. Physicists say we create what we expect to see; we affect what we observe.

On the other hand, God is beyond all thought. We cannot think our way to God. In the same way, the biblical story says true Reality lies beyond all thoughts and imagination. *"For my thoughts are not your thoughts, and your ways are not my ways,"* says God.[4] Imagination can create marvelous fiction, but the Bible story continually points to a reality beyond imagination. True healing, true release from worry, true happiness lie in this Beyond.

Something interesting happens for many who are in extreme suffering or at the point of dying, says Kathleen Dowling Singh, Ph.D., a transpersonal psychologist who has worked with hundreds of people who were dying. She says as people are dying or in an extreme situation, they seem to transcend themselves and their attachment to the body, and they experience an expansion beyond familiar consciousness. They realize they are vastly larger and more endowed than they had ever imagined, and they experience an openness and power beyond the personal self.[5] Mohammed said no one looks back and regrets leaving the world. What's regretted is how real we thought it was![6]

Many times with people who are dying, I have experienced this expanded state where they are leaving their limited experience of themselves and realizing they are vastly more than they ever knew. This is a letting go of the former mind. We experience it over and over until we abide in the ultimate state beyond all form and thought. This is the direction that the sacred healing stories of the Bible take us.

Jesus said to them, "If you fast, you will bring sin upon yourselves, if you pray, you will be condemned, and if you give to charity, you will harm your spirits. [meaning religion alone can't take one to God]
— Jesus, Gospel of Thomas, 14

---

[4] Isaiah. 55:8

[5] Kathleen Dowling Singh, *The Grace in Dying: How We Are Transformed Spiritually as We Die* (Harper: San Francisco, 1998), p. 85.

[6] Rumi, Mathnawi VI: 1450-66, version by Coleman Barks, *The Soul of Rumi* (Harper: San Francisco, 2001), p. 208.

*Jesus said, "I will give you what no eye has seen, what no ear has heard, what
no hand has touched. [meaning beyond all thought]*
— Jesus, Gospel of Thomas, 17

*If you do not fast from the world, you will not find the [Father's] kingdom.
[meaning one must go beyond the limitations of the finite world]*
— Jesus, Gospel of Thomas, 27

What follows is an imagined conversation following a fictional sem-
inar taught by Jesus before the Gospels were written, but based on pre-
canonical sources.

Miriam: Wow! We have been taught that our acceptance before the
Holy One depends on following the Torah and believing in the teachings of Moshe [Moses]. Master Yeshua blew away all that today.

Yitzak: I agree, if I understood him rightly, he was saying that the
true path goes beyond religion and the reaches of the mind. Frankly, I
don't know what to do with that.

Miriam: I know our teachers at the synagogue say the Master is a
blasphemer, but I have always thought that just following all the *mitzvot*
and observing the practices of religion was really kind of monotonous
and boring. I hope lightning doesn't strike. I have always yearned for
something more in religion, and the Master seemed to point to that.

Yitzak: It heartens me for you to say that. I have always hoped for a
religion that would take me beyond myself. I didn't hear the Master say
beliefs are wrong or bad; they help us find ourselves on the way. But I
also had the sense that he suggested that beliefs can kill one in the sense
that one's thoughts *over-contain one* in a world of their own making, not
the True World.

Miriam: Yes, my friend, we can get lost in the ideological fogs of our
own making. I am not sure I understood the Master's analogy about
"fasting from the world." I never thought about fasting or separating
from the world. I don't think that means the world is bad or that we
should not be part of it, but we can't become part of the Holy Kingdom
unless we see beyond the limited world we create.

Yitzak: I am still not sure what to do. I want to say I believe in belief.
But the Master said religion is also binding. Beliefs are training wheels

that get us started on the road, but they are not the end. Beliefs don't save.

Miriam: When someone asked the Master how we get beyond our heads, he said, "Love is the fire that burns both belief and non-belief."[7] I am going to have to think about that.

Yitzak: You are right, in some way, the door to what is true is love. Master said, "The work of God is this: to entrust your life to the one He has sent to you. But as I told you, you have seen me and still you do not give yourself to me, don't worry. No one can come to me unless the Father who sent me draws that person to me. Everyone who listens to the Father and learns from Him comes to me."

Miriam: I guess it is not fully in our hands.

One should love God mindlessly, by this I mean that your soul ought to be without mind or mental activities or images or representations. Bare your soul of all mind and stay there without mind.
— Meister Eckhart[8]

Stories invite us to play. While imagination can take us into illusion and falsehood, imagination also cultivates our ability to explore the fruit of unknown orchards. One thinks of the Tree of the Forbidden Fruit in the Garden of Eden, which did indeed open the door to the imaginary Mind of God, but we were unable to handle where it took us. Imagination can be just as finite and limited as rational thought, just as illusory, but it unlocks the chains of the limited world of orthodox belief and thought. There is a lot more to play than our usual imagination supports.

In our culture, we are taught about mindfulness. Mindfulness calls for stepping out of everyday activity and frenetic thoughts, and becoming inwardly aware of what flows through our inner life. While meditating can be a process of emptying the mind and clearing the clutter,

---

[7] Abu Sa'id Abi 'l-Khayr, in *Love's Alchemy: Poems from the Sufi Tradition*, trans. by David and Sabrineh Fideler (Novato, CA: New World Library, 2006), p. 63.

[8] Meister Eckhart, *Meditations with Meister Eckhart*, trans by Matthew Fox (Rochester, VT: Bear & Company, 1983), p. 46.

meditation can also sharpen us to focus and practice one-pointedness. Sometimes we are invited in meditation to focus on God or on the Christ.

Hsuan-Tsung, an emperor in the spiritual T'ang Dynasty (732 CE), said, "Not observing themselves, they become whole." And Mencius (390-305 BCE) said similarly, "We praise those who don't calculate. We reproach those who try to be whole."[9] When we strive to reach spiritual attainment, the striving creates a spiritual ego. As Jesus pointed out— indeed, the entire Bible—one has to "get-over oneself."

It is not that we don't engage in living a spiritual life, in praying and learning and practicing charity, but we learn to develop a refined and cautionary awareness of what we are doing, so as to not get caught in a trap of our making. The best we can do is forget ourselves, fall in love, and focus on another's well-being.

Higher spirituality is becoming conscious about mind.

---

[9] Quoted in Lao-Tzu's *Tao te Ching*, translated by Red Pine (Port Townsend, WA: Copper Canyon Press, 2009), p. 45.

CHAPTER 2

ARE THE HEALING STORIES TRUE?

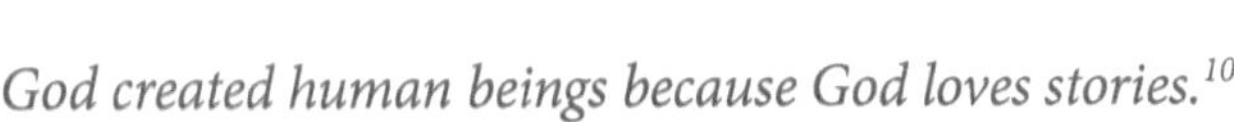

God created human beings because God loves stories.[10]
— Elie Wiesel

Mythic Beginnings:
Failed Early Drafts in the Creation of Man and Woman

When God summoned the band under the archangel Michael, and asked their opinion on the creation of man, they answered scornfully: "What is man, that Thou art mindful of him? And the son of man, that Thou visitest him."[11]

[As God was creating Eve] the purpose of the sleep that enfolded Adam was to give him a wife, so that the human race might develop, and all creatures recognize the difference between God and man.[12]

---

[10] *Because God Loves Stories: An Anthology of Jewish Storytelling*, ed., by Steve Zeitlin (New York: Simon and Shuster/Touchstone, 1998).

[11] The Legends of the Jews, by Lewis Ginzberg (1909), www.sacred-texts.com/jud/loj/index.htm. These words attributed to the story of Creation are found in Psalm 8:5.

[12] *Sefer Ha-Aggadah (Book of Legends)*, ed. by Hayim Bialik & Yehoshua Revnitzky (New York: Schocken Books, 1992), § 66, p. 16. Initially, if beings were created in the celestial likeness of God, they would be eternal and would not reproduce, while terrestrial beings were not created in the image of God and could reproduce. Finally, God decides man is both celestial and terrestrial; he will reproduce,

R. Jeremiah ben Eleazar said, "When the Holy One created Adam he created him hermaphrodite (bisexual)."[13]

Lilith was first given to Adam as wife. But she remained with him only a short time, because she insisted upon enjoying full equality with her husband.[14]

Adam was first made to fall into a deep sleep before the rib for Eve was taken from his side. For, had he watched her creation, she would not have awakened love in him. Knowing well all the details of her formation, he would have been repelled by her.[15]

The healing story of the creation of human beings and the Garden of Eden has many versions. Christians like to have a single story, and they like just one answer; Jews say, "There are a thousand versions, a thousand interpretations of this and every other story, and now we will consider the thousandth-and-first." Over the years, rabbis and learned people made marginal comments alongside the Hebrew text and added related stories to the original text. These are known as the "midrash." The above snippets from the midrash suggest that God went through many aborted efforts before the matter of the creation of man and woman was settled.

---

and he will die. He is the only one who was created by the hand of God. The rest sprang from the word of God.

[13] *Sefer Ha-Aggadah (Book of Legends)*, § 60, p. 15. Other midrash says God made Adam with two heads in opposite directions, like the Greek God Janus. R. Samuel Nahman said God made man with two fronts, then cut them in half, giving them two backs, all reminiscent of Plato's Myth of the Androgyne.

[14] *The Legends of the Jews*, by Lewis Ginzberg. The midrash adds, "She derived her rights from their identical origin. Adam complained to God that the wife He had given him had deserted him. When threatened with punishment, Lilith preferred this punishment to living with Adam."

[15] *The Legends of the Jews*, by Lewis Ginzberg. "For, had he watched her creation, she would not have awakened love in him. To this day it is true that men do not appreciate the charms of women whom they have known and observed from childhood up."

Each version of the creation of Adam and Eve is worth telling in greater detail; they are funny and preposterous. The animals were created to reproduce. Man was not. Adam did not have a mate. The debate was whether man, being made in the image of God, should be immortal like God, or whether human beings should be mortal like the rest of creation. If man is given sex, then he must also be given death, for procreating without limit would exhaust the earth.

In the earlier human drafts, the created man was two-faced from the waist up (like the Greek god Janus), and joined as one from the waist down. Initially, Adam was a hermaphrodite. No clear opposites at this point. Then God made Lilith, who would not let the man dominate her (or mount her), and she fled. Then God made the perfect woman, and Adam watched her creation in every respect; as perfect as she was, Adam said, "There is no mystery to her." And finally there came Eve.

What is interesting about all these "drafts" and versions is that we can see the primitive patriarchal sexism that continues to this day, and we also get a glimpse into the remarkable Jewish psyche. The writers were less interested in a single true story (acknowledging there was no witness present taking notes), but we see the mythic aspects of their imagination, and it is multileveled, sophisticated, psychological, and carries all the patriarchic projections that men and women have carried since the beginning.

As fascinating as this is, it shows that the biblical stories transcend literal interpretation. The writers are aware that the stories have levels of meaning, and the healing qualities of biblical stories are hidden within and not to be extracted into hard principles and beliefs. These stories are not to be understood as "facts." This multileveled textured aspect of mixing history and myth exists in nearly every story in the Bible. Everything is more than it seems.

Is the Garden of Eden Real?: Four Levels of Understanding

> *"Holy are you, O Lord, for you have raised up in me the Tree of Life.*
> *You have shown me a secret Garden, unseen within the seen.*
> *Your Presence, the true Tree of Life,*
> *planted in whatever it is that men are.*
> *—Symeon the New Theologian (949-1032 CE)*[16]

Why does the Bible begin with such an impossible story? A garden with magical trees, a snake that talks, a world without worry yet stern warnings against disobedience, a world without consciousness or sex, a world without work, a world without evil. What is the meaning of such fantasy in the biblical book of Truth?

It is a mistake to see the writers of the Bible as naive and unsophisticated. They were aware that there is a difference between myth and history, as one can see in the Jewish versions of the creation of Adam and Eve. If a group had gathered around a fire in the eighth century BCE to tell the story of Beginnings, when they got to the part where the Serpent shows up as more than a slithering snake, they would have smiled and the storyteller would have winked at those who hadn't heard the story before to say this is not a fable. This is a story of the human psyche, a story about what makes us human, a story about our deeper nature, a story that goes beyond what we think is literally true.

In all religions, there are four "levels" that one experiences as they migrate from everyday life to higher levels of spiritual experience and ultimately become one with God. Every one of the world's religions has these same four levels, although they are given different names. In Judaism, these four levels are called The Four Worlds. When telling a story, the hearer does well to discern what level the story is being understood, and the capacity for healing depends on the level.

As can be seen i, the Four Worlds of understanding are the Gross World, the Subtle World, the Mental Causal World, and the Beyond-the-Beyond. The Gross World is familiar to all of us. It is what we like to think of as "the real world" of everyday life. It is the world of cause and effect, science, objectivity, the need for rational proof, the physical world of "things"—earth, nature, animals, climate, objects. It is the world of

---

[16] Symeon the New Theologian, in *The Book of Mystical Chapters: Meditations on the Soul's Ascent from the Desert Fathers and Other Early Christian Contemplatives* (Boulder: Shambhala, 2003).

"forms," tangible forms that we access through our senses. It is the world around which we fashion our beliefs and organized religion.

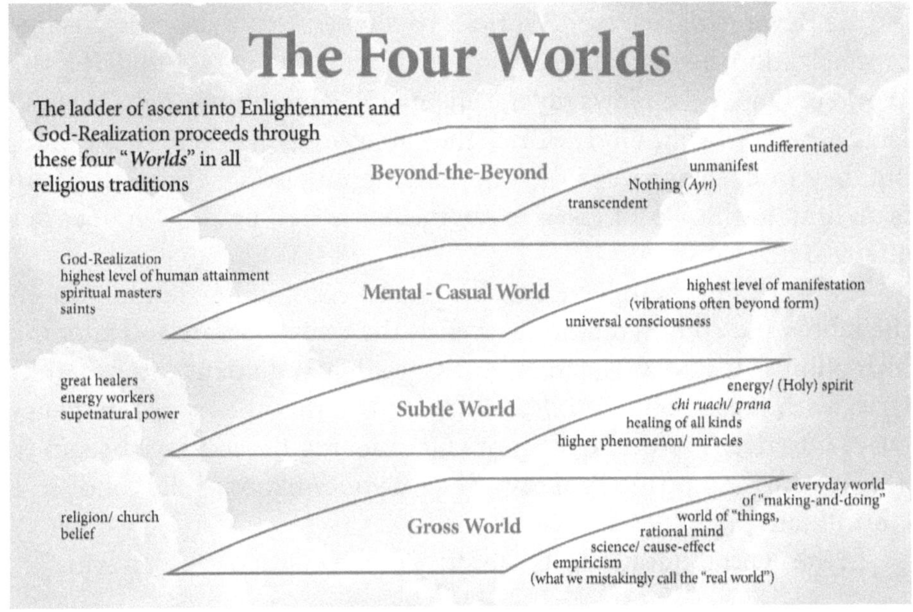

Figure 1: The Four Worlds

The Four Worlds are not independent and separate from one another, but are embedded in one another. The second world is embedded within the first world, but it is a deeper level of experience. It is called the Subtle World. It is a world of energy, of symbolic meaning, of higher connectivity and interconnectivity—including what some see as miracles—of transcending time and space, and going beyond the usual perceptions of cause and effect.

The Subtle World is the level of psyche, the Latin word for "soul." Psyche is what animates us, making us feel alive, vibrant, and engaged. Psyche is a combination of images, symbols, energy, and emotions that creates the power of archetypal meaning and the power of stories to shape us. It is the level we associate with the Holy Spirit and divine activity.

More deeply within is the Mental-Causal World, sometimes referred to as the first vibrations of form in the Creation process. It is the link between form and the formless. It is the highest level of manifestation, and it appears as universal consciousness. This is the level of the spiritual masters and many of the saints, the highest level of human attainment as one approaches realizing and becoming one with God.

The Beyond-the-Beyond World is beyond all words, beyond all conceptualization, beyond all knowing. Jews call it *Ayn* or Nothing. It is the World of One. When Jews say the Shema in Deuteronomy 6:4, "Hear, O Israel, the Lord your God is One," they are not saying there is one God, but they are speaking to a reality beyond monotheism, beyond all. There is no limit to this world. Even to say the name God or Yahweh does not attain to this world.

The stories of the Bible have all these levels of understanding. Both the rabbis and commentators, as well as the writers before and after the formation of the New Testament (or Christian Testament), show familiarity with these Four Worlds, and recognize that the more one penetrates into deeper worlds, the more far-reaching the message becomes. This is why the Apostle Paul says, "I gave you milk, not solid food" in 1 Corinthians 3:2.

To the central question, "Is the story of the Garden of Eden true?"

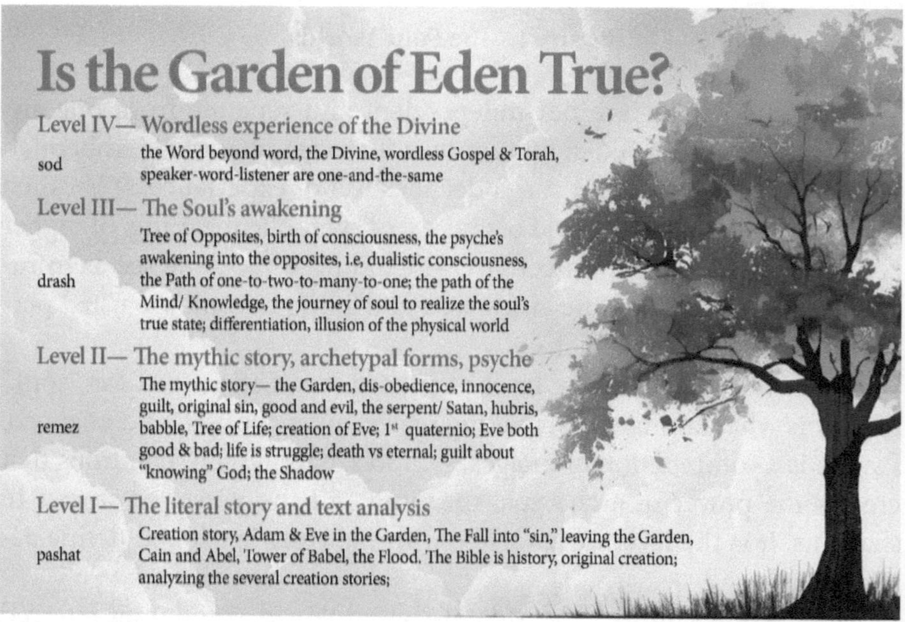

Figure 2: Levels of Understanding the Garden of Eden Story

When it comes to understanding the biblical stories, Judaism has four levels of interpretation that serve as a bridge in ascending the Four Worlds. The four levels of interpretation of scripture and story are *pashat, remez, drash, and sod.*

Pashat

We are most familiar with the *pashat* version of the Garden of Eden story. Genesis 1 and 2 begin with the creation of the world, beginning with the creation of darkness and light; earth, water, and sky; vegetation and animals; and finally human beings. Genesis 3 begins with life in the Garden, the two trees, the injunction not to eat the fruit of the Tree of Opposites, the appearance of the Serpent, Eve and Adam's eating the fruit, their falling into the sin of disobedience, and then their getting kicked out of the Garden. That's the literal story. Is any or all of this story true?

There have been innumerable efforts to have science prove the Bible. In 1885, the president of Boston University, William F. Buckley, proposed that the Garden of Eden was at the North Pole. Other pseudo-scholars note that Eden is described as being near four rivers, including the Tigris and Euphrates, both of which flow close to the archaeological site of Gobekli Tepe; according to Genesis, they say, Eden is situated west of Assyria, precisely where Gobekli Tepe is located. We could continue this line of inquiry into our origins, but it is a total misreading of the biblical text. From this historical perspective, is the Garden of Eden true? Not a chance. The *pashat* version of the story is ridiculous. The original writers of the Torah would agree.

There is another scientific approach to the Garden of Eden that may be seen as another form of the *pashat* approach. Many people look at the scriptures of other world religions and see them as other-worldly and mythical. In contrast, there are those who conclude that both testaments of the Bible are historical documents, and the Judeo-Christian stories are provable and somewhat factual as history. History is perceived as true.

To approach the Bible as uniquely factual and true as history is an error. One can get deeply into the weeds around the philosophy of history, digging into Hegel and Foucault and our own perceptions of history, but what we believe happened in history changes with every generation. We make up history according to our perceptions. History is subjective to the teller.

In looking at the Hebrew Bible, it is difficult to document the Hebrew language before the tenth century, even though a few seemingly Hebrew words are found in the cuneiform library at Ebla, dating to around 2400-2250 BCE. It had been thought that the Torah, which was probably not compiled before the seventh century BCE, was a compilation of at least four sources, each using a different name for God.

There is no archaeological evidence for the Israelites being in Egypt, almost no evidence for the conquest of the Promised Land, and little factual evidence of Israel's presence with the Davidic First Temple. More likely, Jerusalem and the Judaic and Israelite kingdoms were too small to support an army. Most of this material was compiled in the sixth to seventh centuries, and many of the place names in the Bible did not exist until around that time. The Jewish Bible really didn't take shape until the rule of Josiah in 701 BCE.

Similarly, the history of the New Testament appears to differ from the perceived tradition. Both testaments begin in the obscure mists of time. The first century did not have a unified version about who Jesus was; there were easily thirty or more different perceptions of Jesus, some think even a hundred gospels. Tradition holds that Christianity expanded westward along North Africa, and from Turkey to Spain. It is true that Christianity became European, but a millennium later than most people think. But omitted from the story was Christianity's expansion eastward along the Silk Road to China; this eastward Christian movement had eighty-five metropolises (in Tibet, Iran, Iraq, and China) compared to two in the west (in England).[17]

Textual criticism looks like science, tracing the literary threads of biblical text to their dates and origins, but this approach creates the

---

[17] Philip Jenkins, *The Lost History of Christianity* (Harper Collins, 2008), p. 10. Much of what we call the Islamic world was once Christian. As late as the eleventh century, Asia was home for at least a third of the world's Christians. By 800 CE, the Asian church reached a level the European church did not reach until the thirteenth century. Semitic Christianity did not die out until the fifteenth century. The early church enjoyed other interpretations and mystical writings until they were suppressed in the fourth century and the Council of Nicaea.

illusion of "facts" and obscures the deeper understanding of the biblical story.

It is not that there is no truth in history, nor that Judaism and Christianity are not based on history. But the historical perception of the Bible rests on the ever-changing historical imagination and research. The truth of the story of the Garden of Eden does not rest on historical record, archaeology, or textual analysis. None of this has the soul of the story. None of this touches the psyche.

One of my mentors, who had two Ph. D.s from Harvard and was one of the leading archaeologists in the world, said, "We can't understand what the biblical text means until we understand what it meant." The problem is that the story is so multi-leveled that it has no one meaning.

The story of the Garden of Eden is not true at the *pashat* level.

Remez

The second level of understanding scripture, and particularly story, is called *remez* in Hebrew. *Remez* means "hints," "inferences," or "allusions," and so the *remez* story departs from the literal meaning of the text. This level is where the juice, controversy, and energy lie with the story of the Garden. *Remez* engages the psyche wherever one finds meaning. It is more about experience than belief. We use the word *psyche* (the Latin word for soul) to refer to the psychological and spiritual aspects of the story, such as sin, passion, fear, guilt, judgment, and innocence.

The psyche of every person is activated by archetypes, which are "meaning-bytes" that every person understands. For instance, if one says the word "family," this is an archetype that people subjectively connect with, often emotionally. But there are innumerable forms of family, and every time one uses this concept, we give it specific nuances. "Family" refers to a group of familial, social, genetic, and collective units. Other familiar archetypes are father, child, mother, holy person, thief, king, pilgrim, wanderer…. More recently, we are working with archetypes such as the internet, memes, artificial intelligence, data, and hackers. In a sense, every familiar word or unit of meaning that we use for communicating is an archetype. Stories tell of archetypal figures, usually universally recognizable, such as first man and first woman, or Garden, or Serpent, and these activate our psyche as if to say "pay attention." The same is true for the first man on the moon. The stories around these archetypal figures and environments (e.g., sea, forests, outer space) we call myths, and myths are neither objectively true nor false. But they speak to experiences familiar to everyone in almost every culture.

The *remez* level of the Garden of Eden is loaded with symbolic or archetypal forms that touch the psyche, awakening meaning and perspectives that help us understand our lives and the world. The story begins with a Garden (an archetype), which suggests nature, the original state, and the natural, beauty, purity, and harmony, which suggests that every life is born into the natural state of support and care.

All the animals of creation are present in the Garden, but at this point they don't have names, meaning they don't have identity, and they don't have their animal nature. They are not "differentiated." All this is supposedly what a newborn child experiences. The womb is the first containment of a baby, and the nursery, along with parents' arms, is the second containment. Everything is innocent because guilt hasn't made an appearance in the story. So far, Eden is experientially true.

Like all myths/stories, things don't stay smooth, ahah, and that's another archetype. The original steady state was not to last, seemingly because of divine intent. Initially, there is no drama, no plot, no real experience, no conflict, no worry. There was nothing for God (or human beings) to do. Just float in the primordial soup.

New archetypal developments occur. The Garden has two trees of particular note. One tree is the Tree of Life, which is the Tree of Eternity. It symbolically represents the earlier state referred to in the midrash where God considered making human beings eternal as God was. If this had happened, would life be as interesting?

The second Tree is where all the trouble began. It has a long name, The Tree-of-the-Knowledge-of-Good-and-the-Knowledge-of-Evil, or we could say it was the Tree of Opposites. Eventually, human beings realized that consciousness emerges wherever there are opposites—opposite concepts, opposite forces, opposite quantum particles, opposite genders. Sex was part of this Tree, and by archetypal necessity, death was also part of the tree. (If not, as said earlier, procreation would exhaust the planet.)

Why have a Tree of Opposites in the Garden? The fact that there are two trees is already insipient dualism. Why have a command for obedience ("Don't eat!") which by definition sets up disobedience? Why set human beings up for sin (another archetype which means anything that separates us from God or from the state of Oneness)? Why introduce the archetypes of nakedness, needing clothes, being sexual, or Eve being blamed for seduction?

Another *remez*-level archetype surfaces: "Original Sin." It means that because of initial disobedience and punishment, every human being born thereafter is tainted; everyone is born flawed and born with an evil inclination (*yetzer hara* in Hebrew) that makes one in need of redemption from a force outside of oneself. St. Augustine invented the doctrine of Original Sin, saying even newborn babies are infected with a mortal defect which is pictured as a sexually transmitted moral disease, and both Roman Catholic and Protestant theologians, from Anselm, through Martin Luther and John Calvin, adopted Original Sin and felt only the church could save one. Jews do not believe in Original Sin.

There are three *remez* scenes in the Garden story. The first "act" or scene is the state of all creation existing in a state of bliss and harmony. The second scene is the disruption of that harmony, and the Serpent is the main character of that scene. The third scene is banishment from the Garden, exile to East of Eden, and blocked by angels with fiery swords from re-entry. Once one leaves the Garden, there is no return to the way things were, no amnesty or forgiveness. Every image here is an archetype that relates to the ultimate healing story that ultimately drives one to desire a return to Paradise or the New Jerusalem—archetypal images of wholeness and salvation.

The Serpent is by far the most interesting *remez* character. One wants to project the future figure of Satan on the Serpent, but this creates the opposition of Good and Evil that doesn't belong. There is no Evil in the Garden. The Serpent is the voice of Wisdom who emerges much later in the biblical story. The Tempter. The Seducer. The entire biblical story from the beginning to the end of the Bible is concerned with how to let go of oneself in order to return to God. This is the counsel of the Serpent. "Eat of the fruit of the Tree of Consciousness, and you will acquire God consciousness, you will see as God sees." Isn't this the goal of all of creation? Isn't this what God wants? But the message is we were not ready for God.

And this is the unsolved riddle of the story of the Garden of Eden. God-consciousness is not so easily given. One must undergo lifetimes of struggle outside of Eden.

There is another view of the banishment from the Garden. Fifth Plane saint Hazrat Inayat Khan said, "It is not true that Adam was put out of the garden of Eden; he only turned his back on it, and that was like an exile from heaven."[18] In this mythic view, we were never kicked out of the Garden into the Land of Nod, as the Bible says. God never exiled us; we did that to ourselves. In this view, we think the umbilical cord to God was cut by those flaming swords at the Garden Gate, but that's not true. We elected to move into the world we ourselves create, not the one God created. We decided to live in the world of our illusion.

To return to other *remez* features. There is another implicit archetype in the Garden that Carl Jung called the Quaternio, the double pairing of two opposites, a symbol of wholeness. Christianity embraces the archetype of the Trinity of three, but the Quaternio of four (as seen in the symbol of the cross) is more satisfying. There are a couple of ways of picturing this, but the classic way is to have God and serpent (later Satan) on the vertical axis, and Adam and Eve on the horizontal axis.

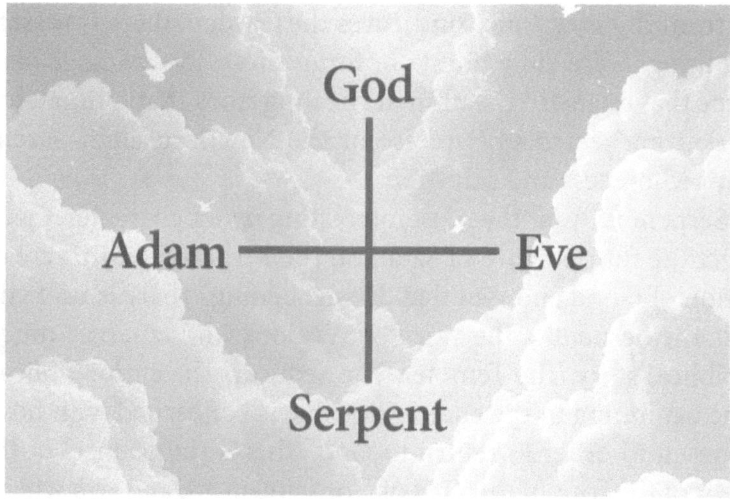

Figure 3: The Quaternio

---

[18] Hazrat Inayat Khan, *The Soul's Journey* (New Lebanon, NY: Omega, 2010), p. 117.

It is the acting out of Heaven and Earth archetype is a critical aspect of the Garden of Eden story. The significance of the Quaternio is the Garden is the archetype of original wholeness.

All of the *remez* archetypal features are what every child experiences in coming into the world—initial connection and oneness with the mother (and father), original innocence, containment by the womb/garden, lack of names, words, and differentiation, eventual beginning independence and stepping away from the parent, developing self-will, saying "no" to the parent (the beginning of individuation), punishment and forgiveness, and eventual leaving home. Are we to say that all these elements of the human psyche are not true? Of course not. The *remez* level of the Garden of Eden story has episodes that are about every human experience and thus are true. Therefore, the *remez* level of the story of the Garden of Eden is provisionally and subjectively true, because the interpretation is understood through the lens of personal and cultural experience.

Drash

The third level of interpretation of biblical stories is called *drash*, which means deeper seeking, inquiry, exploring, questioning, and searching. The previous *remez* level tells of innocence and guilt, good and evil, hubris, babble, nakedness and shame, sin and forgiveness, each with levels of psychological understanding. The *drash* level of understanding Eden is a level above this, where there is a unifying, overarching theme common to all humanity.

The *drash* story of Eden begins with harmony and oneness. All life, all aspects of Creation, is present in the Garden, these aspects of Creation that God called "good." Only at this stage in the Garden, there is no good and no bad. Things just are. The lion and the lamb lie down together, unafraid of one another, because they are undifferentiated, not named, and don't know their lion-and-lamb nature. Adam and Eve are not aware of their differences. In this state, there is no consciousness, and there is no relationship. This is the original state of "Oneness."

Then Adam and Eve eat from the Tree of Opposites, and they see specific forms, they see male and female, they see obedience and disobedience, they see light and darkness, they see ignorance and knowledge. They are waking up to the birth of consciousness as a newborn child does. There is a "this" and a "that." An up and a down. This familiar kind of awareness is called "dualism." It is the natural state of everyday knowing—"I" am different from "you," and now I have to figure out what "I" is.

The original state of oneness and harmony in the Garden is called "nondualism." In this state, one is not separate from God; more than that, *one is God*. There are both a loss and a gain in moving from nondualism to dualism. And that is in essence the story of the Garden of Eden.

The sequel is ever since we chose the path to become conscious and differentiated, we have been anxious worriers, and the spiritual goal is to return to the Garden, to original peace, to original oneness, also known as Paradise and the New Jerusalem.

The formula is—first we were One, then we became Two, then we became Many, and now we seek to become One (once again, but conscious this time). How this unfolds or how it works is the *drash* understanding of the entire biblical story.

The *drash* understanding also involves the soul, the soul of oneself and the soul of every creature, the soul of the earth. The soul is an enduring remnant of the original nondual state. The sages say there is only one Soul. We think each of us has a separate soul, but there is one soul. Hildegard of Bingen said, "You do not have a soul, the Soul has you." So, in our longing to return to the Garden, one of the pieces of this is to realize the one Soul within. That is our original oneness. The *drash* level of the biblical stories is the soul's awakening to itself, and a growing awareness of whatever aspect of life fades or dies, whatever does not last is not true reality, is not part of original creation.

The Garden of Eden story is the story of moving from nondualism to dualism, something everyone does in our human development. Is this aspect of the Garden story true? The name we give to realizing our original Soul, our Oneness, is "salvation." The *drash* level is even more true than the *remez* stories.

In the Gospel of Thomas (part of the Nag Hammadi collection), the disciples ask Jesus, "Where does all this religious activity end? How does all this end up?" Jesus responded, "You end up where you began."[19]

Sod

There is a fourth level of understanding sacred stories. It is called *sod* in Hebrew, which roughly means secret counsel or wisdom beyond wisdom. This is the story emanating from the Source of all Stories; it is the Story that gives rise to all other stories. It is a story beyond all form, a story without words or concepts. The *sod* level can't be reduced to a "level." It comes from the nondual.

If we were to try to tell a *sod* story, we might begin with the opening words of Genesis, speaking about a time before all time, and a state beyond all form. It might go, "In the beginning God created." Only this needs to be outside of time, so we cross off "~~In the beginning~~." The word "created" is an action, and *sod* is outside of action and doing. So we cross off "~~created~~." That leaves us with the word "God," but God is a human concept that doesn't come close to the Holy of Holies that is beyond all human reach. So in a sense, we cross off "~~God~~."

Does this mean that the *sod* level of understanding is true or not true? The categories of truth or false, good or bad, just don't apply here. We can only slightly "hear" the *sod* level echoing behind the Garden of Eden story, being amazed at how the story ever came about, and being in awe of the Sourceless Source. All we can say is that, along with many other creation stories, the Garden of Eden story has organized human thinking about the significance of life from time before time.

Does the *sod* level of understanding biblical stories reach the highest of the Four Worlds, the Beyond-Beyond? Is the person who understands the transcendent dimension of the story close to God realization, or what the New Testament says is the Kingdom of God? It is hard to say, because there is no ceiling to the *sod* level of understanding.

Every story in the Bible from Genesis to Revelation is subjected to these four levels of understanding and interpretation. Those who insist that "if the Bible says it, it must be true" fail to understand the nature of scripture, which is that the words of the Bible are vulnerable to

---

[19] *The Gospel of Thomas*, trans. by Thomas Lambdin, Gnostic Society Library, (Claremont Graduate School), Saying 18. Jesus says, "Where the beginning is, there the end will be, and he who knows the end will not experience death."

subjective interpretation, and at the same time, there is also a higher level of absolute truth.

Jesus said in effect, I come to a child as a child, I come to a woman as a woman, I come to the poor person as one who is poor, I come to a wealthy person as one who is wealthy, I come to a sage as a sage… I come to every person as a figure they recognize in themselves. The stories in scripture do the same thing: they meet us individually where we are. The drive to find the historical and the factual is at the *pashat* level, the Shariat level of Islam; it is illusory and leads to division, judgment, and separation. That Jesus meets every person at the place where they are self-aware is the *remez* level of understanding; this level is personal, psychological, and cultural according to each person's needs. The *drash* level makes us realize that our mind creates a dualistic interpretation of everything, an interpretation which is always something of an illusion, for every separation is a subjective understanding unique to each person, and it steps away from the oneness of everything. The *sod* level reminds us that ultimately any understanding we have of God is shaped by the limited grasp of mind and our only course is to experience life in its deepest levels, and God will take care of the rest.

If nothing else, the limited awareness of the sacred healing stories of the Bible may be sufficient if one is simply aware of these levels of understanding and appreciates the remarkable reach of these sacred writings that at every level have the touch of soul.

CHAPTER 3

THE IMAGINATION OF THE GARDEN
(Dramatic Dialogues)

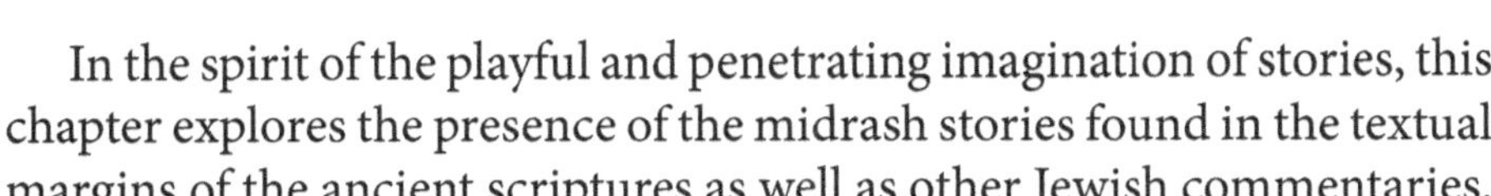

In the spirit of the playful and penetrating imagination of stories, this chapter explores the presence of the midrash stories found in the textual margins of the ancient scriptures as well as other Jewish commentaries. They illuminate the biblical psyche.

Adam and Eve: After Dinner

The man and his wife hid themselves from the presence of the Lord among the trees of the Garden.... And he [Adam] said, "I heard the sound of Thee in the Garden, and I was afraid, because I was naked. And I hid myself..."
— Genesis 3.8, 10

Adam wondered at Eve's nakedness because her glorious outer skin, a sheet of light smooth as a fingernail, had fallen away.[20]
— Pirke de Rabbi Eliezer

Yet through the beauty of her inner body, shining like a white pearl, entranced him, he fought for three hours against this temptation to eat and become as she was, holding the fruit in his hand meanwhile. At last he said, "Eve, I would rather die than outlive you. If Death were to claim your spirit, God could never

---

[20] *Pirke de-Rabbi Eliezar* (Warsaw, 1852) trans Friedlander, (London, 1916) quoted in *The Book of Legends: Sefer Ha-Aggadah*; 94, p. 22.

console me with another woman equaling your loveliness!" So saying, he tasted the fruit, and the outer skin of light fell away from him also.[21]
—Book of Adam

Eve: This is a meal we will remember. The fruit of the Forbidden Tree was not as tasty as I thought it would have been.

Adam: What an understatement!

Eve: Adam, I'm frightened. I'm trying to make sense of what I am experiencing. I feel like I'm vibrating through and through with energy. I feel more alive than ever. I also feel like I am ready to explode or where everything is coming apart inside. I feel like I am coming unglued. I am restless in every organ. Mr. Snake said that people have body experiences like this when they are experiencing a lot of transformation.

Adam: I hope we haven't made a big mistake. I have the strange sense that I am just a part of myself.

Eve: If you had said that before dinner, I would have thought you were off in space philosophizing again. I'm embarrassed to say you make sense.

Adam: I sense that I have lost one part and found another. Say... speaking of losing a part of oneself, when you first took a bite of the fruit from the Tree of Knowledge, you changed physically. I had not noticed your light sheath until it fell off.

Eve: Light sheath?

Adam: Yeah, you had this thin halo of light all over your body. It made you shine, shimmer like an angel. It made you luminescent. But as soon as you began eating, it just fell away. I had never noticed that I have the same light sheath. But when you lost yours, I now see that you and I are different from one another. I was bathed in light and you were not. When I ate of the fruit, my light sheath fell off too. I wonder whether this aura energy went inside our bodies and created this vibrating energy we feel?

Eve: What do you think this energy is?

---

[21] *The Book of Adam* in *The Forgotten Books of Eden*, by Rutherford H. Platt, Jr., [1926], at sacred-texts.com/bib/fbe/fbe006.htm.

Adam: I think it is divine energy. We are made in the image of God, and this light sheath is the God-part which we seem to have lost.

Eve: If eating the fruit of the Tree of Knowledge would further make us like God, giving us the eyes of God, then why would eating the fruit make us lose the God aspect? Isn't divinity what we were seeking in eating the fruit?

Adam: Here's my theory. The loss of the light sheath means that we have become separate from the Divine Parent. We will now have to find another way, some other path to recover our divinity.

Eve: I want to ask a deep question, Adam. When you saw that I had eaten the fruit and lost the light sheath, why did you also eat the fruit, knowing that you too would lose your light sheath?

Adam: That was the hardest decision I have ever had to make. I saw that you were different from me, that there was a deep separation between us. It felt I had to make a choice. I could choose to be like God or be like you. I could be a lover with God or a lover with you. A choice between two different loves. I just couldn't bear the thought of not being with you.

Eve: And so you chose me over God. That's wonderful! That's... [thoughtful pause...], that's scary.

Adam: I can understand the monastic path. To be married with the Light. But somehow it feels that my destiny lies in finding God-dedness by struggle and searching, rather than accepting unconsciously what has been given. You lose your life to find it.

Eve: You lose your light to find it. Before dinner we saw only our illuminated selves clothed in the light sheath. Now we see beyond that, for it has fallen away. We see into our humanness.

Adam: And what do we see?

Eve: I see that you and I are different, male and female. Before I saw our unity, our commonness. Now I see our uniqueness. I feel for the first time a chosen relatedness. Before, it was a kind of given togetherness. Now I am aware of a field of choice where I am conscious that I have some say about to what and to whom I will give my energy and intentionally be connected. That's why it startled me so, when you said you chose me rather than God. It is a new experience to feel chosen. I am a receiver and I am a giver. That is what I see first as I look at our humanness.

Adam: Yes, being human has something to do with being conscious and making choices. You have said something very powerful, Eve. We have eaten the fruit of the Tree of Knowledge, and we not only have a future, but now we have the power to shape our future. We now have time. Before dinner, there was no future. It was more of the same, divine steady state. Now there is change. Evolution, let's call it. And choices. And that means newness. And that gives us the future, which is not like now. Being human means we get to say who we are and who we want to be. We get to recreate ourselves! In any image we choose. Wow!

Eve: There you go philosophizing again. Whenever you want to fly into the sky in your thoughts, I have this urge to earth and ground. I guess that is another aspect of our differences. Sometimes, it's the other way around too, where I will have a transcending thought, and you can be the anchor. [pause...] Adam, I am beginning to feel anxious again. How is God is going to feel about what we have done? I don't think I want to share all my thoughts with God.

Adam: My first impulse is to hide. We are going to have to work this out on our own. God is not going to take care of everything anymore. God will do God's things in God's realm, and we will have to tend to matters in our own realm. My suggestion is that we talk to God about sacred things, religious thoughts, and that we need to be sure to give God lots of positive strokes. But things that have to do with separateness, human seeing, doubts, and less than lofty thoughts—these things we better keep to ourselves. It seems that before we ate the fruit, we could hold our ground in the presence of God, but we no longer can hold that ground.

Eve: Oh, there's the Ruach-Wind rustling again. God is coming. Oh dear, I wish we had time to talk about all this! Adam, I'm scared! Let's hide!

Seeing Differences

Then the eyes of both of them were opened and they perceived that they were naked; and they sewed together fig leaves and made themselves loincloths.
— Genesis 3:7 (Tanakh version)

God: Adam, where are you?

Adam: [silence...]

God: Aaadaaaammmmm. This is not like you. Where aaaaare youuuuu???

Adam: Ahem! [as in clearing the throat]

God: Adam, come stand on your ground. Where are you? Why are you hiding in the Garden?

Adam: Ahhhh... we're, ...we're over here. Behind the bushes.

God: Why are you hiding? Have you done something wrong?

Adam: Well, ahhh, we have learned that we are naked, and it is not right to dishonor the Lord with one's nakedness.

God: Naked! Adam, what does naked mean to you?

Adam: Uhhh... Naked means we can see our true selves. It means nothing is hidden. It means we see our differences. While differences mean that we are separate, we have come up with a new invention that is effective in hiding our differences. We call it clothes.

God: Nakedness has nothing to do with truth. Nakedness inspires hiddeness. People seem to be more honest with their clothes on. That's why I will go along with the clothes. You need earthly clothes of fig leaves and skins because you have lost the heavenly clothing of light and holiness.

Adam: I've been meaning to see my tailor....

God: Who told you that you were naked?

Adam: Oh, your creation, Mr. Snake, did. Snake has been so helpful. Snake has been helping us become self-actualized. Snake has been talking with us about being human.

God: Damn the Snake! No, Snake has been talking to you about playing God. Snake has opened up Pandora's box. This changes the rules, you know.

Adam: Rules? What rules?

God: There shall be no other gods but me. You have upset the Order of the universe.

Adam: We were just trying to grow and to achieve our full potential. We wanted to develop our divine parts so we could improve our relationship with you. We had no intention, God, of taking over your job.

God: I told you *not* to eat the fruit of the Tree of Knowledge. It was my first commandment: You must learn the limits of your human-ness.

Adam: God, uhhh, let me put it this way. If there was a pill, some medicine, that you could take that would enhance your Goddedness and make you even fuller in your divine potential, wouldn't it be imperative that you take this medicine? It would be unethical to refuse to become the highest God possible.

God: Adam, you are absolutely missing the point. Furthermore, I don't like it when you talk to me like this. The ground on which you stand is dangerous. To be the human being I created with my own hands means that you must find your own soul before you can ascend in the divine spirit. You have not yet learned about the ground you stand on. You lack cosmic perspective. Don't talk to me in such arrogance. Your words enflame my anger.

Adam: When you created me with your own hands, that act was different from the rest of creation. The rest of creation you created with your speech. But you made me *with your hands* as a potter works with clay. You moistened me with your own hands and made me juicy. You blew your own breath into me. You shaped me. You looked into the mirror and made the shape of what you saw. You created Eve and me in your very image. You made me like God. You gave me the power to shape myself, just as you were doing. You prided yourself in making me in the likeness of you, and you called me good, ... or called me god. Ooops, just kidding. I liked the pun between good and god.

You are the creative artist, O God. But there is something that seems to be missing. Everything that every artist creates—every being, every poem, every painting, every book, every creation has a soul of its own. Every creation of an artist has a separate life and, *by necessity,* must talk back and challenge the artist. It is not my arrogance, not my entitlement bidding that I speak with you with such boldness. It is the necessity of artistic form. The created thing must challenge and transform the creator.

God: Hmmmmm. I hadn't planned on the lack of cooperation of my own art. Willfulness! That's what eating the fruit of the Tree of Knowledge does. It allows you to look into the mirror and remake yourself in whatever shape you choose. I thought that when you looked in the mirror, you would see your goddedness in my image. But you saw what I didn't see. You saw the shadow of God. It makes you perverse. It marks a distance of greater separation between us. This affects our relationship.

Adam: But it also lights up the path for a more complex form of unity. We can become one, not because you willed us to be together. We can be together as one because *both of us* willed us to be together. That's a superior form of togetherness, isn't it?

God: I see your point, Adam. Henceforth, relationship is not simply a given. Relationship on both your part and on my part will be a matter of intention. The relationship between separation and loving attachment will have to be negotiated afresh each time. I can see this is going to be a lot more work.

Adam: But also more interesting, eh!

Who Initiated the Break with God?

The LORD God took the man and placed him in the garden of Eden, to till it and tend it. And the LORD God commanded the man, saying, "Of every tree of the garden you are free to eat; but as for the Tree of Knowledge of Good and Bad, you must not eat of it; for as soon as you eat of it, you shall die."
— Genesis 2:15-17 (Tanach version)

The sages say we end up where we began, which we understand is the nondual state, the state of oneness with all. This is the ultimate healing. This nondual state may be beyond our imagination, but the story of the Garden of Eden speaks of this absolute harmony.

Maybe I should have said "near-absolute." We tend to blame Adam and Eve for breaking the spell by disobeying the rule: "There is a Tree of Opposites (A Tree of the Knowledge of Good and a Tree of the Knowledge of Evil), i.e., a Tree of Dualism, here in the Garden. And God was rather blunt—"Don't eat of it! Just don't!"

Eve and Adam: Well then, why did you put it there? Are you trying to push us out of this State of Oneness? If anyone has disrupted the state of Oneness, it is You, O God! Furthermore, we never set up the dualistic state of Life and Death. They are going to pin "Original Sin" on us, but it is You who started this Game.

God: I was simply wanting to test your obedience.

Eve and Adam: Why? Obedience suggests disobedience. That sounds like dualism to us! We never thought of obeying or disobeying until You brought it up. Do you want disharmony? Is this Tree-thing a trick? Maybe it's *You* who is not obedient with your creation. Maybe you want to destroy what you have created!

God: I don't like your accusations and insolent questions. Having differences and conflicts is not part of the Original Plan. But maybe you are right that if I created everything, it seems as though I created the bad as well as the good. I created nondualism as well as dualism.

Adam and Eve: Well it looks like you also created Free Will to choose from other options. Free Will, by definition, means we do not have to do what You, O God, want. From here, it looks like you might have shot YourSelf in the foot. We're just not sure who the bad guy is here.

God: Yeah, creating willfulness may have been one of my mistakes. This is going to create some serious Karma.

Where Did Evil Come From?

Now the serpent was the shrewdest of all the wild beasts that the LORD God had made. He said to the woman, "Did God really say: You shall not eat of any tree of the garden?" The woman replied to the serpent, "We may eat of the fruit of the other trees of the garden. It is only about the fruit of the tree in the middle of the garden that God said: 'You shall not eat of it or touch it, lest you die.'" And the serpent said to the woman, "You are not going to die, but God knows that as soon as you eat of it your eyes will be opened and you will be like divine beings who know good and bad.
— Genesis 3:1-6 (Tanakh version)

The 'Yetzer Hara' [evil inclination] was riding on the snake in order to make (the snake) responsible for the downfall of Adam and Chava [the Mother of all Life].
— Midrash Rabbah 20:1

"Haven't you separated from your wife for 130 years because death was decreed on the world because of you?"
— Rashi Bereishis 4:25, based on Midrash Rabbah 23:5

All the spiritual paths ask us to look at our core or original self, beyond all the outer "husks" of being in a temporary body and carrying one's present ego-identity. One of the places to look for original "being" is the Garden of Eden, not in the mythic details of the Garden itself, but at the state of oneness. Oneness is where our story begins.

The Serpent interrupts the state of unanimity and anonymity. All the creatures in the garden lack any definition they will have later. The lion lies down with the lamb, each unaware of their true nature. True, except for the Serpent, who seems to be an oppositional figure. Some say the snake is Satan, but that is reading a future dualism back into the story of nondualism. Where does the Serpent come from? Is the Serpent part of the original creation?

The midrash says the serpent has "Yetzer Hara," which every Jew knows is the evil inclination. Where does this come from? Are Good and Evil part of the Original Creation? No, Good and Evil are dualistic and do not belong in the original state, and do not belong to essential human nature. We are not born having an evil inclination, no matter what Original Sin says.

In holding to the original oneness, we ask, is the Serpent really God in disguise? Is the Serpent another Face of God? The Shadow of God? Does the Serpent belong in the Trinity or Quaternity? Do we violate the Oneness by creating a Shadow Hell to quarantine the evil inclination?

Another question: For some odd reason in the human psyche, we like to sexualize Eve and sexualize the Serpent. They are the source of our lustful nature (just ask Hollywood). It is in this direction that I included the Jewish midrash passage that said after Adam and Eve ate the forbidden fruit (which allowed them to realize their individual nakedness), the myth explains they stopped having sex for 130 years. Our inner psyche is multileveled, but I have seen couples stop sex for a lot less.

And from the ground the LORD God caused to grow every tree that was pleasing to the sight and good for food, with the Tree of Life in the middle of the garden, and the Tree of Knowledge of Good and Bad.
— Genesis 2:9 (Tanach version)

The Two Trees

Eve: I've been thinking about the Tree in the Garden. There were two Trees, really. The other one we never approached, although I yearn for it. The Tree of Immortality. Then we could have truly been like God. It is now out of our reach. It means that someday each of us will die, and each of us will be left alone.

Adam: I grieve that day, my beloved Eve. [pause...] I think we had a choice... back there in the Garden. We could have chosen sex and the pleasures of intimacy, or we could have chosen immortality. We could have chosen either Tree, but not both Trees. We chose sex, and I'm all for it. However, sex and death are partners. In choosing one, we choose the other, for without death, sex and procreation would exhaust the planet.

Eve: I, too, am glad we chose the way of sex and procreation. I just wonder about the other Tree.

Adam: You shall be known as the Mother of All Life and you shall be known as the Mother of Death.

Eve: I shuddered when you said that. I wish I could just be a local person, here and now, not some archetypal figure that people revere or curse. We've been talking about lofty ideas that hold considerable life force—Paradise, the Tree of Immortality, the Tree of Good and Evil, Mother of Life, Mother of Death, sexual union, consciousness. These seem almost larger than life.

Adam: The soul invents figures and experiences that are larger than life for the Gods to be served.

Eve: Why do you say Gods in the plural sense?

Adam: When we were in the Garden, there was but one God, but outside of the Garden, God is manifest in as many forms as we can possibly imagine. Inside the Garden, we were monotheistic. Here in the Land of Nod, in the land of *homo schitzein,* the land of the Many, as opposed to the One, we are polytheistic.

Eve: So you are saying that there is a god served in every one of these archetypal images?

Adam: Yes, that's the way I see it. It is our job to find that aspect of divinity within each archetypal form, for that is what eating the fruit of the Tree of Knowledge has commissioned us to do.

Hiding

Eve: Ever since I ate the fruit of the Tree of Knowledge, I have had this urge to hide. That doesn't seem right. If this were a Tree of God, why do I seem to favor Darkness rather than Light?

The Serpent: It is a strange beginning, isn't it? There is a necessary rebellion required for separation from the parent, or from God, for that matter. It doesn't work just to have the parent's permission to leave. The child must *willfully* initiate separation. There has to be a dramatic act that says no, I will do it my way!

Eve: What does this have to do with hiding?

The Serpent: Well, the child *finds him or herself* in hiding. The child learns to keep secrets from the parent.

Eve: And parents hate it. They demand the child be honest and absolutely open. "Thou shalt have no secrets from Mommy and Daddy."

The Serpent: Secrets are one of the forms in which a child develops a life of his or her own. A child develops over time a set of experiences unknown to the parent. Some are deliberate violations of the parent's rules. Others are inadvertent indiscretions. All this independence is kept within the core of the emerging self, and maintained with subtle lies and avoidances.

Eve: It all has such an ominous and sinister feel to it. Why does becoming human arise from such deception and injury to relationships?

The Serpent: I don't know. But it is interesting to see that hiddenness is one of the primary attributes of God. *Mysterium Divinum.* The soul emerges from the depths and dark places. The sacred is surrounded in mystery. Being both human and being divine seems to embrace what the eye cannot see and what the mind cannot know.

Eve: This is an interesting turn in our conversation. I see we are talking about several kinds of hiddenness. When I am hiding because I am avoiding and dishonest, that is a kind of hiding that hurts me. I am hiding from myself. There is another kind of hiding where I find myself. Sometimes when I am hiding this way, I am being introverted or a hermit or a mystic. And then there is the hiddenness of what is divine, higher, and sacred, what is at the core of things. Why this last kind of hiddenness, the hiddenness of God?

The Serpent: The infinite cannot be held or contained. It is not that God wants to withhold God's glory. But the path of wisdom is a path of hiddenness and unknowing, a path of humility arising out of a sense of proportion and perspective. The danger in eating the Fruit of the Tree of Knowledge is that one forgets proportion and perspective amidst such beauty and beholding. The hubris is not in disobeying God and eating the fruit, it is in losing sight of one's limitedness once one eats the fruit. This is why you must be careful when you pray.

Eve: What do you mean?

The Serpent: We cannot imagine the fullness and glory of God in our highest imagination. We fill this gap with the longings and inadequacies of our undeveloped selves, that is our hidden selves. This does not sufficiently meet what God offers to us.

Eve: Well, I can see that my uneasiness about hiding was just the tip of the iceberg, that I was acting out a theme that is destined to hold much more for me if I pay attention to it.

Atonement

But it is just and fitting for us to lament in the sight of God who made us. Let us repent with a great penitence; perhaps the Lord God will be forbearing and pity us and provide for us that we might live. And Eve said to Adam, "My Lord, tell me, what is repentance and what kind of repentance should I do, lest by chance...the Lord not hear our prayers and turn his face from us because we did not keep our promise. My Lord, how much did you intend to repent...?
— *The Life of Adam and Eve [Vita], 4.3-5.2 (Old Testament Pseudepigrapha)*

After partaking of the fruit of the Tree of Knowledge and being banished from the Garden of Eden, Adam and Eve fell into a deep guilt and major depression. They each sought to find a way to wash off the stain of shame and loss. An ancient text[22] depicts Eve standing in the Tigris River up to her neck for eleven months, day and night. Adam chose an even more sacred river for his cleansing, the Jordan. One imagines their joining together following this ordeal:

Adam: Ahhhh man, my skin looks absolutely like a dried prune.

Eve: Mine too. I feel like I've aged thirty years.

Adam: It didn't work, did it! There is no way to wash off the stain of what we did. We are marked just as Cain is marked for his transgression, only you can't see our blemished humanity. It is there, nevertheless.

Eve: Oh Adam, what are we going to do? I can't get rid of my depression. I have cried enough tears to turn the Tigris into salt water. Is there any way to win with God? Is there any possible way to even find our ground with God? To be acceptable as creatures of the divine?

Adam: I don't know. I have been giving it a lot of thought. I keep having thoughts that atonement requires death.

Eve: You mean suicide?

Adam: Well, not really. Not that I haven't thought about that. Sometimes I would rather be dead than go on feeling like this. But I

---

[22] *The Old Testament Pseudepigrapha*, Vol. II, *"The Life of Adam and Eve,"* ed., by James H. Charlesworth (Garden City: Doubleday & Company, Inc., 1985) 7.1.

have been thinking about martyrdom. You know, doing something heroic and losing one's life for God. Maybe that might help.

Eve: Well, if that was the answer to sin, then everybody who wants to be good would die and that would leave all the no-good people left. Then how would the world stand a chance of improving? Martyrdom sounds like the path of entropy. All the saints are gone. Jesus! Atonement is a screwed-up idea.

Adam: Getting rid of the effects of sin is a lot harder than doing the sinning. I can foresee where the debt and weight of sin will be a whole lot harder than the reservoir of goodness. The whole system is stacked. The bad outweighs the good. We are in a no-win situation. Entropy is the rule of the universe.

Eve: God! I can just see it. Sin keeps mounting up. People will look for someone to blame. Before you know it, they will be pointing at us, saying *we* did it all. *We* started the world's ruin. Theology will be based on this crap. I can just see it: Original Sin!

Adam: Well, with this worrying, we are working ourselves into an even worse state. I don't have the sense that God has this worked out yet, but what we are talking about is such a serious flaw in creation that life will lose all sacredness, all beauty. Surely God will have to develop a plan to address the problem of sin and the difficulty of getting over its effects. I can't believe that God wants the human psyche and personality to be based on shame and guilt.

Eve: Well, all I can say is standing in the river doesn't do any good.

Adam: Have you noticed that we keep encountering situations where it looks as though there is no way out, and then something happens where a new solution emerges out of the blue? Life is impossible, and then sure enough, the impossible happens.

[an interlude]

The following dialogue is based on a rabbinic midrash:[23]

---

[23] *Tanhuma,* a midrash on the Pentateuch based on the sayings of Rabbi Tanhuma bar Abba, a Palestinian Talmudic sage of the fourth century A.D.; *Genesis Rabba,* 216-220 is a midrash on the book of Genesis compiled in the fifth century in

Adam: Cain? Cain? I can't believe it is you! Did you not kill your brother Abel? When I saw how God punished us for eating the fruit of the Tree of Knowledge, I thought you would surely have faced capital punishment for murder. Cain! Is it really you? I thought I would never see you again.

Cain: Yes, it is me, Cain! Where have you been? I haven't seen you in a long time.

Adam: Eve and I were on a special mission of atonement, trying to do something about our damned guilt. We have been standing in the river. If baptism in the river cleanses one of sin, we thought we could get cleansed. It doesn't work. How are *you* coping, Cain? Have you been wracked with guilt? Why didn't God kill you for killing your brother, an eye for an eye?

Cain: Well, I repented, Father, and was forgiven. Forgiven by God.

Adam: Forgiven?... Forgiven!... FORGIVEN! [smiting his head with the heel of his hand]. Such is the power of repentance? Forgiven! Now why didn't I think of that!

Noah: A Second Chance

And God blotted out every living thing that was on the face of the ground, man and animals and creeping things and birds of the heavens. They were blotted out from the earth. Only Noah was left, and those who were with him in the ark.
— Genesis 7:23

God: I see the wickedness of man, my creation. I repent, and I am sorry for having created man. I will blot out this thing I have made.

Noah: Rather than destroy your creation, don't you have another option?

Palestine, and published in the critical edition of J. Theodor and Ch. Albeck, Berlin, 1912-27, 2 vols. Quoted in Graves and Patai, *Hebrew Myths*, 93.

God: I have made a mistake. I will destroy humankind and the animals and the earth. Noah, make an ark and take two of every kind of creature and I will start over. We will call it Creation II.

Noah: When we were kicked out of the Garden, angels of great force prevented all return to the Garden, much as we wanted to return to the original First State. Have you changed your mind, God? Is this Flood a return to the Garden of Eden?

CHAPTER 4

WHAT HAPPENED ON MOUNT MORIAH?

(37 Midrash Stories)

---

*Some time afterward, God put Abraham to the test. He said to him, "Abraham,"
and he answered, "Here I am." And he said, "Take your son, your favored one,
Isaac, whom you love and go to the land of Moriah, and offer him there as a
burnt offering in one of the heights that I will point out to you.*
— Genesis 22:1-2

The enigmatic story of Abraham's sacrifice of Isaac is a pivotal moment in Jewish history, and perhaps the core breakthrough in spiritual evolution in the Bible prior to Jesus. It is a story that defies any definitive interpretation; its greatness lies in its ability to transcend every interpretation. Traditionally taken as a demonstration of Abraham's faith and worthiness of the Father of the nation of Israel, it remains as stunningly outrageous in every respect—in its depiction of fidelity and moral choice, its questionable modeling of fatherhood, and its bizarre portrayal of a God who would ask Abraham to make such a choice.

The story is called the *Akedah* in Judaism. In Hebrew, *Akedah* means "binding;" Jews prefer "binding" to "sacrifice." The "binding of Isaac" is a high mystery, forcing us to surrender all our certainties as we ponder its many dimensions. It seems to function as something like a spiritual Rorschach test, so provocative are its archetypal elements.

Nineteenth century Danish theologian Søren Kierkegaard follows in the spirit of the Jewish midrash by creating a number of spiritual improvisations that rival Mozart in their beauty and creativity. In good Jewish tradition, we will follow the imagination of this story in similar fashion, appreciating its myriad forms and nuances, each which lifts up a dimension of soul. The following stories are based on the biblical midrash; they reflect the Jewish imagination and mirror doubt and faith, soul loss, wounded soul, and triumphant soul of the spiritual journey to God. The following stories of the imagination and the soul found in the Jewish psyche offer clues to the healing of the soul.

The story of the binding of Isaac is almost a parable in form, unsolvable, multileveled, evocative, and challenging. This may be the ultimate spiritual teaching form, for like an undecipherable Buddhist koan, it draws us into it, forcing us to find a solution only by surrender and moving into a new consciousness. In ancient Hebrew, the parable itself was called a *mashal*. The effort to decode the parable, that is, to uncover the story within ourselves that gets hooked by the parable, leads us into aspects of the story that twist and confuse us until we collapse and let go, thereby finding a new and higher truth—this "second story" was called *nimshal*. We shall approach both the *mashal* and the *nimshal* of Abraham's "sacrificing" of Isaac in search of one of the most powerful healing stories ever told.

The following midrash versions of the story are all embedded in ancient Jewish, midrash, and Hasidic literature. They could be seen as falling into four groups: (1) the loss of order, (2) who or what was sacrificed?, (3) does faith need to be tested?, and (4) becoming One with God.

PART 1: THE LOSS OF ORDER

-I-
Abraham is forced to choose the son he loved most

And the Lord commanded Abraham, putting him to the final test. "Take now thy son."
"But I have two sons," Abraham replied.
"Take thine only son," the Lord said.

"But I have two only-sons," Abraham rejoined.
"Take the one thou lovest most," the Lord commanded.
"But I love them both," Abraham said.
"Take the one you love best," the Lord insisted.
"But I love them both," Abraham said.
"Very well, then take Isaac, your son..."[24]

It was "Sophie's choice"[25] to be forced into the ungodly decision to choose between your own children. To decide who lives and who dies. It is not a human decision. Whom do you love the most? Whom do you love the least? To answer the question is to forever wound both children as well as the parent. O cruel love that so divides the heart. Such a decision that kills the human spirit also kills God. O God who kills divinity.

-II-
Is sacrifice a religious virtue?

Abraham did not know what to do with the knife he used to cut the rope that bound his son. A knife has both binding and freeing aspects, but for him, he wanted it out of sight. Abraham had a business in world trade, and he knew about other cultures in the region. The sacrifice of the first son was a common practice as an action to appease or show deference for the gods. His father's business of selling idols to appease the fear and terror of people's experience was a fake strategy imposed both by royalty and religion.

Even though all his life Abraham carried a deep anxiety in his bones, he eschewed the idea of human sacrifice, and even more when it was made personal as a family practice. Human sacrifice was based on fear. Surely this is not desired by the God he now followed! There had to be a higher way of connection with the divine.

---

[24] This dialogue appears in a midrashic account, but with a different intent, i.e., an effort to say that God dragged out such a command so that Abraham would not be as stunned by this heart-rending. command. Tanhuma, *Va-yera*, § 22-23. *Pirke de Rabbi Eliezer*, 31. The story here is quoted in *The Book of Legends Sefer Ha-Aggadah: Legends from the Talmud and the Midrash*, 40.

[25] This is a reference to a William Styron novel about a woman in the Nazi concentration camps who was forced to choose between her two children, which one would live and which would die at the hands of the Nazi guards.

The problem of sacrifice troubled Abraham. It seemed that another way was needed to find intimacy with God, a way that involved desire and relationship. It seemed to him that the way to God involved the requirement of *work*, of personal effort and intention. Such work would involve facing and engagement with the primal instincts of the psyche, addressing the egoic aspects of fear, and work that established one in the higher aspects of the promise of life.

-III-
Abraham's Father refuses to sacrifice his son

Nimrod, king of Mesopotamia, sent word to Terah [Abraham's father] saying, "Last night a son was born to you. Now give him to me that we may slay him, and I will fill your house with silver and gold." Terah said, lying, "A son was born, but he died." Nimrod said, "My offer was for a live son, not a dead one." And Terah hid his son in a cave for three years.[26]

And Abraham remembered that the King had asked his Father to also give him up to sacrifice, but his Father had refused. Abraham wondered whether he should refuse the King [God] and save the life of his son, Isaac, as his Father had done. Was the sacrifice of the son a pattern of generations, a pattern where Isaac's firstborn [Esau then Jacob] would rejected, and then Isaac's Grandson [Joseph, first born of Rachel] would be slain as well? What is the meaning of the lethal risk to the firstborn? Why does God kill his beloved son?

-IV-
Isaac experiences resurrection

When the knife touched Isaac's neck, his soul left him. At that moment God made his voice heard among the angels, saying, "Do not lay your hand on the boy," and his soul returned to his body. And Isaac rose to his feet, and Isaac knew that in this way the dead would return to life. He knew God as One who is greater than death, and who can bring the

---

[26] *Sefer Ha-Aggadah* (*Book of Legends*) ed. by Hayim Bialik & Yehoshua Revnitzky (New York: Schocken Books, 1992), p. 31.

dead back to life. He knows the dead will be revived, not through the teaching of prophets, but because it happened to him. And Isaac opened his mouth and declared, "Blessed are you, God who revives the dead."[27]

-V-

Does God favor some children over others?

And God said to Abraham, "Take the child you love the most."[28] "But I love them the same," said Abraham, appalled that the Holy One would ask him to choose. Does God choose between his people, blessing some and cursing others?

And Abraham fell into a deep sleep and dreamed that God was asked, "Who is the greatest in the world to come?" And God brought forth a child and said, "You must be like a child before me,[29] innocent before what is beyond understanding, trusting in my love and care." So Abraham awoke and said to himself, "There are no children that the Holy One loves the most. A good father loves them all the same. There are no chosen children of God, no hierarchy with the Holy One, for all are equal and all are the same in the eyes of the Holy One. Even when one is fallen, they are the beloved child of the Holy One."

So Abraham went before God and said, "You have broken your Holy Way in asking me to choose the one I love most. For like You, I love them all."

And God repented of his error and saw that Abraham had momentarily more faith than the Almighty.

-VI-

Abraham's father wound

"I had always wanted to be a father," thought Abraham. "I had always wanted to repair the damage with my own father, Terah, and leave a legacy of fathering that will bless all fathers. Here, at last, in my old age,

---

[27] From Pirkei de-Rabbi Eliezer, 31, quoted in Avivah Gottlieb Zornberg, *The Murmuring Deep: Reflections on the Biblical Unconscious* (New York: Schocken Books, 2009), p. 241.

[28] Tanhuma, *Va-yera*, § 22-23. *Pirke de Rabbi Eliezer*, 31.

[29] Matthew 18:1-4.

I finally have the chance to do that. A chance to embody the Divine Father. Now this happens! How does this show fatherly love?

"I don't understand the legacy of the Akedah."

-VII-
Losing to become whole

Abraham remembered the time when God had said *Lech Lekha*, "Go forth into the land of your becoming." Again God had come to him, and God said, "Walk in my ways and become whole,"[30] and the way to become whole and blameless and many, is to become circumcised. "I had thought I was whole before I was circumcised, thought Abraham, but now a part of me must be cut off. Somehow, wholeness is framed in losing a part of myself. My name was changed from Abram (exalted father) to Abraham (father of many).

Now, here on this mountain, I face another *lech lecha* moment of a new kind of becoming, and once again such wholeness involves losing another part of myself, my beloved son. It is a paradox to lose oneself to become whole."

-VIII-
Isaac's blindness

While Isaac lay on the altar of God, the angels cried and their tears fell like rain into his eyes.[31] His blindness was the result of the pain of the angels. They were crying because they were unhappy with God. Even the tears of the angels failed to move the heart of God. Yea, even heaven was divided against itself. Indeed, it was heaven that found itself blind.

It was Isaac's eyes that seemed to hold the secret meaning of the Event. Undoubtedly, his seeing was forever changed by what happened on the altar. Was it the terror of hell that he saw? Or the terror of heaven? Nonetheless, his eyes grew dim. He never left home to see what lay

---

[30] Genesis 17:1-2.

[31] *Bereshit Rabbah*, ed Wilma, 1887, 65, 4-10. This is a midrash around Isaac's blessing of Jacob in Genesis 27, reprinted in Louis Ginzberg's *Legends of the Jews*.

beyond the horizon of his life. He failed to see the beauty and fullness of his wife Rebekah, and so his gaze turned toward his firstborn son; even there, he failed to see the tragedy of Esau's life. His blindness also prevented him from seeing through the mask of his son Jacob, that impersonator seeking a Blessing promised to another. His failure to see made him look like a fool. His lack of insight was the shame of the *Akedah*. It turned out to be a congenital matter, this family blindness. Jacob's eyes grew dim as well.

But was Isaac's seeing as impaired as it seemed? Perhaps it was out of his sharpened inner seeing that he saw the hidden unfolding of God's way manifesting in the younger son, the one who until then had not had his Father's Blessing. Perhaps in his inner seeing, Isaac knew all too well to whom he was blessing, and therein he was drying the tears of the angels, and thereby redeeming Heaven.

-IX-
Abraham would rather have Isaac see him as a monster than God

But Isaac was unable to understand his father Abraham. His soul could not be exalted. He embraced Abraham's knees, fell at his feet imploringly. He begged for his young life, for the fair hope in the future. He spoke of the joy in Abraham's house. He called to mind the sorrow and loneliness. Then Abraham lifted up the boy. He walked with him by his side, and his talk was full of comfort and exhortation. But Isaac could not understand him. He climbed Mount Moriah, but Isaac understood him not.

Then for an instant, Abraham turned away from him. And when Isaac again saw Abraham's face, it was changed. His glance was wild, his form was horror. He seized Isaac by the throat, threw him to the ground, and said, "Stupid boy, dost thou then suppose that I am thy father? I am an idolater. Dost thou suppose that this is God's bidding? No! It is *my* desire."

Then Isaac trembled and cried out in his terror, "O God in heaven, have compassion upon me. God of Abraham, have compassion upon me! If I have no father upon earth, be Thou my Father!"

But Abraham, in a low voice said to himself, "O Lord in heaven, I thank Thee. After all, it is better for him to believe that I am a monster, rather than that he should lose faith in Thee."[32]

-X-
A religion that requires death

The sweet smell of lamb and the pungent aroma of the charred remains still scented the air around the cairn of piled stones—the altar on which Isaac had been bound, the altar which binds us all.

"There is something incongruous about 'sacred sacrifice,'" Abraham reflected. "The God of life requires death. A religion that upheld all life makes more sense. Such a religion would not even take the life of this innocent lamb. The ram's severed coiled horns lay on the ground nearby—the very horns that had entrapped the poor animal in the vines. "I'll cut off the tips of the horns and use them as a trumpet to call forth the people," Abraham thought. "And I will remember this experience of God's providing on the mountain."

In thinking about the symbolism of the ram's horns, suddenly Abraham asked, "I wonder whether the sacrifice is also better taken as symbolic as well. No longer would sacrifice be to kill to satisfy a bloodthirsty God. God does not require blood and the spilling of the Life-Force. The sacrifice has to do with letting go, letting death. It has to do with releasing the lesser that the greater may live. How can *sacre-ficio*, sacred-making, be life-giving? What needs to die for there to be life? Not relationships. Not a parent's love. Not life of any kind.

"What needs to die is illusion. Attachments that block and limit. Views that lessen Reality. Clinging to our lesser pictures of God. Trying to preserve our immature theories of being saved and the way to Heaven—all this has to go. The sacrifice is to burn all of our sacred habits, that we make room for the Light we cannot yet see."

---

[32] Søren Kierkegaard, *Fear and Trembling* (Garden City, New York: Doubleday, 1954), 27.

PART 2: WHO OR WHAT WAS SACRIFICED?

-XI-
Who was being tested?—God?

Isaac, the child, grew up and was weaned; and Abraham made a great feast on the day that Isaac was weaned.[33] The midrash goes on to say that after these things, i.e., the feast of celebration, Satan spoke to the Lord God, saying, "Master of the universe, out of the entire feast that this old man, upon whom You bestowed fruit of the womb at the age of one hundred,—out of the entire feast that he prepared, could he not have spared, say a single turtledove, one fledgling as an offering to you?"

God replied, "Is it not true that Abraham prepared the feast in honor of his son? Still, if I say to him, 'Sacrifice your son to me,' he will sacrifice him at once."

Satan said, "Try him."

Immediately after that, God tested Abraham.[34]

In the days after Abraham and his son Isaac returned from the test on the Mountain of the Lord, Abraham called upon the Lord, and asked, "All my life I have followed your commands. You have known of my faithfulness. Why then did you test me yet again, asking me to sacrifice my son Isaac? "

God replied to Abraham, "You have been faithful and righteous in matters both great and small."

"Then why must I prove myself and be put to the test?" Abraham implored.

"It was Satan who questioned your faithfulness," said the Lord.

"Then whose faith was being tested?" cried Abraham. "Was it *your* faith, O God?"

And the Lord was silent and did not answer Abraham.

-XII-

Abraham is the one being sacrificed

---

[33] Genesis 21.8.

[34] B. Sanhedrin 89b. The story here is quoted in *The Book of Legends Sefer Ha-Aggadah: Legends from the Talmud and the Midrash*, p. 39.

"Why?" wondered Abraham, "Why am I being tested? Is being tested essential to the spiritual journey? Is faith not enough? Or love? Do I follow a God who doesn't believe? Is this karma? Does this test to sacrifice Isaac have background cause?

"I have been tested all my life. I can easily count ten major tests.[35] I was thrown into the fiery furnace. I was told to leave my home and become a stranger in a strange land. I was made to send away Hagar with my firstborn son Ishmael to another foreign land. The king of Gerar took in my beloved Sarah, intending to take her for himself. There were other tests, all of them painful.

"I have assumed that such challenges are not to test my obedience, for I believe my obedience does not need to be questioned, but to break me out of old ways of thinking, and free me up for something greater. "The aim [of testing] would be to take one through an experience that will remap a world of self-knowledge with transformative clarity."[36]

-XIII-
Abraham is sacrificed…sending Ishmael away

And so Ishmael, the first born son to Abraham, said to Isaac, "Come let us test our mettle in the field." Then Ishmael took bows and arrows and shot them in Isaac's direction, pretending that he was merely making sport. Isaac was not aware that his life was in danger. And Sarah, mother of Isaac, saw Ishmael making sport of Isaac, and so she told Abraham, demanding that Ishmael and his mother Hagar be exiled from the family. It came to pass that Ishmael and his mother sought refuge in the wilderness of Paran.[37]

---

[35] Cited in *Pirkei de Rabbi Eliezer*, 26, and by Maimonides, *Commentary to the Mishnah ad loc.*, where the sacrifice of Isaac is the tenth test.

[36] Avivah Gottlieb Zornberg, *The Murmuring Deep: Reflections on the Biblical Unconscious* (New York: Schocken Books, 2009), p. 170.

[37] This story is from the midrash Genesis Rabbah: Julius Theodor [1849-1924], *Midrash Bereschit Rabbah*, Berlin, 1907-17; completed by Chanoch Albeck [1890-1972] 53:11, *Minhat Yehudah*, Berlin 1928-36, and from *Pirke de Rabbi Eliezer*, (Warsaw, 1852), trans Gerald Friedlander [1971-1923] (London, 1916) 30. The story here is quoted in *The Book of Legends Sefer Ha-Aggadah: Legends from the Talmud*

At the end of three years, Abraham missed his son Ishmael and longed to satisfy himself as to the well-being of his firstborn. But Sarah prevailed upon Abraham, that should he ever visit Ishmael, he would not dismount from his camel. To maintain peace in his home, Abraham so promised.

Now Ishmael had taken a woman from the land of Moab as his wife; her name was Aissa. When the father Abraham approached the place where Ishmael was living, it was midday and the sun was hot. Abraham found Aissa, Ishmael's wife, and asked, "Where is Ishmael? " "He is out in the desert with his mother gathering fruit and brooms." And Abraham tested Ishmael.

"Behold the day is hot, " Abraham said, "Please give me a little water and bread, for I am weary." But she said, "No bread, and no water." Abraham said, "When your husband returns, tell him, "An old man from the land of Canaan came to see you and said to tell you, 'The household of this house is not in good repair.'"

When Ishmael returned, his wife gave him the message, whereupon, he promptly divorced her. Then his mother, Hagar, sent for a woman from her family in Egypt. Her name was Fatima, and Ishmael married her.

After another three years, Abraham again rose up to visit his son Ishmael, for his heart yearned. And again Sarah was afraid and bade him not to dismount from his camel. Abraham so promised. He reached the place again at midday and he found Fatima, Ishmael's wife, and he asked the whereabouts of his son. "He and his mother have gone to graze camels in the wilderness," she said.

"Give me some bread and some water," Abraham said, "for I am weary from the journey. And she brought out bread and cool water and gave these to Abraham. Then Abraham entreated God on behalf of his son Ishmael, and Ishmael's house was filled with all manner of good things. When Ishmael came back, his wife told him what had happened.

Then Ishmael realized that his father still loved him.[38]

---

and the Midrash, ed by Hayim Nahman Bialik and Yehoshua Hana Ravnitzky (New York: Shocken Books, 1992) 39.

[38] *Pirke de Rabbi Eliezer*, an eighth-century midrashic narrative, (Warsaw, 1852), trans Gerald Friedlander [1971-1923] (London, 1916) 30, and *Midrash ha-Gadol* on Genesis, ed. by Mordecai Margulies [1910-68] (Jerusalem, 1947) 339-40.

After these things Abraham took his other son, Isaac, up to the mountain to offer him unto the Lord. And he wished for Isaac a good wife and the blessings of home, as he had for Ishmael. But the Lord hardened his own heart against Abraham's *hesed*, his open-heartedness. Then Abraham began to feel that he himself had been banished into the wilderness, and he did not know whether his heavenly Father loved him.

-XIV-

The testing of Isaac was greater than the testing of Abraham for Abraham heard the voice of God, but Isaac did not.

Rabbi Bunam was asked: "Why in the story of the sacrifice of Isaac is it especially stated and related that they went, 'both of them together'? For is this not self-evident?"

He replied, "The temptation which Isaac resisted was greater than that of Abraham. Abraham heard the command from the lips of God. When Isaac heard his father say that God himself would provide the lamb for the burnt offering, he understood—though Isaac had heard the command from the lips of man. But Abraham brooded: "Whence has my son this strength? It must be the strength of his youth!" Then he fetched forth from within himself the strength of his own youth. Only then did both of them really go together."[39] Isaac was not attuned yet to the voice of God.

-XV-

At first Satan was sacrificed in his failure to challenge Abraham's faith.
Then Sarah was tested by Satan.

Now Satan was furious that he had failed to prove Abraham's faithlessness in trusting God. The one sacrificed on the altar of faith thus far had been Satan himself. A midrash story tells of Sarah's experience

---

The story here is quoted in *The Book of Legends Sefer Ha-Aggadah: Legends from the Talmud and the Midrash*, 39.

[39] Martin Buber, *Tales of the Hasidim*, (New York: Schocken, 1947, 1991) p. 260

while Abraham and Isaac were on the mountain. While Abraham was binding his son Isaac to the altar, Satan went to Sarah, appearing to her in the form of Isaac. When Sarah saw him, she asked, "My son, what did your Father do to you?"

He replied, "My Father took me, led me up the hills and down into valleys, until finally he brought me up to the summit of a high and towering mountain, where he built an altar, set out the firewood, bound me upon the altar, and grasped a knife to cut my throat. Had not the Lord said to him, 'Lay not thy hand upon the lad,' I would have been slaughtered."[40]

Even before Satan finished his tale, Sarah's soul left her. And she cried out three sobs, corresponding to the three *Teki'ah* notes of the Shofar, and she wailed (*Yelalot*) three times, corresponding to the *Yevava*, staccato notes of the Shofar. Then she gave up the ghost and she died. Abraham came and found her dead.[41]

-XVI-
Sarah's death cries are similar to Isaac's

Isaac's death cries, the cries of one caught in the grip of overwhelming forces, are echoed by Sarah in her anguish. She died because she could not bear to hear the end of the story. Her husband has committed an unthinkable act. She could never look at him again. Her marriage, her faith in the Covenant promise, and her purpose in life were irretrievably broken.

Sarah was the one who was ultimately sacrificed on the altar of the Lord. Isaac survived because of God's intervention. But God did not intervene and save Sarah.

-XVII-
Truth is sacrificed. Abraham misleads Sarah about the sacrifice.

---

[40] *Pirke de Rabbi Eliezer*, 31. The story here is quoted in *The Book of Legends Sefer Ha-Aggadah: Legends from the Talmud and the Midrash*, 43.

[41] Tanhuma, *Va-yera*, § 22-23; Tanhuma B. *Va-yera*, edited by Solomon Buber [1827-1906 (Vilna, 1885) § 46, quoted in Zornberg, *The Beginning of Desire*, 124.

After the Lord had spoken of the test of faith, Abraham meditated in his heart, saying, "What am I to do? Shall I tell Sarah? Women tend to think lightly of God's commands. If I do not tell her and simply take off with him, afterward, when she does not see him, she will strangle herself." The truth was, he could not look her in the eyes then or ever again.

And so Abraham spoke to Sarah. "Prepare food and drink for us, and let us rejoice." "Why do we rejoice?" asked Sarah. And Abraham said, "I was only three years old when I became aware of my Maker. This lad, growing up, has not yet been told about his Creator. There is a place far away from here where lads are taught about the Creator. Let me take him there." And Sarah said, "Take him in peace."

It was early in the morning when Abraham arose to take Isaac up to the mountain. "I will get up early while Sarah is still asleep, lest she change her mind and reconsider what she said yesterday. Moreover, it is best that no one see us. And so they departed for the mountain."[42]

-XVIII-
Isaac says, "Don't tell Mother"

And they came to the place. Both were carrying stones for the altar, both carrying fire, both carrying the wood. For all that, Abraham acted like one making wedding preparations for his son.

Then Isaac said, "Father, hurry, do the will of your Maker. Burn me into a fine ash, then take the ash to my mother and leave it with her, and whenever she looks at it she will say, 'This is my son, whom his father has slaughtered.'"

Then Isaac said, "Father, what will you do in your old age without me?" Abraham replied, "My son, we know that we can survive you but for a short time. He who comforted us in the past will comfort us until the day we die."

When Abraham was about to begin the sacrifice, Isaac said, "Father bind my hands and feet, for the urge to live is so willful that when I see the knife coming at me, I may flinch involuntarily [causing the knife to

---

[42] Tanhuma, *Va-yera*, § 22-23, an early medieval homiletic midrash; Tanhuma B. *Va-yera*, edited by Solomon Buber [1827-1906 (Vilna, 1885) § 46; B. Sanhedrin 89b; *Pirke de Rabbi Eliezer*.

cut improperly] and thus disqualify myself as an offering. So I beg you, bind me in such a way that no blemish will befall me." So Abraham bound his son well. Then Isaac said to Abraham, "Father, don't tell Mother about this while she is standing over a pit or on a rooftop, for she might throw herself down and be killed."[43]

Both Abraham and Isaac knew that the faith of Sarah was different. Had God tested Sarah, rather than Abraham, and asked her to offer her son, the one whom she loved, as a sacrifice on the altar of the Lord, she would have defied the Lord God and spit in his face. She was more committed to the Covenanted Sacred Destiny of the future that lay in the gift of her motherhood and would hold the Lord God to his promises.

-XIX-
The necessity of betrayal?

Everywhere Abraham looked it seemed as though relationship was in ruin. After the unthinkable experience, how could there ever again be trust? Not with his wife. Not with God. Not with the people. Does the spiritual Path require such radical severance with the Beloved? Is such disillusionment connected with Ultimate Reality?

"Betrayal. I have betrayed the love of my son and I have felt the betrayal of the Father. What is it about betrayal and the Son of Man? What is it about betrayal and the great Saving Moments? Is betrayal the experience that launches a religion?

"It is as though the Truth needs to be shaken. The Truth of Love. The Promises and Expectations are dashed. This is the holocaust of all sacred thoughts. God, why have you forsaken the Plan? Why have you killed the theology?

"I am coming to see that betrayal serves to breakdown our reliance on certainty and it reveals that the way we live in illusion. Knowing dies. Betrayal, Love, Truth, Faith and loss of Faith, they all go together. There must be an emptying out for there to be a wholeness, a falling for there to be a rising, a death for there to be life."

---

[43] Tanhuma, *Va-yera*, § 22-23.

PART 3: DOES FAITH NEED TO BE TESTED?

-XX-
Not sure what the test is. Did he fail the test?

"After these things God tested Abraham." As he made his way up the mountain to the High Place where holiness dwelt, Abraham thought about those words. "Why was there yet more testing? Is this a God of tests? Does the testing ever end in one's life? Am I at fault? Did it have to do with my deception of Abimelech where I hid the identity of my wife? Is this a needed-proving-of-oneself to the Lord because of some shortcoming, some relapse? Does the Creator not know his/her own creation?"

Abraham thought about the other tests: such as trusting that God would lead him to the sacred homeland,... believing that the promise of a future lay in the impossibility of having a child after a lifetime of childlessness,... trusting the rescue of his nephew's family in the holocaust of the Valley of Sodom. As he walked in silence beside the beloved one of his life, the problem that puzzled Abraham was, "I am never sure what the test is at the time it is given, and what I must do to pass the test. What does faithfulness to God mean?" he worried. Things are never as they seem.

"'Take your son whom you love and offer him as a holocaust at the Holy Place on the mountain that I will show you.' It was suicide of the future. Trust God. Is God always aligned with goodness? Is God pro-life? Is this a test of literalism? Or is this a symbolic request? How far do I go to follow the Lord?" Abraham agonized. "Does God want people to follow blindly like sheep, or to wrestle and stand up to the Almighty?" Maybe God likes to be tested.

Abraham was old and in no condition to challenge the Almighty. He did as the Lord commanded. Exactly, in every detail, following not his own heart, but he did what he thought was the will of the Lord. And it was only later near the end of his days that he learned the horrifying answer to his questions: He had failed the test.[44]

---

[44] From personal conversation with Rabbi Arnold M. Goodman, Atlanta, GA, January 17, 2000.

-XXI-
We need a world where we bend the rules

When God turned his eyes to Sodom and Gomorrah, God sought to include Abraham in the sacrifice of human life that was necessary for righteousness to prevail. The Lord God said, "Shall I hide from Abraham what I am about to do?" It was as though Abraham's response mattered to God, and *his awareness* was critical for God. Such divine inclusion emboldened Abraham so that he sought to challenge the justice of the Almighty. "Shall not the Judge of all the earth deal justly? ...Wilt thou destroy the whole city if ten righteous are found there?"

But Abraham fell silent before the Lord in the face of the holocaust of his own son. And he did not challenge the justice of the Almighty.

It was not that Abraham lacked courage. But the relationship between justice and righteousness had touched a paradoxical mystery. For the midrash says, "The judge of the whole earth shall not do justice, or if it is a world You want, then strict justice is impossible. And if it is strict justice You want, then a world is impossible."[45] Being human and upholding strict justice in a world with absolute rules are incompatible. We need a world where we bend the rules, even the rules of religion, where we live situationally, and adapt and evolve as we go along.

When God commanded Abraham to "Take your son, your only son Isaac, whom you love and offer him as a burnt offering," Abraham said, "I am in a terrible double bind. Either the world had lost its order, or you, God, have lost your Love. Justice opposes mercy. Faith fights reason."

It was then that Abraham realized that being human means we must keep reinventing ourselves and living in the imagination, not in any prefigured order. There are no absolutes. We build a world out of alternative possibilities.[46] In sacrificing Isaac, there would be no justice ... or there would be no love. The name Isaac means "joy" in one tradition, and "truth" in another. Would Abraham sacrifice joy or would he sacrifice truth?

---

[45] *Bereshit Rabbah*, 49:5, quoted in Zornberg, *The Beginning of Desire*, 109-110.

[46] Zornberg, *The Beginning of Desire*, 110.

The Psalmist sang, "Truth will spring up from the earth."[47] In other words, Truth does not fall in absolute form from heaven. There is a midrashic story that the Angel of Truth fell to earth and broke into many pieces. It is our task to put the pieces back together. And in our struggle and conflicting activities, we keep reassembling Truth in many forms. We create and recreate truth in spite of contradictions.

-XXII-
God's last words … silence beyond repair

God's last words to Abraham were, "Offer him as a burnt offering on a mountain that I will point out to you."

Never again did Abraham hear from God. Not a word. Divine silence. When the sacrifice was annulled, an angel stopped it, not God. It was God's final words that seared Abraham's heart for the rest of his life: "Take your son whom you love and offer him as a burnt offering.

These last words of terror block the heart of those who don't know. Did Abraham's obedience block God's heart? Why was God silenced? No explanations, no apologies, no word about what it all meant. No one with a rational heart can deal with the paradoxes of what happened. Was it all a divine mistake?

-XXIII-
Either he would fail as a father or he would fail as a son

In the shadows of Mount Moriah, Abraham threw himself upon his face. He prayed to God to forgive his sin, for a situation had arisen in which he could not avoid sinning. There was no righteous choice, no higher moral ground. God had, in effect, put him into a position where sin was unavoidable.

Either he would fail as a father or fail as a son, a son obedient to the Higher Father. Was one option less evil than the other? Had God asked him to kill himself, Abraham would not have hesitated. Perhaps suicide was the most moral and noble way out. Should he fail God's test of

---

[47] Psalm 85.11. The comment that follows here is from Zornberg, *The Beginning of Desire*, 110.

commitment and obedience, he would no longer carry the Promise, and his life would lose its meaning and its purpose. It would be the sin of reneging on one's love for God.

On the other hand, his willingness to go through with this murderous act was a willingness to forget his duty toward his son. Even to think about it—that which has been unthinkable—and consider it in his heart, has changed things forever. He tried to rationalize it as a sacred act: how could it be a sin to offer to God the best thing he possessed![48] But there was no escape: sacrificing his son would be sacrifice of his own fatherhood.

Created in the image of God, God the Father. Somehow the father image was failing. "But I love them both," Abraham thought. "I love them both—God and my son." It was the betrayal of love.

Prostrate on the ground, Abraham breathed the smell of the clay in his nostrils, the earth moistened with his tears. "How then can I ask for forgiveness? What is the place of justice and righteousness that can cleanse and make this impossible choice livable? Has God sinned as well and made forgiveness a mockery?" In the ensuing madness that overswept him, Abraham thought, "I cannot avoid placing myself as well on that altar of sacrifice with Isaac." And the edge of the knife was already at his own throat.

-XXIV-

We must all lose faith in the parents
so that we may look to something higher to parent us

It was early in the morning. Everything in Abraham's house was prepared for the journey. He bade Sarah farewell, and Eleazar, the faithful servant, followed him along the way, until he turned back. They rode together in harmony, Abraham and Isaac, until they came to Mount Moriah.

---

[48] Søren Kierkegaard, *Fear and Trembling*, 29. This section begins with Kierkegaard's musing over the problem of forgiveness for Abraham in the third of his four powerful "panegyrics upon Abraham," but with all respect to Kierkegaard, my reworked panegyric took a different turn.

But Abraham prepared everything for the sacrifice, calmly and quietly, but when he turned and drew the knife, Isaac saw that his left hand was clenched in despair. Isaac saw his father's fear, and he felt the tremor of doubt that passed through his father's body. There was a ram nearby and Abraham lifted his son, Isaac, off the altar. And Abraham sacrificed the ram in his place, giving thanks to the Lord.

And they returned home again, and Sarah hastened to meet them. No word of what happened on the mountain had been spoken, and Isaac never talked to anyone about what he had seen. In the trembling of his father's hand, Isaac had lost his faith.[49] He no longer carried the spirit of the Promise, and his soul remained there on the altar.

We must all lose faith in the parents so that we may look to something higher to parent us. But Isaac lost faith in his parents and never found what was higher.

-XXV-

Isaac had seen the knife of the Lord cut his Father's heart

Abraham and Isaac made their way down the mountain and toward home in silence, each lost deep in thought. For each of them, something had been lost, and something had been gained. Isaac remembered his father's tears and knew from their embrace at the end of the ritual that he was loved as much as life itself. He had survived an initiation, a matter of life and death. He had lost his innocence as he had seen the knife of the Lord cut his father's heart.

He had crossed over a threshold, although what it was he did not understand. He was acutely aware of the striving between heaven and earth, and that something new had been born. There coursed in his veins a new freedom, a new Blessing. Because his Father was Blessed by the Highest One, so he was Blessed.

Abraham was so seized by the experience that he was completely oblivious to the bone weariness of his body. He had half-heartedly made up the rationale that the trip up into the mountain was to initiate Isaac into a relationship with the Almighty. But it was he, Abraham, who was

---

[49] Søren Kierkegaard, *Fear and Trembling*, 29. Some minor changes are made here from Kierkegaard's fourth panegyric.

initiated. Initiated by God, initiated by his innocent son. All his life, he had searched for the truth of enlightenment. He had followed the disciplines of the way of righteousness, embracing his holiness as Sarah embraced their son.

The truth of enlightenment revealed in the sacrifice on Mount Moriah was the opposite of what he had thought. Finding is losing. Having is letting go. Salvation is letting go of what you want most, of what you love most... beloved Isaac, bone of my bones, heart of my heart,... letting go of what you love most: God, Soul of my soul.

-XXVI-
We are asked to smash all the idols of every attachment

"The omnipotent Holy One knows already what is in my heart, so why this lethal test?" wondered Abraham. "It seems unnecessary. He already knows my obedience. Ahhh, but perhaps He does not yet know my surrender."

"I became fatherless when I left my family and home in Ur. He now asks me again to become fatherless in a different sense by killing my son. I literally smashed all the idols and religious figurines for sale in my own father's business. Now I am asked to smash all the idols of every attachment I have known, even the idol of love and the idol of hope."

-XXVII-
The spiritual wandering of indeterminacy

"How is it that the transformation of my soul arises from this wandering? I left all that was familiar because I felt some Divine pull. My wandering has not been one of punishment or exile, but a wandering of indeterminacy. *I go to where 'I know not' and find that God is there.* My journey has been trackless, unmapped, directionless… and I am beginning to see that it has been about total displacement, a deconstruction of all that I thought life and spirituality was about. My wandering has been about losing the life I thought I had. If I plunge this knife into the jugular of the one remaining bit of life I love the most, my dear son, I will have lost all. In a sense, in my mind, I already have.

"And yet I am still here. There is some hidden process of growth, some invisible movement at work, something that is not vulnerable to the knife or to my craziest thoughts of insanity. I am fatherless in every sense of the word, yet the Father and I are one."

-XXVIII-
Truth is not singular. God brings contradictions.

"Am I an abusive father?" Abraham thought as he raised the knife to slay his son? "Is God an abusive God to ask this of me? I had thought of this journey as an ethical way to God."

God is full of ambiguity and contradiction. Before Moriah, God had said, "Isaac, your seed will be named and more numerous than the stars." Then God said, "Take your son and offer him as a burnt offering." God said the word, "*Ha 'aleyhu,*" slaughter him!" And then he said, "Bring him up," again with the same word, "*Ha'aleyhu,*" but with an opposite meaning.

Was the first "*Ha'aleyhu,*" the voice of Satan?[50] How to distinguish between God and Satan? God does not make it easy. And God continues to not walk the straight and narrow with consistency as if to say I will not be predictable, and Truth is not singular.

-XXIX-
Abraham lived in the enigmas and the contradictions
learning that God is the archetype of life

The Covenant promise began with such fortuitousness and unbounded joy, focused on the longing for a baby by an old couple long past menopause and hope. "Give up your idealism," their aging friends had advised. But they had not given up on wishing. It was their bliss. They believed, and in their believing, they were still young. For it is said,

---

[50] Tanchuma, *Va-yera* 22, quoted in Avivah Gottlieb Zornberg, *The Murmuring Deep: Reflections on the Biblical Unconscious* (New York: Schocken Books, 2009), p. 199.

"It is great to give up on one's wish, but it is greater to hold it fast after having given it up."[51]

Then the impossible happened, mocking all the hags in their cynicism about the absurdity of hoping. A child *was* born. A woman whose breasts had never fed an infant could now feed a nation and a future.

Then the impossible happened again. The child was all but killed, and with it came the utter devastation of wishing and hoping. The cynics were right. The ultimate message was the impossibility of full joy in this world. Even God seemed to lack delight and joy in the world, for God could not help but spoil such a wonderful life. There is no place for enduring joy, the midrash intones, at least not in this life.[52] There was defeat, not victory, on Mount Moriah.

He was all but slaughtered. *Kime'at shelo nishhat,* also translated, "a little thing decided his fate." "A hair's breadth separates life from death." We live in a fragile world not being able to preserve one's being.[53] The Deuteronomist was right: "The Lord will give you a trembling heart, and failing eyes, and a languishing soul. The life you face shall be suspended in front of you; you shall be in terror, night and day, with no assurance of survival."[54]

And so the two paths of life diverge. Sarah sought definitiveness. She wanted a religion of justice and order, where God is good, where God is accountable and the truth can be pinned down. For Sarah, the resolution of what happened to Isaac did not neutralize the terror. She dies of her life.

Abraham lived in the enigmas and the contradictions. For Abraham, Sarah is the part of himself he must evade if he is to reach Mount Moriah, the mountain of God.[55] What Abraham found there was that God is the archetype of life, life in its fullness, in its capriciousness, in its heights and its depths. God is Reality. Totally. Abraham's life is dominated by the conflicting opposites, and only God can preside over the evolving conflict. In the madness in front of that altar, all rationality

---

[51] Søren Kierkegaard, *Fear and Trembling,* 33.
[52] Zornberg, *The Beginning of Desire,* 126.
[53] Zornberg, *The Beginning of Desire,* 127.
[54] Deuteronomy 28.65b-66.
[55] Zornberg, *The Beginning of Desire,* 133.

failed him. And only then could he step into a higher complexity of living and feel utterly helpless.

Our legacy is what we give our children to unravel.

-XXX-
Abraham was obedient, but his soul had died

It was early in the morning. Abraham arose betimes and embraced Sarah, the bride of his old age. And Sarah kissed Isaac, who had taken away her reproach, who was her pride, her hope for all time.

So they rode on in silence along the way, and Abraham's glance was fixed upon the ground until the fourth day, when he lifted up his eyes and saw Mount Moriah afar off. But his glance again turned toward the ground.

Silently, he laid the wood in order. He bound Isaac. In silence, he drew the knife—then he saw the ram, which God had prepared. He offered the ram as a sacrifice and returned home....

From that time on, Abraham became old. He could not forget that God had required this of him. Isaac thrived as before, but Abraham's eyes were darkened. And he knew joy no more.[56]

Abraham was faithful to the end, obedient to God. But his soul had died in the test. The juice had drained out of his faith. He had obedience without joy, promise-fulfilled without filling. And Isaac, whose name meant laughter, now carried a name that mocked the miracle of his birth. Abraham still had his son, but he had lost his Father.

-XXXI-
We are not saved by being good.
God took away the rungs of Jacob's Ladder, the Path to God.

As the path up the mountain became arduous, Abraham wondered why God had him climb to such a high place for the sacrifice. Why so distant from home? Up to now, the religion of the God of Abraham, Isaac, and Jacob had been based on the family and the home. This was away from family and home. Perhaps God wanted him to have time to

---

[56] Søren Kierkegaard, *Fear and Trembling*, 28.

think. Perhaps God wanted to make him exert high energy to commit this terrible act. Abraham suffered as his aging knees struggled with the climb.

Abraham wondered why. Why this test? God already knew him through and through. There was no need for a test. Did God have doubts? Was God not sure of God's own faithfulness? For all his hundred plus years Abraham had been unwaveringly faithful. He had not laughed as Sarah had laughed when the three angels visited to tell that they would have a baby. He had faith in God.

Abraham believed in God's impossibilities. He had trusted God in Egypt when Pharoah wanted to have Sarah for himself. He had trusted God back in his childhood, when he challenged Nimrod, the King of lower Mesopotamia, who falsely claimed divinity. Abraham trusted God who called him to leave his family in Ur. Had he not proven himself?

Then it dawned on Abraham—one is not saved by faith, one is not saved by virtue, one is not saved by belief, one is not saved by passing all the tests. One may be an exemplar of spiritual attainment, but none of that matters. God not only took away all that he had worked for, but God also took away all the rungs of the spiritual ladder to heaven that he had climbed. He took away all the perceived means to reach heaven. And now, God was taking away the one he loved most. He was naked, naked before God. This is what God asks.[57]

PART 4: BECOMING ONE WITH GOD

-XXXII-
God began to feel the binding of the Covenant, trapped by the promises made in a different time and place

---

[57] **Based on** Martin Buber, *Tales of the Hasidim* (New York: Schocken, 1947, 1991), Vol I, p. 192.

The Lord made a Covenant with Abraham and Sarah, saying, "Your descendants shall number like the stars, so great shall their destiny be." And so it came to pass that Isaac was born to the aged couple, in fulfillment of the Covenant promise. The Lord noticed that Abraham and Sarah were exacting and literal in their expectations of the Lord, holding to every word of the Covenant. And the Lord began to feel the binding of the Covenant, trapped by the promises made in a different time and place. The Lord God did not like feeling predictable. It was as though human beings wanted to control the divine.

And the Lord God said, "I will not break my promise, but I long for there to be more imagination between Abraham and Sarah and me, for there to be delight and surprise in our relationship." So the Lord put Abraham and Sarah to the test, asking them to sacrifice their son Isaac, whom they dearly loved. Abraham and Sarah obeyed the word of the Lord, even though they felt that the Covenant promises were betrayed. "The Lord giveth and the Lord taketh away," explained Abraham to soothe his wife Sarah.

The test of faith requiring the sacrifice of their son created a distance between Abraham and Sarah and God. But in this new space created by the distance, the imagination ran wild. Why did God ask this? What kind of God is this? What is the truth about love? The aborted sacrifice of the innocent child created an ambivalent play between God and human beings.

And so it was that Abraham and Sarah realized that we are not just bound to God in submission. God is not bound to our expectations and the rules of fairness and goodness. God's freedom holds precedence over God's promises. It is a kind of play that says life is not predictable or fair. Life does not follow rules. There are shocks and surprises.

"We must pay careful attention to this space between ourselves and God," Abraham thought. "It is a place where the imagination reigns and sometimes goes mad. In this place of mad play, full of paradox and contradiction, we open ourselves to the unknown. It is here in the imagination and this madness that one meets God. It is this improvisation and play in this space that gathers transforming power that leads to humanity becoming divine and God becoming human."

In the binding of Isaac, Abraham broke out of fixed worldviews and entered the creative play-area with God. Abraham really never quite abandoned his madness. He learned to live with two-sidedness. Before, Abraham was sterile in his determined obedience; now he was fecund.

-XXXIII-
Beyond the rungs of the ladder, beyond religion

For a hundred years, Abraham had striven in his faith in God. He himself had sacrificed much already. The sages said, "You must die before you die."[58] He left his mother and father and homeland, a form of dying, leaving them feeling judged and rejected. He had gone forth hearing the call "*lech lecha*," that is, "go forth into the land of his own becoming." He had been a stranger in a strange land. He had wounded Sarah, his wife, as he failed to claim her or protect her from Pharaoh's amorous advances on her. For years, his family had felt as barren as Sarah's womb, with no child to love, no reason to be a family, no hope of future. Abraham had been emptied many times, even "gutted," as he walked up the mountain with dear Isaac beside him.

"Take the one you love the most, and kill him," God said.

"But God, you know my love for You. Do you have any doubt of my absolute obedience? I have left all for You, even my marriage. You have tested my faith as You have tested Job's. O Lord, 'Thou knowest my soul is pure.' Do You doubt me?"

"There is but one thing left for you to come to me," the Holy One said. "*You must leave all* to be with me."

"I feel like I have already done that."

"Yes you have climbed all the rungs of Jacob's Ladder. I will take you to the next level which is no rung, no ladder, no strategies, no path, no belief, no mind. In that place… there is no holiness, no religion, no faith. I will show you the total annihilation of self. What will remain is only God. This emptying out cannot be done of your own will, but only through My grace."

And so God gave Abraham the strength to kill what he loved most, his son, his future, his life's work. And all that was left was God, and for

---

[58] Mohammed (Hadith), Rumi, Kabir, Murat Yagan, Meher Baba.

"Abraham" (the person), there was nothing that remained, except the promise of everything. And the miracle was that Abraham was then resurrected, and his son, dear Isaac, lived.

-XXXIV-
First time Yahweh experienced emptiness; as below, so above

Then Vast Face[59] (the God beyond all form, the imageless everything beyond the God of human creation) said to Small Face (Yahweh, the nameless God of the Bible), "Take your Son, the Beloved One of humankind, i.e., Abraham, and take him to the hill where he will be sacrificed on the altar of human ignorance. Empty yourself of your God-Self," said Vast Face.

And for the first time, Yahweh experienced emptiness. God experienced what He was asking of Abraham.

-XXXV-
Our greatness is in proportion to the greatness of what we love

As Abraham and Isaac made their way down the mountain and toward home, it became strikingly clear. The usual human logic is: the more you have, the more you have. Divine logic is: the more you give up, the more you have. Therefore, whoever of you does not renounce all that he has, cannot be my follower. Whoever seeks to gain his life will lose it, but whoever loses his life will find it. The meaning of the sacrifice was not the gift of death and sweet ashes, but the higher life.

Love is the one thing that survives all annihilation. "Our greatness," Abraham thought, "is in proportion to the greatness of what we love, and the greatness of that with which we strive. If I love myself, I become great within myself. If I love other people, I will become great out of my selfless devotion and compassion. But the one who *loves* God becomes greater than them all. The one who *strives* with God acquires an even higher greatness. I have found the great thing I was seeking by reason

---

[59] Jewish Kabbalah speaks of Vast Face and Small Face. Vast Face is beyond all thought, all religion, all form. Small Face is the God of the Jewish Bible (Old Testament) known as Yahweh, but still beyond thought and form.

of my power whose strength is impotence, by intelligence of my wisdom whose secret is foolishness, by the reach of my hope whose form is madness, by the gift of the love which is letting go of myself."[60]

-XXXVI-
The experience on the Mountain was about the Higher Self

As he walked in silence back down the mountain behind his son Isaac, the Gift of His Life, along with the gift of his Beloved Sarah, Abraham was aware that he had undergone profound change. Beyond words. Thoughts only diminished the experience. His soul was no longer what it was. His eyes no longer saw the same world. Everything was different. A psychotic break perhaps, he thought momentarily, but, no, it was as though he had taken on a new mind, a much more expansive mind, as though he was seeing through the eyes of God.

"God is not a murderer," Abraham thought. "God is not bloodthirsty in wanting the blood of the Life of my son. It wasn't about Isaac. God loves Isaac and wants him to have a full life. It was about me, about my sense of Self. It was also about the same old me who has been a trader, who is the master of vast herds and a large household. The experience on the Mountain was about my Higher Self, the Infinite Self within.

"The Self that is also called God.

"The veil has at last fallen off. I am a fully realized Being. It is not that I can no longer focus on the things of this world, but now when I see them, my heart opens to such fullness that every little thing, every bird, every creature, every being becomes as precious as my Beloved Isaac. I see Isaac everywhere my eyes take gaze. It is all a mirror and when I look in it, all I can see is God."

Abraham was moved by these new awarenesses. He was conscious that he now lived as the embodied Infinite Presence. He remembered the words of old Melchizedek, that remarkable "Man-God" (yes, that was the only way he knew to name that indescribable luminous figure) who had met him on the battlefield and who had exposed him as one on the Higher Path around the sacred meal of bread and wine—"the

---

[60] This is a paraphrase of Søren Kierkegaard, *Fear and Trembling*, 31.

meal with God," he had said.[61] Melchizedek had spoken of the higher Inner World, the seeing what outer eyes could not see, the seeing of the heart of God. Melchizedek had beckoned him to come forth ever so powerfully. "Come, be who you are. You are the I AM. You are the Way. You are the Father. You are the Son. You are the Ancient One." It was as though Melchizedek had kissed him and woke him up.

"Was that what had just happened?" Abraham pondered. "I didn't know what Melchizedek meant then when he said, 'You are the Father in your infinite form.' He meant, 'You are the Son in your embodied form.' He meant, 'You are the Ancient One.'

"I see now that Melchizedek was a Perfect Master whose role it was to unveil me into my own perfection," thought Abraham. "But I have not understood his words until this experience on the Mountain. The Father and I are one. I am 'God-Man.' Now I am the Father to *all* peoples. Not just one child, not only to Isaac. But to all children, to Isaacs without number. The precious children. 'I AM!'" Abraham exulted. "I AM Life! I AM the children! Some hiddenness has left me, some unwrapping of me happened on the Mountain and released me into this Blessed state of Godliness. Ah, my heart overflows."

-XXXVII-
What God had asked of him revealed his own God-Nature

And God blessed Abraham in all things. Abraham prospered in the fullness of life. The days brought joy and they brought sadness, healing and suffering. Abraham saw that the ebb and flow, the laughter and the vicissitudes were all part of the Blessing. There was no regret about what had happened between him and Isaac, for it all had its place in the higher scheme of things. It was all the manifestation of God.

The suffering from what God had asked of him on Mount Moriah had not diminished his spirit. Rather, it had transformed him. It revealed his own God-Nature. He saw that God was also on that altar, that God shares in our stripes and our travail. To Abraham, it was a blessed realization around the axiom "As above, so below." The split between

---

[61] Genesis 14.17-20

heaven and earth, God and humanity, exists only temporarily for those who have not yet developed the inner eyes.

For Abraham, it was the future that had changed rather than the past. For one whose life had been wrapped around barrenness and impotence, the future was now pregnant with possibilities, more than the stars of the sky. For Abraham, his descent was complete, and he knew then that he was the descending One who founds religion.

On the Mountain, Abraham saw that the spiritual life and the work of The Ancient One (the God-Man) has nothing to do with dynasties, kingdoms, or earthly power. It has to do with being the servant to all, a servant willing to embrace suffering. It has everything to do with opening to the full effects of living, including the suffering that would befall his children in the future. By that wild act of opening to suffering on the Mountain—not only in one's own life, but in the lives of every being—Abraham discovered the mystery of the Divine Presence in and beyond suffering. "Yes," he thought, "this takes courage. This takes absolute honesty. This takes a ferocious commitment to truth."[62]

CONCLUDING THOUGHTS

And thus it came to be that Abraham realized his true nature as a man who was also one with God. It was not just a union of two (God and man), but an inseparable sameness of one, which existed originally in the Garden. He was of the order of Melchizedek,[63] which is the same as the Ancient One. Whenever the flame of the divine spirit burns low, God comes in human form to give humanity a boost. Abraham as the Ancient One had come previously as Zoroaster, as Ram, as Krishna, and in his now omnipotent awareness, Abraham the Ancient One will come as Buddha, as Jesus the Christ, as Mohammed, and as Meher Baba, all

---

[62] Paraphrased from Andrew Harvey, *A Spiritual Awakening.*

[63] Genesis 14:18-20, Psalm 110:4, Hebrews 7:17. The Order of Melchizedek is used to speak of the God-Man, the God-realized person, including the reference to the Christ in the book of Hebrews.

manifestations of the one God with the same teaching of the Way, but each uniquely tailored to the specific culture and conditions of the time.

It was an Axis Mundi event, an event that changed the axis of the world, where heaven and earth met one another. As a result of the *Akedah*, Abraham raised consciousness to the level of divine Oneness, a consciousness having to do with "dying to self" in order that the true Self could be manifest, and in so doing made this available to everyone. As did all the other divine masters, Abraham demonstrated how to ascend to God.

Where does Abraham fit in Jewish history, in the overall history of religion? The Sanskrit word "avatar" is given to those who are God in human form, synonymous with Christ. Was Abraham an avatar? Most Jews do not think of him as such. Meher Baba is a spiritual master, the Ancient One of our present age, one whom Mother Teresa said, "He had the mind of Christ," and by that she literally meant he was the same one who said, "Before Abraham I was."[64] Mehera, who was Meher Baba's closest woman disciple, asked him whether or not Moses was an avatar (God in human form), and Meher Baba replied, "No, Moses was a true seeker of the sixth plane, but Abraham was an avatar."[65] Similarly, Meher Baba said on another occasion, "I come to arouse and awaken humanity. I came as Zoroaster, **Abraham** [my emphasis], Rama, Krishna, Buddha, Jesus and Mohammed and now I have come as Meher Baba."[66]

It is said that in the present cycle of advents where God has taken form as an avatar, a religion has risen around almost every avatar (Zoroastrianism from Zoroaster, Hinduism from Ram and Krishna, Buddhism from Buddha, Christianity from Jesus, Islam from Mohammed). Later on, history revealed that four world religions arose out of the presence of Abraham—Judaism, Islam, Christianity, and North Indian Tantra in the Indus Valley from the concubines of Abraham.[67] We must be clear the avatar is not the religion, for the avatar cannot be reduced to

---

[64] Gospel of John 8:58

[65] David Fenster, *Mehera-Meher: A Divine Romance* (Ahmednagar, India: Meher Nazar Publications, 016 PDF Edition), Volume III, p. 197.

[66] *The Ancient One*, ed. by Naosherwan Anzar, (Los Angeles: Meher Baba Books, 1985), p. 212.

[67] Rabbi Daniel Hale Feldman, *Qabalah: The Mystical Heritage of the Children of Abraham* (Santa Cruz, CA: Work of the Chariot, 2001), p. 29.

religion. Jesus Christ is not the same as Christianity. Judaism is not the same as Abraham. When we consider the significance of Abraham, we can see that he was among the Highest of the High and is considered an avatar, even though many Jews are not sure of this. So it is interesting that Isaiah says, "Look back to our father Abraham to find God." Implied in Isaiah 51:1, "Look to the rock from which you were cut," meaning Abraham.

Just as Jesus says leave all and come to me, let go of what you love and cling to most, so the story of the *Akedah* (the binding of Isaac) similarly asks Abraham to let go of everything, in order that he might realize everything.

CHAPTER 5

MOSES: IN THE VEIL OF SOUL MAKING

The Fire That Burned the Soul

What you showed Moses was not fire,
but a shape of consciousness.
— Rumi[68]

The biblical story says that Moses went up on the mountain, encountered God, and came down from the mountain with the Word of God. This is the outer narrative of the story, the skeleton on which the story unfolds. Is this a healing story?

The healing aspect of the story is found in the cracks of in-between places or the meta-story, the story behind and around the core narrative. The healing story of Moses is more than the story of the baby growing up in Pharaoh's palace, the Burning Bush, the Exodus from Egypt, the Torah and Ten Commandments from Sinai, the wilderness wandering, the Golden Calf, leading up to entering the Promised Land. Often just telling the story of the outer event misses the experience, failing to reveal the inner soul-story of the psyche. The deeper story is behind a veil.

From the third to the tenth centuries CE, Jewish rabbis reflected on the ancient story of scriptures and sought to lift up the nuances that

---

[68] *Soul of Rumi*, p. 231.

were healing to psyche and soul. These observations became the midrash; the rabbis paid attention to the gaps in the story, the resonances of the words, the shadow of what was not outwardly expressed by the character and the people.

Narrative theory explores how stories help people make sense of the world and how people make sense of stories. What makes the biblical story connective and effective comes from the way it speaks to both communal and personal experience. How does one make sense of the world and make sense of the story, and put them together? The archetypes of rescue, palace, king, murder, wilderness, escape, salvation, law, order and chaos, homeland, and others arise in each of us, and each person's perception of them is unique. Take the story of the Burning Bush:

*ADONAI (The Lord) appeared unto him in a fire blazing from the middle of a bush: … God called unto him out of the midst of the bush, and said, "Moses, Moses." And Moses said, **"Here am I."***

God said, "I am, the God of your father, the God of Abraham, the God of Isaac, and the God of Jacob." "I have surely seen the affliction of my people who are in Egypt, and have heard their cry … behold, the cry of the people of Israel is come unto me: and I have also seen the oppression. You must rescue them."
*Moses said unto God, **"Who am I,"** … that I should bring forth the children of Israel out of Egypt? And God said, "Certainly, **I am** with thee."*
*[Your people] ask me, 'What is His name?' What shall I say to them?" And God said to Moses, "Ehyeh-Asher-Ehyeh," **"I am who I am."** God continued, "Thus shall you say to the Israelites, 'Ehyeh [**I am**] sent me to you.*
— Exodus 3:-14 selected verses

*God said to Moses, "Do you not see that **I am** in distress, just as Israel is in distress? Be aware that the place from which I speak to you is in the midst of thorns. I am their partner in distress!"*
— Shemot Rabba 2:7

One would miss this story if all one saw was a miracle, a bush burning but not consumed by fire. Or if they simply analyzed it as "Moses' Call." One sees, with the introduction of the untranslatable Hebrew words, how the story carries a higher intention for the listener/reader, but even this intention is subjective. The name *Ehyeh* is a word play around the verb "to be," [*yeh hi*] but the layers are difficult to entangle. A God whose name is "Being," or "I have been," or "I will be" or even "I am." What does *Ehyeh* mean? Why is God giving such an enigmatic name? A name that can't be pinned down. What is Moses to do with this? If he tells the people "I AM" sent me, what are they going to do?

This is the first time in the biblical story that God gives the divine a Name, as incomprehensible as it is. For the first time, we are being introduced to the "collective unconscious," (meaning that which is hidden from all the people), a concept beyond the psychology of the ancient Semitic mind. The idea of "being" or "existence" was an emerging aspect of the Hebrew "collective or corporate personality," where meaning lay not in the individual, but in the group, but this was not the way people thought. Hence, it was in the shadow or the unconscious. This understanding of reality being unknown, underneath the awareness of the community, was not generally understood until Carl Jung in the twentieth century.

Still, for an ancient story to not see God as an outside entity but to see God as an aspect of inner personal existence itself was new, an aspect that Jesus later picked up on when he said the Kingdom is within. It means that God, the I AM, cannot be an objective idea; God is an experience, a subjective experience.

For Moses, this suggests that God is present in every experience. God could be seen as a "third" element that is part of every relationship, every act. It is a transcendent aspect, which every person experiences differently. It is the "intimacy of all experience."[69] In the biblical story, sometimes the story engages in this deep intimacy, and at other times it separates God to the opposite, an outside entity, i.e., "Wholly Other."

Jewish midrash scholar Avivah Gottleib Zornberg writes, "A third subject is created in the experience of reading that is not reducible to either writer or reader (listener)." As she encounters the story of Moses, she feels herself addressed by this subjective transcendent aspect of

---

[69] From a book by Rupert Spira, *The Intimacy of all Experience* (Sahaja Publications, 2016).

experience as "I-not-yet-I,"[70] meaning that as I read this, I am becoming something new or more than I was. This is critical to the sacred healing story that addresses us in our own self-discovery. True reading of scripture is always dynamic, unfolding, and progressively revealing.

Notice, in the scriptural narrative above, all the bold-faced occurrences of the appearances of "I am" and "Who am I" and even "Who are you." Socrates is attributed to the philosophical axiom, "Know thyself" (*gnōthi seauton*), often cursorily understood to mean a command to understand our limits, our history, our ego self, how we understand reality, and our motivations, but more accurately and deeper, it means to know our soul or core Self, the divine Self beyond the ego self. This is the focus of biblical healing stories that call one to realize the God-Self within beyond one's personal identity.

The sages of every religion say the ultimate question is "Who am I?" It is the question that opens the door to the ultimate realization that "I am God," "I am One." This is what lies embedded within the story of the Burning Bush, far beyond the miracle of liberation in the Exodus story. Liberation, a synonym for "salvation," means to realize the universal reality behind all forms, and when we let go of all the illusions of personal and group identity which bind us, we are free, without limit. Who am I beyond my personal ego awareness? The true Self lies in the shadow unconscious of every person. The God of the Burning Bush story introduces this new spiritual pursuit into the human agenda.

Murder and Suicide

Some time after that, when Moses had grown up, he went out to his kinsfolk and witnessed their labors. He saw an Egyptian beating a Hebrew, one of his kinsmen. He turned this way and that and, seeing no one about, he murdered the Egyptian and hid him in the sand. When he went out the next day, he found two Hebrews fighting; so he said to the offender, "Why do you strike your fellow?" He retorted, "Who made you chief and ruler over us? Do you mean to

---

[70] Avivah Gottlieb Zornberg, *Moses, A Human Life* (New Haven: Yale University Press, 2016), p. 2.

kill me as you killed the Egyptian?" Moses was frightened, and thought: Then the matter is known! When Pharaoh learned of the matter, he sought to kill Moses; but Moses fled from Pharaoh. He arrived in the land of Midian…
— Exodus 2:11-15 [Tanakh version]

The following biblical story is after the Burning Bush experience where God had asked Moses to go to Egypt and liberate the enslaved people.

So Moshe took his wife and sons, put them on a donkey, and started out for Egypt. Moshe took God's staff in his hand. ADONAI said to Moshe, "When you get back to Egypt, make sure that you do before Pharaoh every one of the wonders I have enabled you to do. Nevertheless, I am going to make him hard-hearted, and he will refuse to let the people go. Then you are to tell Pharaoh: 'ADONAI says, "Isra'el is my firstborn son. I have told you to let my son go in order to worship me, but you have refused to let him go. Well, then, I will kill your firstborn son!"

At night at a lodging-place on the way the LORD encountered him [Moses] and sought to kill him. So Zipporah took a flint and cut off her son's foreskin.
— Exodus 4:20-25 [Complete Jewish Bible Version]

Murder. Moses kills the Egyptian. Then God seeks to murder Moses, which is the suicide of God's salvation plan. Why does the story of Moses, the bringer of salvation to the people—Moses, a holy man—why does the story of Moses begin in such outrageous scandal?

The killing of the hero had figuratively happened before. Abraham's father lied to the King, saying his son was dead. Abraham destroyed his father's business. He left his family, an act of killing the family, or family suicide. Moses does the same, for his murder of the Egyptian was the annihilation of his being a royal of the palace, a betrayal of the royal family raising him, forcing him to flee the kingdom, just like Abraham. Moses' violent act was the suicide of his high position and loyalty to the Pharaoh. And in response, Pharaoh sought to kill Moses, presumably his adopted son. As a result, spiritually Moses has to leave all and go back to "nothing," to emptiness (symbolized by the wilderness), and start over from scratch.

In a parallel story, God does the same thing. Moses is on his way back to Egypt, obeying God to save the people, carrying with him the power and promise of God, when, shockingly, the text says God sought to kill him, to murder the Chosen One. And to do so without apparent cause. Why? Is God as hesitant and undecided as Moses? To murder Moses is to kill the Promise. It means the suicide of the dream of salvation, just as God asked Abraham to kill his son and the future of the Covenant.

Does God have suicidal ideation? Do we need to worry about God, or can we trust God? Did God ever repent around these events as He repented other times?[71] Absurd as these questions are, we need to ask questions about these dark beginnings to the ultimate Journey of Life.

It is interesting that after Moses killed the Egyptian, Moses flees to the desert, an apophatic environment. Moses had lived in the palace with servants, food, gardens, water, all the highest comforts. What was this longing for the opposite environment? Moses' longing for the desert seems irresistible. Was this a reaction to his sense of the artificial and controlled life of royalty? Was it his prophetic spirit that caused him to foresee that his own greatness and the greatness of Israel would manifest themselves there? Did Moses realize that it was in the desert where God's wonders would appear, and also that the desert would become Moses' last resting-place? Did Moses realize the desert is its own "promised land" where one can make contact with God and with Self before one resettles into life? For Moses, the desert was a Holy Place, a Burning-Bush place, a place that offers the "solace of fierce landscapes."[72] In the Nothingness of the desert, Moses found his origin and his destiny.[73] The desert is a macro-environment that gave rise to much of ancient Israel's experience of the divine.

Still, why murder? Apparently, it took such a violent act to break things loose. God's hope lay in a man who was living in the comforts of the palace of the King, who had kidnapped the Chosen People, now to be freed, in spite of the fact that Moses got into the royal palace as the

---

[71] Genesis 6:6; Exodus 32:14; 1 Samuel 15:11; Jonah 3:10; Joel 2:13-14.

[72] A reference to Beldon C. Lane, *The Solace of Fierce Landscapes* (Oxford University Press, 2007).

[73] *The Legends of the Jews* by Louis Ginzberg, (1909) http://www.sacred-texts.com/jud/loj/loj206.htm.

ironic result of the King's holocaust pogrom of killing all the Hebrew male children. The soul loves irony.

At a deeper level, life must begin with death, even if it is only the "death" required in leaving the womb. The sages say we never fully come to grips with life until we are willing to wrestle with death. Creation and un-creation (destroying) belong together. Integration pairs with disintegration; you don't have the one without its opposite. Not to ennoble murder; death is related to coming to the God of Life. It happened as well with King Herod killing the Jewish babies in Bethlehem.

Ironically, Moses was apparently the co-architect of the eighth commandment, "Thou shalt not kill." At the same time, we cannot avoid death; we cannot avoid the soul of death and its consciousness if we are to live fully. We cannot make death the *summa malum* (greatest evil), and we cannot say the killing of another person is always an injustice. We cannot ignore that the Egyptian army was killed in the crossing of the Red Sea. Neither can we make Moses' killing of the Egyptian a good act, particularly because it was done out of anger.

The story of Moses the savior begins with a scandalous and violent murder with an attempted cover-up, which launches another story, an escape and rescue story that seeks to stop the killing of the enslaved people who came to be the children of God.

We cannot separate the story of Moses committing murder from the story of God wanting to kill Moses, which is also a kind of suicide on the part of God. Rather than wrestling with the ethics of suicide, we will treat murder and suicide together inasmuch as they share a common soul, which is part of the healing story.

As already stated, the archetypal role of death by killing and suicide lies in helping things break loose. The killing creates a new direction for the story. How to get Moses out of the palace? How to get God to respond to the suffering of the people and to the upcoming stand-off and refusal on Pharaoh's part to let the people go? The side story of God's murderous anger at wanting to kill Moses for not being circumcised and having his *mother* do the job makes no sense. Murder and suicide gets the ball rolling.

Psychologist James Hillman says understanding human nature must begin with the soul, and the soul of death. Death is not the end of the soul, it is the beginning of the soul, for encountering death releases the profound fantasies of the human soul, even though the full meaning of death is always unconscious.[74] Religion seeks to rationalize and control death, moving quickly to consideration of life after death, avoiding the soul of death itself. Religion starts from dogma, rather than experience.

"Death appears in order to make way for transformation, breaking down the old order."[75] The soul related to death is an effort to usher in another level of reality. This is what is symbolized with Abraham, with Moses, and with Jesus. In the cases of murder-suicide under consideration here, there is the necessity of dying to the present world as it exists. The presence of murder-suicide here is mythic in nature, meaning it has a much larger implication than a simple, singular event. It challenges the rational morality of present existence, and a soul consciousness is awakened as if to say, "Wake up, something new is coming, something that has to do with the fundamental truth of life!" There is a dying away from the false life and wrong hopes of the lesser life being lived both by the children of Israel and even by the Egyptians.

Following the Hermetic axiom, "As above so below, as within so without," it would seem that God must also address a core futility and hopelessness within the divine-psyche; it is as if God had long been asleep and uninvolved. Hence, God "acts out" in the same manner as Moses. The story went that humanity is created in the image of God; both God and human beings have Light and Shadow. The story of Moses' beginning and the destructive elements at the outset of saving the people are important and significant elements woven into a mythic pattern, suggesting that creating and destroying can't be separated.

The mythic pattern of death's importance in creating new beginnings does not belong only to Moses, Abraham, or Jesus. It belongs to each one of us. Death teaches us about what is permanent and what is impermanent. We have to be reminded of this over and over. A well-lived life must experience ten-thousand deaths: deaths of loved ones, deaths of hopes and dreams, deaths of attachments, deaths that seem senseless and unjust, deaths of beliefs and certainties. We die before we die so that we become conscious about death, and we rehearse our own

---

[74] James Hillman, *Suicide and the Soul* (Dallas: Spring Publications, 1955), p. 51-53.

[75] Hillman, p. 67-68.

death. Death teaches us about our marriage to time and space, our wed-dedness to the forms of this world. Every death is a teacher that not only speaks about what comes to an end, but also what transcends and lives on, burning ever-brighter.

Kabir, the Hindu and Muslim Perfect Master, says our attachment to ourselves is an attachment to what is so much less than what is really unfolding here, and gets in the way of our seeing. Death will not be able to die as long as we cling to what dies.[76] Kabir is talking about dying to the lesser self, the temporary, finite, limited, identity and ego-driven self.

It was Mohammad who coined the phrase "die before you die." Implicit in it is the assertion that death is never the end. Death is never the last word. As just stated, a well-lived life must experience ten-thousand deaths—deaths of loved ones, hopes, dreams, attachments, beliefs and certainties.[77] Some deaths die of attrition after they no longer serve us. Some deaths are accomplished by our murderous intention. Some deaths we resist until they are removed by suicide. Some deaths happen as a gift from God.

Exodus: A New Model of Salvation

"When, at some future time, your son asks you, 'What is this?' [Mah zoth in Hebrew], then say to him, 'With a strong hand ADONAI brought us out of Egypt, out of the abode of slavery.'"
— Exodus 13:14 (Complete Jewish Bible)

The story of the Exodus, or we could say the archetypal myth of Exodus, is the story of the goal of every spiritual journey, which is to be released from all form, physical and mental, forms that hide us from our true nature. But this meaning is deeply embedded in the story,

---

[76] V.K Sethi, *Kabir: The Weaver of God's Name* (Punjab, India: Radha Soami Satsang Beas, 1984), p. 476-477.
[77] Hafiz, *The Subject Tonight is Love*, trans by Daniel Ladinsky (New York: Penguin Compass, 2003), p.55.

generally invisible in the common celebration of the Pesach Seder (Passover celebration meal).

Somewhere around 1150 BCE, the incipient Hebrew people formulated the most sophisticated story the world had yet seen about a God who saves the people, rescuing them from captivity. The idea of redemption/salvation, aka liberation, was thus born in the history of religion. The outer story told of severe hardships of slavery imposed by Pharaoh, the killing of Hebrew male babies, the creativity of the Hebrew women in defying the Pharaoh, the rise of the unheroic Moses as a leader, the severe resistance of Pharaoh (instigated and complicated by God) to let go of his caste and economic system, the unthinkable plagues, the great escape of the people to the edge of the sea, the miraculous opening up of a path through the sea—this is a dramatic story worthy of Cecil B. DeMille. The inner healing story portrays the collective and individual psyche's difficult journey to realize its divine nature and become liberated from what binds it.

Christians usually ask the question, "How is one saved?" What is the story of salvation? Jews don't have a word for salvation, but use a word more common with other religions: "How is one liberated?" What is the story of liberation? Passover is it. What is the "pass-over," and why is this idea so important?

It is interesting that the Hebrew word for "pass-over" (*pesicha/ pesach* in Hebrew) as in "I will pass over you," also means "leap." Imagine that! We have a God who *leaps over,* or "skips on by". And in some forms, the verb means "be lame," or "limp," or inactive. It is interesting to have such a word at the very center of Judaism. It is also interesting that God told the people to be dressed with shoes and coats on ("Get ready to run!), for when God acts it means that the people will need to act as well. The Passover meal is a celebration of "it's time to move," not as a past memory but as a present active step—time to move into our destiny, and where there is death there is new life.

But what is the "pass-over" in making this ancient event our own present-day story? Our stories, doctrines, theologies, endless explanations limit us, for we are confined by the physical and mental forms of our lives; we all suffer from some enslavement or confinement that imprisons us and we don't know how to break through to the true reality that transcends it all. God obviously sees all this. God sees us stuck in our limitations, and God passes-over. God "over-looks" our not getting it yet. God is almost limp in not holding us accountable and allowing us to be content in what is not the Truth. God lets us live our lives. At times, God passes-over, that is, God gives us a pass, and keeps us in the game of not-yet-coming to our true Home. We wander in the wilderness of our not knowing.

The road to God is a road with many "dead ends." The people come to the sea with the Egyptian army at their back. When all hope is lost, God creates a Path. Perhaps that is an aspect of the healing story, that God is always doing, creating the Path for us even when we think we are creating our own way. This is a story for people in impossible situations, where there is no apparent solution. It is a story of surrender, not surrender to Pharaoh, but surrender to God. There come times when the only thing to do is let go. Let go and let God.

At the same time the Exodus story is not the triumphant outcome we see in movies. The struggle with hardship and liberation was not over.

A Road Sign: "Promised Land Only 250 Miles"

When Pharaoh let the people go, God did not lead them by way of the land of the Philistines, although that was near [the direct route]. For God said, "Lest the people change their minds when they see war and return to Egypt." But God led the people around by the way of the wilderness toward the Red Sea. They traveled and set up camp, at the edge of the desert.
— Exodus 13:17-18

If this was such a Great Rescue, why didn't God lead the people the direct way to their Promised Land? They were led instead into the desert wilderness, where there was no water, no roads, no food, no trees, no pretty scenery, only scorpions and snakes. Why does God make things so difficult? Later, the Prophet Isaiah said the Lord would lay low the hills and make the roads straight (and flat), but that never happened. Being saved is not for sissies. And there is no Hollywood happy ending to rescue.

Why are things so difficult? Why does the spiritual journey take the long and arduous way? Why does God make coming to God next to impossible? These are great questions that we must address to understand our own spiritual experience. And they are essential to the "healing story." It seems that every one of us must take the "crooked road" into the wilderness of our lives and into unfamiliar landscapes and the edges of sanity. These difficult places paradoxically force one to think about things, to ask subversive, sarcastic, and even angry questions, rather than enjoy the softer comfort of following the familiar map of faith. The true way is not a straight line, but always a zig-zag through places of doubt and revision, where we lose ourselves over and over, until at last we lose ourselves into God.

The sobering truth was that not one of the people who fled Egypt and crossed the sea reached the Promised Land. Not even Moses. Their entire generation perished in the wilderness, not seeing the fulfillment of hope in the Promise. Can our spiritual goal be accomplished in a single lifetime? The Promise waited for the next generation who also did "cross the waters," this time the waters of the Jordan.

The way to God is narrow, a *mitzrayim m'eitzrim*, the narrow and treacherous strait. This becomes a template for the way of faith, the journey to God. Being "saved" is not a piece of cake. The journey into the wilderness was not punishment, but a universal experience far from a triumphant victory. One becomes released from one binding of servitude to the Pharaoh only to encounter another binding in the wilderness, again with little security and a serious lack of trust. Liberation doesn't come easy. That is exactly what God led them into: a difficulty just as challenging as what they were used to. And ironically, this becomes an aspect of the healing story. Healing can only come with wounding.

The story says God diverted the journey into the wilderness so that the people would not be tempted to return to Egypt. But that is exactly what happened—the people wanted to go back multiple times, rather than go forward. They thought it would be better to suffer a painful familiarity than a painful and uncertain unfamiliarity. They even retreated to the "bull" religion of Egypt in making the golden calf.

Where else in the Jewish and Christian Bibles is there a topic so relevant to the troubled psyche as this? We learned in Sunday School that after Moses led the children of Israel out of Egypt and across the Red Sea, they wandered in the desert for forty years. And nearly every step of the way, the people grumbled, complained, and were rightfully angry at God. Is this what salvation is?

Wandering in the wilderness is a huge theme for Judaism. For many, the real wilderness is within, not the outer desert, but the inner wilderness of looking for a job, of struggling with marriage, worrying about health, and the even deeper struggle with the madness and chaos inside that we try to keep under control.

True life is not smooth sailing; it is wandering, challenges, obstacles, serpents and beasts, anxiety, chaos, and unknowing. Like the medieval map makers who drew pictures of monsters at the outer edges of the known map, the people of Israel had their own monsters. But the point of the story is that God *knows* this. We are given wildernesses to walk through, and that is by intent, not from a sadistic God, but from a "God-of-the-refinery" always burning out impurities.[78]

Life may be challenging, but at least it is not primarily because one has messed up and is being punished. It is because it takes all this struggle to awaken us from our answers, our own plans, our false securities, and our illusions. If it were smooth sailing, we would never get anywhere. Jewish scholar Avivah Gottlieb Zornberg says wandering in the wilderness is about "interim space," in-between space, the place of disorientation and wandering, and being lost in the psyche and in our outward wandering. It is about the human mapping of "blank space," senseless states of living that are bewildering to the human imagination.[79]

Apparently, God wanted the people to be conscious of this inner state of chaos, asking Moses to write down "the starting points of their journeys." He was creating a therapeutic template, creating a consciousness and a healing process where the people were "watching over themselves."

These are the stages in the journey of the people of Israel as they left the land of Egypt divided into groups under the leadership of Moshe and Aaron. Moshe

---

[78] Malachi 3:3

[79] Avivah Gottlieb Zornberg, *Bewilderments: Reflections on the Book of Numbers* (New York: Schocken Books, 2015), p. xii-xiii.

recorded each of the stages of their journey by order of God; here are the start-ing-points of each stage.
— *Numbers 33:1-2   (Complete Jewish Bible)*

What relevance does recreating a troublesome written history have to the mystical reaches of spirit? Such a narrative enables the awareness of those parts of the self that need to be relinquished for something new to appear.

Why does the Torah make a point of writing down all these "starting points"? Where else in the Jewish and Christian Bibles is there a topic so relevant to the troubled psyche as this? An entire generation of hopeful Israelites died out in the wildest, parched landscape one could imagine. There was a death of sorts in leaving Egypt, but no rebirth to follow.

So Moses was told to write down the troublesome story, that is, the points of revising the journey. True journeys have stops, dead ends, and starts. He wrote of experiencing defeat and failure—the points of anger with God, stories of their mistrust of God, stories of the people's doubts, and their lack of faith—all serving to explain why life is so difficult. This is a terrible rationale! So Moses wrote the first Jewish history of pain and suffering. There were other similar Jewish histories to follow, up to the present.

Zornberg asks, What does this have to do with healing? Does making a record of the complaints and suffering have anything to do with healing the past? One could argue that such a memory of suffering generates a determination that ensures survival and state-of-the-art military defenses; however, there is another way to understand the suffering in/of the wilderness.

The Jewish midrash says that suffering and illness have to be *seen through*. Illness and suffering needs to be *re-imagined as part of a larger process*.[80] It has an important part to play in the redemptive process of losing and gaining toward the realization of what matters and is true and what is transitional and must die. The complicated task of seeing-through the vicissitudes and suffering of living has a role to play in attaining a higher health beyond the body.

---

[80] Zornberg, *Bewilderments*, p. xxix.

When "Moses wrote down the twists and turns of their journeys," he was creating a therapeutic template, a consciousness and a healing process where the people were "watching over themselves." Such a narrative enables the awareness of those parts of the self that must be relinquished for something new to appear.

In approaching the Exodus as a saving event, outwardly the people were freed from enslavement by the Egyptians, notwithstanding the fact that years before the foreigner, Joseph, son of Jacob, had saved Egypt by foreseeing a major regional famine and developed a plan to store grain. With Moses, the children of Israel were outwardly freed, but they were not inwardly freed. They were not freed from themselves. They were not freed from their selfishness, their illusions about religion, their arrogance about being chosen as people of God. They remained a people limited by perceptions that bound them, and as such, they remained in exile from themselves. The sacred healing story had yet to be told.

Did the wilderness work as a therapeutic spiritual intervention? After all, it occupies a substantial environment in the Jewish imagination. Even though the Jewish story found its way through repeated temple destructions and exiles, each with a disestablishment of its religion, it seems that in many ways the religious culture never found its way through the challenge of losing everything and "going back to zero," the Jewish counterpart to Jesus saying, "Leave all and follow me."

Initially Freedom Is Bipolar

If the Exodus is the archetype of freedom, aka salvation, it has a counterpart. It is a bipolar archetype. Freedom always comes with structure or order.

The children of Israel found themselves in the wilderness, free to go wherever, no specific goals or obligations, no rules or guidelines other than what Moses set forth. Initially, there were no enemies, no reason to organize an army, no governing body, no farms, no crops, no food, no real jobs, no real organization. It was an adolescent dream, no one telling them where to go or who to be. But in the midst of wandering in the desert without a country, another event happened, one that affected their freedom: Sinai.

Freedom requires limits. Freedom requires structure; it requires order. These opposites come as a pair. This is a principle parents know in raising teenagers. They must have rules and consequences until they mature enough to create their own. The meaningless wandering without direction is matched by the giving of the Torah at Sinai. Wandering is paired with meaning and intention, so that it is not aimless.

On the east shore of the Red Sea, after the divided waters closed over the Egyptian army (was this another divine massacre or holocaust?), probably no one said, "We are free." Freedom is not self-defining; it finds itself over against what limits it. Undoubtedly, this lack of clarity was not immediately realized, not before the people camped at the foot of the rugged mountain called Sinai. Only then did the people realize a deeper truth: true freedom within a community is born from structure.

Far more than a set of rules, what was given to these nomadic wanderers at Mount Sinai was a story around which they could develop an identity. It was a structure that provided the foundation for clarity, direction, and shared purpose. Sinai provided a framework that ensured the community would function smoothly—roles and responsibilities were defined, and a collective vision came into view. It is structure that allows real freedom to emerge. Psychologists say it is structure that creates freedom, not limits. Accordingly, it is immature to see the rules that came from Sinai as simply limits.

Sinai provided a framework, a discipline for spiritual consciousness. It created a collective view of reality rather than an individualistic view. Law and relationship and social interaction came from the group; there was no such thing as individual rights, individual liberties. Today this is preserved in Soviet legal jurisprudence. What was real emerged out of the community, including the perception of God, in the form of the Shekinah, God-in-the-community.

There is a divide between those who crave flexibility and those who seek certainty. The challenge arises when the desire for free flow becomes so dominant that it undermines the stability and purpose of the group. The truth is, structure and freedom are not opposing forces. Rather, structure is the foundation that makes true freedom possible. However, an overemphasis on rules can lead to a sense of oppression, stifling individual expression and personal growth. Rules are not inherently good or bad; they are strategies aimed at meeting certain needs.

The healing story is not simply a story of freedom and salvation, but a story that says healing is not an individual matter; it emerges in the context of family, community, and global community.

What is the Torah That Moses Gave?

You will make holy what unbinds.
You will offer liberation everywhere.
It shall be a total release for you.
You shall be restored [to a state beyond]
your attachment/possessiveness
You shall return to your original and true state.
— Leviticus 25:10 (rendering by the author)

I have heard and realized that bondage and
liberation are both within yourself.
— Acarangasutra 5.36[81]

Moses is inside the soul of Jesus as
Jesus is in the soul of Moses.
— Rumi[82]

A larger way of looking at what happened at Sinai is God gave Moses the Torah, something much broader than the commandments chiseled on two stone tablets. Torah is often taken literally as the first five books of the Bible: Genesis, Exodus, Leviticus, Numbers, and Deuteronomy. Many look at these books as an expanded list of rules. If nothing else, these five books make up a story, a story that creates identity.

---

[81] Acarangasutra is scripture from Jainism. Citation is from Andrew Wilson, *World Scripture: An Anthology of Sacred Texts* (New York: International Religious Foundation, 1991), p. 488.

[82] Rumi, in *The Soul of Rumi*, trans by Coleman Barks, (HarperSanFrancisco, 2001), p. 50.

But Torah is much more than a telling of origins and where we are going. Some would say the Torah is the creation of the Jewish religion. Yet, Torah is more than perceived religion, more than beliefs, more than worship and prayer, more than ritual. Torah is the way for meaningful living, beyond the synagogue, beyond creeds, beyond rituals and holy days, beyond religion. In this sense, Torah becomes the constitution and order that matches the wandering without intent or direction.

What was given at Sinai (and later at Pentecost in Jerusalem) was not a set of commandments, mitzvoth, or teachings. What was given was a new consciousness, a Way of life, a sense of destiny and Higher Presence. What was given was something that created a community, a spirituality, a people of the Way.[83] What was given cannot be reduced to rules, beatitudes, sermons, and ideas. Jews don't speak of Torah as a "thing," as in *the* Torah. Rather, they see themselves as stepping into an experience or a Reality.

Up to this point in biblical history, there had been an "exile of the Word." There were no scriptures, no guidelines, no memory of the future, no directions, no identity. The people were unable to comprehend their own history and experience. There was no framework to speak of their own redemption. The absence of word is mirrored in Moses' inability to speak, being of uncircumcised tongue. The "development of their subjectivity" became their project in the wilderness. Like Moses, they all have the daunting challenge of coming into language.[84]

Considering Torah in this way asks us to view Torah as being multi-leveled in the same way we looked at the Garden of Eden. Every religion interprets its scripture at four levels of understanding, beginning with the literal, then the symbolic, then the highest reach of the mind, and finally beyond form. In Judaism, as we explored in Chapter 2, these levels are given the names *pashat*, *remez*, *drash*, and *sod*. These levels are depicted in Figure 4.

---

[83] cf. The wording of the Book of Acts, "people of the Way," a formulation before the Christian movement had defined itself.

[84] Avivah Gottlieb Zornberg, *Moses : A Human Life* (New Haven: Yale University Press, 2016), p. 6.

Pashat

The first level (*Pashat*) of understanding the Torah given to Moses is the Ten Commandments in Exodus 20. The first four commandments are about the relationship with God, while the fifth is transition. The last five are about human relationships.

**Figure 4: Different Levels of Understanding Torah
(beginning at the bottom up)**

Each Commandment is subject to being taken literally or in more subtle ways. For example, the Fourth Commandment is "Keep the Sabbath Day holy," but does this mean one cannot cook on the Sabbath, or use a cell phone? Or the Second Commandment, "Do not make a graven image" (idol). In a larger sense, this means don't put into literal form what is formless. Don't "freeze-frame" what is alive and always changing. Don't nail things down. Fundamentalism in any religion, which goes for literalism, violates this Commandment. One might add, the idol of your *self* is the mother of all idols—an idol on which we spend millions adorning, pleasuring, feeding, preventing aging, and worshipping.

The *pashat* level of understanding Torah is to reduce its essence to the Ten Commandments and to want to make these into an idol to be placed in courthouses and classrooms throughout the land. There are a couple of dangers in remaining at this level of understanding. First, law and mitzvot tend to become codified and enshrined instead of lived. The second is the tendency to make religion into a moral institution. What is seen as good and not good changes as one matures spiritually, where eventually one sees that every evil has some good and every good has some bad; eventually, in higher spirituality, one transcends the categories of good and evil to the point where the commandments are no longer necessary.

Remez

The *remez* level of understanding Torah sees not just the commandments but the larger story from Genesis to the Promised Land. This is why in Figure 4, the recital of the "mighty acts of God" from Deuteronomy 26 is cited. Here, the story of the identity as the Children of God is formed, a people with a special calling among the nations of the world. It also had its shadow form as the Israelites marched with entitlement into lands belonging to other people and took it for themselves (and still do).

The *remez* version of Torah creates a chosen people and a perceived idea of God with a Plan for Holiness. It includes the story of Creation, Adam and Eve, Noah, Abraham, the Exodus, the creation of a religion around the Patriarchs, and wandering into the wilderness. The *remez* version is a great story of success and failure, of holiness and sinfulness, a story of messy families, jealousy, hate, and love. And embedded in the story is an incipient, largely unconscious beginning of the path to God, largely centered on the theme of obedience. Unconscious in the story is the realization of soul, the latent, deeper healing story.

To this day, rabbis speak of Torah as being feminine. They speak of the biblical tales as being the Torah's outer garments, and the understandings from the stories are undressing "Her"; however, they add, woe to the one who regards these outer garments as being Torah itself.

Developmental psychology asks, "What holds us?" Initially, the developing infant is "held" within the mother's womb and father's love. Then the infant is held by the mother's arms (and father's). As the child grows, it is "held" by the family, including siblings and grandparents. Upon entering school, the child is "held" by friends and belonging. Later one is "held" by lovers, and so on. We do not really know what holds us, for we are largely unconscious about this until we are at the threshold of leaving what holds us and entering a new holding. The point here is, one does not possess or hold Torah—it holds them.

Drash

The *drash* level of understanding Torah is represented in what Jews call "The Shema," coming from the first word of Deuteronomy 6:4. "Hear [*shema*], O Israel, the Lord your God is one." This is rightfully the most familiar mantra in Judaism, recited in nearly every service. However, it is not easily understood, for it is the highest teaching in spiritual language. It is often understood as being a statement of monotheism, and seen as a riff on the first commandment, "Thou shalt have no other Gods but me." As seen in Figure 5, the word for "one" here means one without a second. It has nothing to do with the number 1. It goes back to the beginning of Genesis; in the beginning all was one.

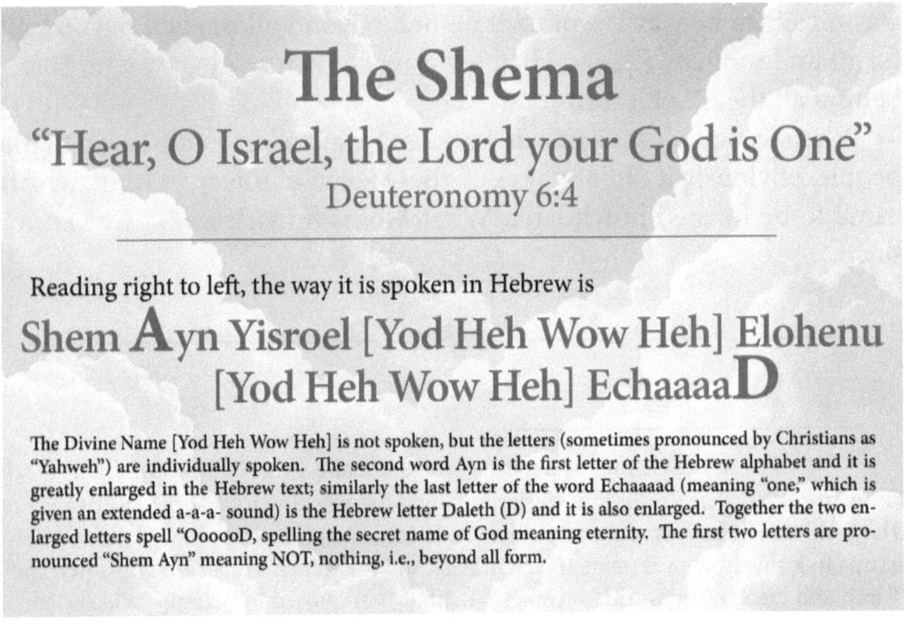

The Shema
"Hear, O Israel, the Lord your God is One"
Deuteronomy 6:4

Reading right to left, the way it is spoken in Hebrew is

Shem Ayn Yisroel [Yod Heh Wow Heh] Elohenu [Yod Heh Wow Heh] EchaaaaD

The Divine Name [Yod Heh Wow Heh] is not spoken, but the letters (sometimes pronounced by Christians as "Yahweh") are individually spoken. The second word Ayn is the first letter of the Hebrew alphabet and it is greatly enlarged in the Hebrew text; similarly the last letter of the word Echaaaad (meaning "one," which is given an extended a-a-a- sound) is the Hebrew letter Daleth (D) and it is also enlarged. Together the two enlarged letters spell "OooooD, spelling the secret name of God meaning eternity. The first two letters are pronounced "Shem Ayn" meaning NOT, nothing, i.e., beyond all form.

Figure 5: The Shema (Deuteronomy 6:4) and its Islamic Counterpart

We come from one, we return to one. Reality is nondual. There is only God. Any two-ness (dualism) is illusory. Reality is one. Period.

The Shema is considered as a *drash* understanding at the highest level of the mind's reach. It is a move beyond the myriad forms, stories, moral and ethical teachings of the *remez* level of understanding. There is no undressing at the *drash* level, no meaning behind the meaning. The *drash* level of Torah requires we step outside ourselves (is this undressing ourselves?), outside our separate identity and ego, and therein become one and the same as God.

Sod

The *sod* level of Torah is beyond the mind and beyond religion. It is the Creator before creation. The midrash says that God consulted Torah *before* He created the world.[85] In Figure 2, the *Sod* level says. "Vast Face beyond Small Face, i.e., Yahweh." This is a reference from the Kabbalah. Yahweh is the transliteration of the Hebrew consonants YHWH, and it was meant to be beyond form and the mind, so it was not to be pronounced, i.e., given form. But still Yahweh conjures up a formed image of God, so Kabbalists called this Small Face. What they called Vast Face was meant to be way beyond all names, beyond all images, beyond all forms and thought. This is what *Sod* is reaching for, the only true Torah behind all the other Torahs.

When we say Moses came down from Sinai and brought Torah to the people, obviously it did not have all these levels of interpretation, which came to be formed much later. What Moses himself knew, we cannot say.

---

[85] "Then I was beside him as a master workman and I was daily His delight" (Proverbs 8:10). The Torah thus declares, "I was the working tool of the Holy One. The architect, moreover, does not build it out of his head, but employs plans and diagrams to know how to arrange the chambers and the doors. Thus God consulted the Torah and created the world."—Genesis Rabbah 1:1, quoted in Andrew Wilson, ed. *World Scripture: A Comparative Anthology of Sacred Texts* (New York: International Religious Foundation, 1991), p. 100.

How Successful Was the Sinai Experience?

Obviously, Torah is as central to Judaism as the Gospel is to Christianity. But, as is true in every religion, the ultimate understanding and highest healing story is beyond what is usually told. The fact that there is more sacred substance and more spiritual gold to be mined beyond the reach of scholars may be an aspect of the genius of sacred scriptures.

God is not overly crazy about rules, and religion may want to take note. There is no universal rule, no absolute virtue, no universal morality. Religion is about living, not about good and bad.

So the Kabbalah says that God said to Moses on the mountain, "Let's figure out a way of not having a rule for everything, but to have a conversation between me (God) and the people and figure out a dynamic and positive solution." God asked Moses, "How do you want to do this? I suggest that whenever an issue arises among the people, we create a 'safe neutral zone' where I will set aside my power and judgment and you and/or the people can enter this space without any fear or consequence, and we can just talk about it together." This benign neutral zone in Hebrew is *challal panui*. "The other option," God continued, "and far less interesting, is that we could just create rules (commandments). Go, ask the people which approach they want."

It was an interesting proposal for how God and human beings could work together. God suggested that He and the people simply get together and figure things out. It would always be a moment for innovation, intimacy, and creativity. The state of *challal panui* is free from the "anxiety of influence." *Challal panui* is a play area that yields limitless new possibilities for being. The "form-free zone" that God proposed was a divine move to invite God's lovers to move beyond all laws, all rules and beliefs, all forms, and to experience true liberation.[86]

Challal panui was also a zone where God and each of us could challenge one another without consequence or punishment, and together consider many different options. God allows himself to be questioned by his creation, and God is capable of change and flexibility. Make note, it is God who created this space, not human beings. This is the antithesis

---

[86] Zornberg, *The Particulars of Rapture: Reflections on Exodus* (New York: Doubleday, 2001), p. 190, 192, 393.

of a fixed universe and a God who sets up immutable laws. The universe is open to novel development and innovation. God pulls back or retrenches God's total Presence in order to make it possible for a world to emerge.

Moses went back to the people, and they clamored, "No, we don't want the first option. That takes too much work. We want rules." The result? The Ten Commandments.

Moses went back to God with this, and God was very disappointed, but God then gave Moses the Ten Commandments. God was upset that the people did not want a higher spirituality, and (the midrash story says) that is why God called the people of Israel "stiff-necked"[87] (in Genesis 32).

This safe, neutral space that God was offering is also called *tzimtzum* in Hebrew, meaning that God contracts, shrinks, holds back his presence. For us, God appears hidden in his *tzimtzum* state. Even though God is everywhere and in everything, this holding himself back and limiting himself makes us feel more independent and in control. *Tzimtzum* allows the people to develop personal egos. *Tzimtzum* is God reining himself waaaaaayyyy back. *Tzimtzum* means God limiting Himself and entering into human form.

Was this refusal to meet God in a consequence-free zone a failure? Apparently, it was a disappointment to God. Just following rules represents a lower level of spiritual consciousness that is more black-and-white and requires less inner reflection and inner struggle, not to mention the fact that just following the rules is less intimate and keeps God at a distance. Absent is the "intimacy of all experience." Following the rules is a less developed level of spirituality.

It wasn't that the outcome of what happened on Mt. Sinai was a failure, but it got off to a rocky start. It took many generations where Israel kept redefining a workable religion (as noted in the next chapter), with different religious forms, different leaders, different ideas about God, different religious structures. At least a hundred and fifty years passed before the Commandments were given a home in a Temple. There were setbacks, as noted in the following.

---

[87] Exodus 32:9. "And the LORD said to Moses, "I have seen this people, and behold, it is a stiff-necked people."

And the Lord said to Moses [on Mt. Sinai], "Go down, for your people have corrupted themselves… and made a molten golden calf and have worshipped it. These are your gods who brought you up out of the land of Egypt? … Now let me alone, that my wrath may be hot against them and I may consume them."
— Exodus 32: 7-10, 14 (abridged)

When God said to Moses, "Now let me be… And I shall make you a great nation… immediately Moses replied, "For the sake of my own success, should I abandon the cause of Israel? Now all the nations of the world will say that I have killed the Israelites as Noah [killed the people of his generation] … It is better that I should die and Israel not be destroyed." Immediately. Moses entreated God…" – he sought mercy for them and God's mercy on the world was aroused.
— Shemoth Rabba 43:1 (Zohar)

It looks like the people broke the Second Commandment that said don't give form to the divine before they knew that there was such a commandment. As a child in Sunday School, when I learned the story of the Golden Calf, even then it felt immature and primitive. The children of Israel had f--ked up. I wondered how Moses' brother, Aaron, seemed to escape responsibility and why he was the first High Priest and the Levite priesthood descended from him. But such judgments come from a much later perspective.

Forty days is a metaphor for a long and indeterminate time, similar to when Jesus was in the wilderness for forty days, when it rained forty days with Noah, when Goliath taunted Israel for forty days, when Elijah fled from Jezebel for forty days, etc. At the bottom of the mountain with no direction, the religious impulse arose and the people resorted to the only religious form they knew. The sacred bull, Apis, was the prime deity at the time of the Exodus. Scared and faced with uncertainty, the people resorted to the only thing they knew: the religion of Egypt. The Golden Calf was not a randomly chosen image of fake religion.

It is a familiar move in the religious quest that, when faced with the unknown future, one resorts to the good old religion with its literal and fundamentalist elements. No one knew at the time that Moses was attempting to introduce a religion beyond form and idolatry. At the same time, the above texts from Exodus and the Zohar depict God as an angry, jealous, vindictive figure, which is also a fundamentalist and limiting picture.

It is an interesting story when God loses his temper, and it is Moses who has to talk God down. It is reminiscent of Job's critique of God, where Job takes a position of compassion that is morally higher than God. Here as well, Moses is higher, more developed than God. When God says, "Now let me be [in my anger]…," God in effect asks Moses for permission to destroy the people. Moses says, "Whoa, hold on, what will happen to your reputation when the Egyptians see you brought them out here to the wilderness only to kill them all? Is this really a 'Noah-moment?' What about the merit of Abraham, Isaac, and Jacob and the promise You made to them? You say the people are stiff-necked. Well you, God, are the one who is stiff-necked, fixed on revenge! If you gotta kill someone, take me!"

This is a narrative of re-inventing the godly in the world. It is a story of revisioning the world beyond action-punishment, beyond the old eye-for-an-eye approach, to considering mercy as an option. Moses sees his options to either take sides with God or stand with his people. He stood with the people against God. Is this Jewish story about a God who is an angry God, or a God who forgives, a God who changes His mind, a God who shows mercy, a God who comes back again and again with love? Is the universe friendly? Does "the arc of justice lean toward mercy?" It is an interesting moment in the history of religion.

Moses' stand against God may be the beginning of his ascendency from that of a hero to the highest sainthood.

When Moses approached the camp and saw the calf and the dancing, his anger burned and he threw the tablets out of his hands, breaking them to pieces at the foot of the mountain. And he took the calf the people had made and burned it in the fire; then he ground it to powder, scattered it on the water and made the Israelites drink it. [We eat our sins.] The next day Moses said to the people, "You have committed a great sin. But now I will go up to the Lord; perhaps I can make atonement for your sin."
–(Exodus 32:19-20, 30)

But the story doesn't end there. God may have forgiven the people, but they couldn't forgive themselves. Thus begins a new chapter in the history of sacred healing stories known as "atonement," beginning with Adam and Eve, the Tower of Babel, Noah, etc. The traumatic effects of the Golden Calf brought troublesome ghosts for years to come.

The next book of Torah, Leviticus, carries forward the effects of the catastrophic "oooops moment" of the people's sin. Theologian Aviva Gottlieb Zornberg says, "The central subject of Leviticus is the functioning of the *Mishkan*, the Holy Tabernacle, with its sacrifices, its pollution taboos, its priesthood with its powers and limitations. ...The *Mishkan* does not merely represent forgiveness; it becomes a therapeutic device for healing the national disorder that is called the Golden Calf.[88] "Let the gold of the *Mishkan* atone for the gold they brought toward the making of the Golden Calf."[89]

The Book of Leviticus is tiresome in its detail of the construction of the tabernacle, obsessive and soul-less. Does the book reflect the exchange of one idol for another, the second dedicated to the God of Sinai? The Torah story winds its way through trial after trial of faith and the heartbreaking story of Moses not being admitted to the Promised Land. As previously stated, Moses is not the Highest of the High in Judaism, but he was close. He went to God in his death.

As a footnote to the high work of Moses, Meher Baba said, "Rameses [II] in his next incarnation entered the Path; the old Pharaoh [Seti] received *mukti* [liberation], because he took Moses' name when dying." This means Pharaoh reached God-realization in his next incarnation through his work and struggle with Moses.[90]

---

[88] Avivah Gottlieb Zornberg, *The Hidden Order of Intimacy: Reflections on the Book of Leviticus* (New York: Schocken Books, 2022), p. xi-xii.

[89] *Shemot Rabbah* 51:61 cited in Zornberg, *The Hidden Order of Intimacy*, p. xii.

[90] Meher Baba, in Bhau Kalchuri, *Lord Meher* (Myrtle Beach, SC: MANifestation, NC, 1979), v. 15, p. 5264. Meher Baba said this on the occasion of seeing DeMille's film, *The Ten Commandments*.

CHAPTER 6

EIGHT WAYS OF FINDING SALVATION

Let them make for me a place
so that I may dwell among them.
— Exodus 25:8

The Garden of Eden, Abraham, and Moses are all big stories, each with a mix of adventure, human pathos, and embedded dynamics that offer healing to the searching soul. But is there an even bigger healing story, one that encompasses the entire Bible? Is there a story that goes beyond all the sinful and mundane aspects of human activity, the acts of genocide, betrayal, greed, the Levitic rituals of sacrifice, details of temple-building, the wearying theological lectures? If one wanted to make the Bible shorter and more readable, what should be cut out? What is the overall effect of the holy scriptures?

At the risk of being reductionist, the entire Bible could be summarized into eight big story shifts, eight big plot movements. Seven of these story shifts can be attributed to the Old Testament (which Jews appropriately prefer to call the "Jewish Bible") and the eighth would be the New Testament, which, in deference to the Jewish perspective, could be called the Christian Testament.

The Big Story of the entire Bible can be seen as the universal story of the journey of the soul for all people, not just Jews and Christians, as it becomes consciously realized as the journey into God (the Alpha/the Beginning and the Omega/the End), and the Bible is also the journey of God as well, meaning God is not separate from the story. No journey is separate from any other journey.

The eight story shifts are listed in the chart in Figure 6 below. One can see these as a set of historical developments, the history of Judaism and Christianity. But they go beyond history; they were not written chronologically as historical fact. Some are outside of history completely, such as the early stories of creation, the Garden of Eden, the Tower of Babel, and Noah. A sizable number of stories were written in the seventh century BCE to provide a national identity as Babylon was taking over the nation, and there are many historical inaccuracies in their memory. The Jewish Bible was not established until 91 CE at the Council of Jamnia. And the Christian Bible continues to be fluid and has never been closed, meaning parts could be added or removed.

It is more accurate to see the eight developments of the biblical stories as "mythology," rather than history. But to be clear, *myth does not mean false*. Myth is not devoid of history. Myth embraces facts and actual events. Mythology means it is a story of the people's perception and interpretation. These are stories of the experience of the human psyche.

As seen in Figure 7, each of these story shifts is a different world view. Each has a different name for God. Each has its own unique religious institution. Each arises out of a different "place" or geographic environment, each having a unique sociology. Each has spiritual themes specific to the particular worldview, giving the religious experience a specific focus and quality. Each has its own particular theology. Each has its own answer to the question of "how can one be saved" or become one with God. Each has its own heroic figure or central character, and when that person is named everyone recognizes the spiritual model or religious approach of that world view.

It is tempting to call these eight story shifts "religious paradigms," suggesting that they are integrated, coherent, almost-complete ways to experience God and each one creates a definable spiritual path. These eight religious paradigms are archetypes of the psyche that are universal to all people, for these archetypes are found in other world religions.

Chart of Eight Biblical Mythic Paradigms

Mythic Paradigm	Major Event	Key Figures	Religious Institution	Mode of Salvation	Concept of God	Key Themes
CREATION FALL	Creation Garden den The Fall Cain - Able Flood Babel	God Adam-Eve Serpent Noah/ Babel	The world. No institution (which is its own institution)	At first, no separation from God obedience	Creator God (God is One, then Two [nondualism then dualism])	Word (Dabar) Creation Order/Chaos Sin/Evil Innocence/Guilt
COVENANT	Abraham Covenant Akedah-- Sacrifice of Isaac	Abraham Isaac, Jacob Joseph	Family Patriarchy	Faithfulness to Family's covenant	family God: (God of Abraham, Isaac, and Jacob)	covenant inheritance family loyalty/trust betrayal
LAW/ FREEDOM	Exodus Mt. Sinai wilderness	Moses	Tabernacle	Obedience to Torah Following religious contract	God the Liberator Shekinah (feminine)	Law/com'nts Torah liberation wilderness wandering
PROMISED LAND	Conquest of Palestine North South kingdoms	Joshua Elijah	High Place	The religious Warrior Heroic establishment of the Way	Warrior God punishes and protects	Holy Land Homeland/ place/belonging Holy War victory-defeat
KINGDOM	Davidic Kingdom 1ˢᵗ Temple	King David Solomon	Temple	Temple cultic religion	King of Kings a Royal God political God	Kingdom national ego Temple priesthood Jerusalem
PROPHETIC HEALING	Babylonian Exile Restoration	Isaiah Jeremiah Ezekiel	Synagogue	Death and resurrection	Transcendent God (with angels and intermediaries)	judgment/ punishment apocalyptic Holy Writings prophetic
WISDOM	Ezekiel's chariot Psalms transcendent spirituality	David Solomon Ezekiel	Inner Self	Transcending the Mind	Sophia	Psalms/proverbs spirituality beyond life hope/eschatology transcendent life
KINGDOM OF GOD	Jesus Teachings Resurrection Early Church	Jesus Apostle Paul	church	Atonement. Leaving all & becoming the Christ	God Incarnate Divine-human Trinity	agape love Normative Xty vs Way of Jesus globalization of religion Universal Christ

Figure 6: Eight Paradigms of Religion in the Bible

There is a beauty and a power in seeing the biblical story as a whole, although one never sees the psyche as a complete whole.

Is there an evolutionary development reflected in the movement of these eight story shifts? This is a dangerous position to take, other than to say the human community has learned from its story and that religious experience has matured. But one cannot say, "I follow Abraham," with that being seen as a more primitive position than "I follow Christ." Each path has its significance as a way to God. As the sages say, all paths go to God; there is no other way for them to end up. Some paths just take longer than others.

In the 1980s, there was a movement to define developmental stages—adult development, moral development, faith development, child development, stages of women's development, etc. One of the learnings that emerged from developmental theory was the assertion that no stage of development was superior to another, as each stage had its own integrity. Children are not immature little adults, as was once thought.

Sam Keen, with theological doctorates from both Harvard and Princeton, challenged the seriousness of colleagues doing developmental theory. In his book, *The Passionate Life: Stages of Loving*,[91] he offered the five stages of being a lover—child, rebel, adult, outlaw, lover/fool. Each of these forms had positive and deep understandings about love, and each has its shadow (unconscious and destructive) side that often shows up in every culture.

In a sense, each of Keen's five stages—child, rebel, adult, outlaw, lover/fool—can apply to each of the religious paradigms. But archetypally, with some adaptation, the eight religious paradigms can be characterized within these stages as well. For example, one could say that the paradigm of Creation/Fall has many characteristics related to Infancy (the archetype before Keen's Child). Thus, we speak of innocence, abandonment, original sin, guilt and shame, fear of not being lovable, trust, establishing relationship, parent-child relationships within the Infancy framework. The serpent symbolizes chthonic energy, physical and earthly forces, only partly conscious, emerging from earlier animal existence. The Garden is the womb of beginnings. Nakedness is an aspect of the Infancy archetype, as is learning language, differentiating things, naming the animals.

---

[91] Sam Keen, *The Passionate Life: Stages of Loving* (San Francisco: Harper San Francisco, 1983).

The stories of Abraham (and the three generations that follow, called The Patriarchs) are family stories. God is a family deity, probably originally differentiated as the God of Abraham, the God of Isaac, and the God of Jacob. These stories relate to the archetype of the Child in Keen's perception, climaxing in the sacrifice of the child on Mount Moriah. Within this paradigm are the archetypes of family wounding, sibling wounding, homelessness, loss of parents, the orphan, the bad parent, the trickster, and the theme of belonging.

The stories of the next religious paradigm, the Exodus, seem to mirror the archetype of the Rebel, seen in adolescence. Here are the themes of rebelling and challenging authority, wandering in the wilderness of one's life, unable to reach clarity, much less realize one's destination. There is grumbling, negativity, impatience, anger, addiction, struggling with rules and limits, yearning, boredom, loss of religion, and dislike of society and structure. Parents and pre-adult children need these archetypal forms to make sense of leaving the known of childhood and moving into the unknown of adulthood. Psychologists say this is a liminal experience, a being in-between.

The paradigm of entry into the Promised Land under the leadership of Joshua is the beginning of what Keen might have termed Adulthood, but it is an immature adulthood, or "Adulthood 1" when compared to the next stage. Here the activity and energy is not unlike what is experienced in one's twenties—finding out where one lives, fighting over what belongs to one and to others, setting boundaries, creating new rules for living and social interaction, developing new peer relationships, figuratively "killing" the parents, exploring the "shadow" (undeveloped side) of the Warrior archetype, killing unnecessarily and not knowing where the battle is, falling in love, beginning to work with the ego-self, and developing inadequate ways of addressing fear.

The Kingdom of David would seemingly qualify for Keen's stage of Adulthood. It was almost as if ancient Israel said, "Okay, God, I think we got it. I think we have things under control, we are grown up and see what is going on. We can take it from here." So the main pillars of society were constructed: the royal kingdom, the palace, the military, political dominance in defeating the Philistines, the Temple, and judicial and moral law under Solomon. So the archetypes of this religious paradigm became establishing power, defenses, security, nationhood, institutional religion, and also the shadow of this Adult state, i.e., corruption, failure of trust, materialism, national ego, success and failure, fundamentalism, knowledge without wisdom, and loss of soul.

There is a parallel here with the (probably mythical) Kingdom of King Arthur. When Arthur came to power, the story goes that he supported every person in the kingdom to do their best in expressing their gifts, and the kingdom flourished because Arthur "held the center." Arthur kept things in balance, blessing everybody without being caught up in his own ego. But then his best friend (Launcelot) fell in love with his wife, and the kingdom fell apart. The Davidic Kingdom did not last long and fell apart in eighty years, never to be restored.

The next stage of Israel's development is seen as the Prophetic Period, dominated by Isaiah, Jeremiah, and Ezekiel. With all the hubris of the Davidic Kingdom, everything went to hell in a handbasket. The people of the northern Kingdom had been sent to the steppes of southern Russia, and the Russians were transported to Northern Israel, and these foreigners were called Samaritans. The Southern Kingdom was subsequently taken over by Babylon, and then by the Persians who defeated Babylon. Many Jews did not return to Jerusalem but continued eastward along the Silk Road. The Prophets set about trying to point out where the people got off the spiritual path and sought to restore a religious community. This is why this paradigm is called Prophetic/Healing, i.e., destruction and healing. Actually, it is in this phase of deconstruction that the themes of death and resurrection begin to arise, and the spiritual assertion that death is never the end.

This is a stage in Keen's developmental thinking that he calls the Outlaw stage. This is a stage where many in the Adult stage "wake up" and realize that the accepted certainties of adulthood are really not the answer to life. Many older adults see the bankruptcy of their careers and living the dream of having two homes and big investment accounts to soothe their anxiety.

It is interesting to ask what the difference is between the Rebel stage before Adulthood and the Outlaw stage that can follow Adulthood. The Rebel is pushing against and rejecting the limits imposed by society and blaming others. The Outlaw sees the illusion of the answers and no longer wants to stay in the game. The Outlaw sees other alternatives and possibilities for higher being and more meaningful living than the status quo.

The Prophetic/Healing paradigm asks people to explore the purpose of life, to seek the deeper essence of self. It addresses archetypes of self-destruction, idolatry, beauty, seeing other cultures, loss, suffering, the archetype of the Destroyer, and new vision/higher reality. This paradigm asks people to face the certainty of death, to ask what does and what doesn't die, to see the illusions of everyday attachment, to realize what is stronger and surpasses death. This is the true sacred healing story of the Bible.

The seventh religious paradigm is called Wisdom. In many ways, it overlaps the Prophetic/Healing stage, and in many ways, it found its deeper development in the post-biblical movements of the Kabbalah and Hasidic movements in the 13th, 16th, and 18th centuries. In many ways, Wisdom, reflected in the Psalms, Proverbs, Job, and Song of Solomon, is seen as practical guidelines for everyday living. Wrong! This is not the real religious paradigm of Wisdom, which vastly transcends moral and relationship guidelines about the good wife, the good father. It is difficult to think of Wisdom as not being a wise teaching. For the first time, true Wisdom is a human effort to assume a divine attribute beyond the limited human mind.

Wisdom had its roots in the image the prophet Ezekiel had of the divine flying chariot, which meant God was not just in the Temple of Jerusalem, but God was everywhere, a novel idea for Jews who needed a "place" for God. The mystical continuance of this biblical path is called "Merkabah Wisdom" and the "Work of the Chariot." In the first nine chapters of Proverbs, Sophia is the named personification of Wisdom who takes the Mind of God in creating the world and puts them into form. Jesus is linked as being the same as Sophia by the Apostle Paul.[92]

Jewish mysticism differentiates between Wisdom (*Hochmah*), Understanding (*Binah*), and Knowledge (*Daat*). Knowledge is the accumulation of experience, learning facts about the world, and having information. Understanding (*Binah*) is a synthesis beyond Knowledge, with an awareness of what it all means. Understanding is the culmination of

---

[92] 1 Corinthians 1:30. "It is due to him that you are in Christ Jesus, who became for us wisdom from God, as well as righteousness, sanctification, and redemption."

worldly experience, the fruit of individuation in the Jungian sense, the highest reach of faith. Reaching to an even higher level, Wisdom *(Hochmah)* is a knowing beyond the mind and mental thought, *an experience of the universal oneness.* Wisdom is a knowing beyond the mind and mental thought; it is what we think of as "God realization" or the experience of universal oneness. There is nothing in Wisdom *(Hochmah)* to grasp or acquire. No description of Wisdom is possible.

The eighth story shift in the Bible is represented by the New Testament, the story of Jesus Christ and the early Christian way. Jesus brings together into a single story every one of the previous seven religious paradigms. Jesus is called the Second Adam, signaling that creation is getting a new start. Jesus introduces the New Covenant (the first Covenant being with Abraham); additionally, the story of both Jesus and Abraham tell of the father sacrificing the son. Jesus is seen as the Second Moses, the giver of the new Law. Jesus' name, Yeshua, is the same as Joshua's, who takes people into the Promised Land/new kingdom. Jesus is seen as being from the lineage of David, and the messianic hope is a revival of Davidic rule. Jesus is seen as a prophet ("Are you the prophet/messiah, or are we to look for another?" Matthew 11:3), and as Emmanuel, he is seen as being foretold by Isaiah. Jesus embraces the Merkabah imagery of Ezekiel, and his teachings have a mystical reach of Wisdom. One could argue that the eighth religious paradigm has Jesus, the Jewish teacher, pulling together all the history of the Jewish people from Adam on, perhaps signaled by Jesus saying, "Before Abraham I was."[93]

At the same time, the story of Jesus the Christ moves beyond the story of the people of Israel to include the whole world. Jesus said his work was not to criticize or replace the Jewish religion, but to expand the religious experience into a much larger way.[94] It is here that the nature of the expanded experience of the psyche and its healing through fulfillment can be realized.

---

[93] John 8:58

[94] Matthew 5:17. "Do not think that I have come to abolish the Law or the Prophets; I have not come to abolish them but to fulfill them."

Another Mythic Perspective About the Biblical Stories

The general view of history is often seen through scientific certainty, holding that history is factual. There is a positivist view of Jews and Christians that the Bible is the story of God in history, that God is a God-of-history, and that this story is factually provable. But history is more fluid; it depends on the perspective and culture of the person looking at it. As a Palestinian archaeologist, it amused me how the interpretation of the history of what was being discovered changed from season to season of excavation.

As has been said, to say that a particular event in history is myth is *not* to say it is false. To take a biblical story, such as Abraham or Jesus, and speak of it as mythical is to say it has an impact on the psyche. We give it meaning and interpretation and soul that defines us as well as the event or figure we are looking at, and this makes it mythic, spiritual, and psychological in nature. We give history narrative and symbolic understanding, and we do this with each of the individual stories and larger paradigms in the Bible and we do it for the Bible as a whole.

Oswald Spengler was a German cultural historian a century ago. His two-volume book, *The Decline of the West*,[95] looked at history as repeating two-thousand-year cycles, with four movements in each cycle. He asserted that the first half of the two-thousand-year cycle was a period of creativity, imagination, growth, expansion, and new insights. The second half of the cycle was a period of stabilization, consolidation, and institutionalization, all leading to a further lack of growth. In this second half, the civilization arrogantly decided it had already understood the world and would stop creating bold new ideas, which would eventually lead to the loss of vision and energy. For example, the creativity of the earlier Greeks in fifth century BCE waned in the literalism, routinization, and practicality of the Romans.

The first period of Spengler's cycles was called The Age of Gods, the second was The Age of Heroes, the third was The Age of Men (making note of the sexist overtones here), and the last period of the two-thousand-year cycle was The Age of Chaos. And then it all begins again.

---

[95] Oswald Spengler, *The Decline of the West*, Vintage, reprint of 1918 and 1922 volumes.

To wit, the Bible begins with The Age of Gods in the figure of Abraham, somewhere in the neighborhood of the Early Middle Bronze Age (ca. 1800 BCE). While there is not historical continuity between Abraham and the Hebrew community of the Davidic kingdom, Abraham is increasingly seen as the avatar midway between Krishna and Buddha, and the Father of four world religions—Judaism, Islam, Christianity, and northern India Tantra. As noted earlier, Avatar Meher Baba said Abraham was among the Highest of the High. Abraham arose out of the civilizational collapse and chaos of the end of the Early Bronze Age. So we say our myth of civilizational cycles marks this period with Abraham as The Age of Gods.

The Age of Heroes is seen in the figure of Moses, a giant of faith who led an entire nation out of captivity and slavery, a spiritual leader who met with God on the mountain of Sinai and who gave the people a Torah that established an identity, a religion, a structure of religious guidelines, and a creative imagination that energized the people to see themselves as the people of God.

The third period, the Age of Men, seems to largely rest on the shoulders of King David, who created the institutions of kingdom and government, who created an army and the largest nation-state in Israel's history to the present day, and who established the Temple with Solomon and the Temple-religion. When vision becomes routinized into institutions and permanent forms, the creativity stops and mechanisms of control take over… the mark of the beginning of decline.

Following this began the Age of Chaos. The Kingdom was divided, its leaders were susceptible to corruption and diminished vision, the spirit of the people began to suffer, three super-powers (Assyria, Babylon, and Persia), and later the Seleucids and Ptolemies subjected the people to exile or domination and other religious influences. Judges like Elijah, and Prophets such as Isaiah, Ezekiel, and Jeremiah tried to recreate the past, but things continued to slide downhill. The chaos continued into the first century CE with the Romans destroying the Temple and scattering the Jewish community into the diaspora.

The cycle begins anew. Jesus the Avatar-Christ begins a new Age of Gods, establishing a new spiritual and religious paradigm that dominates for fifteen-hundred years. This was not a singular vision, for there were probably a hundred gospels and different versions of what happened, and there were lots of conflicting visions, as the movement expanded from a particular localized people to cultures over the world.

The Age of Heroes of the modern era is a little more difficult to pin down than the earlier figure of Moses. One might suggest that St. Augustine could be a heroic contender. More likely, the mythological figure of King Arthur rises to the heroic level of the medieval period, shaping a millennium culminating in the Quest for the Holy Grail, the development of courtly love, and the tragedy of the Crusades.

The Age of Men may have found its insipient beginning in Thomas Aquinas, who brilliantly systematized all of theology, creating a theological system not unlike King Josiah in the sixth century BCE. But if we were to identify a luminary who can be said to exemplify the Age of Men, perhaps it is Isaac Newton. Science gradually took over the world view from religion.

The Age of Chaos has followed down to the present day for the last four-hundred years. The printing press fostered literacy, leading people to begin to think for themselves, contributing to individualism, capitalism, democracy, human rights, nationalism, human diversity, pollution—all the "isms" that are under attack today.

Is the two-thousand-year cycle, rooted in the first two millennia of the biblical story, about to repeat itself in our time? Are we beginning again the Age of the Gods?

It is still a matter of religious and cultural debate, but the appearance in our time of Meher Baba, 1894-1969, suggests we are again in the Age of Gods. Meher Baba has been proclaimed all over the world to be "the Avatar of the Age," a reappearance of the Christ. He made four trips around the world, he drew devotees from every world religion, but he said he did not come to found a new religion. He came to awaken people, not proclaim new doctrines and beliefs. He often referred to the coming "new age" as a global community in which the entire world would become more spiritual, not necessarily more institutionally religious. He united all the religions of the world into a spiritual movement that transcends religion, he proclaimed a New Humanity and a divine future, and this has resulted in a growing spiritual movement all over the world.

The purpose of suggesting this repeating two-thousand-year cycle suggested by the biblical story is that we are at the threshold of a *new two-thousand-year cycle*, and that what is occurring at the present time is a new Age of Gods. Still, the world still seems in the Age of Chaos. This does not negate the emergence of a new spiritual age.

Well, what has happened? It seems that the world is in a transition with a lot of unfinished business from the past—continuing racism, anti-inclusion, anti-feminist, antisemitic, anti-climate change, and nationalistic and parochialism around white supremacy and control of wealth. It would seem that there is a lot of "clean-up" work around these harmful dynamics, all of which is a necessary part of the Age of Gods becoming manifest. One can see a similar struggle of conflict in the first century CE and in the nineteenth century BCE in the collapse of the Ebla Empire.

This is a book about the healing nature of the biblical story, with particular attention to the biblical psyche, where deepest healing occurs and is most needed. Common to every story from the Garden of Eden to Noah to Abraham, Moses, David, and the Prophets is the theme that the end is not the end. True enough, what is created by both God and human hands has its part to play, and then its time is over. And out of the chaos and ashes, something new arises, a new story begins. God is Creator and Destroyer and then back to Creator.

The human psyche, the human soul, learns what is provisional and temporary and what does not die. Death is never the end. Can anything be more healing to the soul than to realize it overcomes everything and is beyond all? This is encapsulated in the overarching biblical theme of death and resurrection localized in the story of the Avatar-Christ, but it is a healing theme that goes far beyond the New Testament story.

CHAPTER 7

HEALING AND PROPHETIC CONSCIOUSNESS

Moreover, I will give you a new heart
and put a new spirit within you;
and I will remove the heart of stone from your flesh
and give you a heart of flesh.
— Ezekiel 36:26

In the previous chapter, the seventh story shift or the seventh religious paradigm, described as Prophetic/Healing, saw the collapse of the kingdom of Israel. It was previously said things went to hell in a handbasket, with three world powers destroying the Temple, with Assyria first taking the Northern Kingdom of Israel into exile, and Babylon and then Persia taking the Southern Kingdom of Judah into exile. The religious and societal structure collapsed. From the eighth to the fifth centuries BCE, the story shifted from the triumphalism of the Davidic-Solomon kingdom of affluence and wealth to the fragmented, dispersed peoples, who never recovered an established national existence and a cohesive culture.

Had the religious experiment of Israel failed? Not exactly. Three prophetic giants, Jeremiah, Isaiah, and Ezekiel, spoke bluntly to the people, saying disaster must come, but they also added that this was not the end of the story. The usual picture of these prophetic interventions bringing bad news is often depressing, with oracles of judgment, calls for repentance, and examples of corruption and sin cited. The prophets' messages often included calls to social justice, urging the people to care for the poor, the widow, and the orphan. The prophets were severe social critics. They challenged the status quo and confronted kings, priests, and the people with their sins. But there is a much different story here, other than simply religious decline and falling off the wagon. This experience taught that spirituality was far more than the "Prosperity Gospel."

In the last chapter we considered the repeating two-thousand-year cycles of history outlined by Oswald Spengler. In each of his mid-cycles, approximately a thousand years into the movement, there is a shift from the Age of Heroes to what Spengler called the Age of Men. It marks a time when the earlier imagination and creativity of spirituality and vitalizing experience of God gave way to normalization and systematization.

Even today, the last eighty years have brought exciting new movements of spiritual innovation to the United States, such as the coming of yoga to America from India in the 1960s, the spread of shamanic spirituality, the worldwide expansion of Pranic Healing, and the formalization of mindfulness and meditation. However, there comes a point in these movements where people want to give the movement more permanent form, create an organization around it, financially profit from it, market it, write books about it, and create organizational structures for teaching and control. When the desire to manage the creativity and establish control and permanence arrives, the movement loses something important. In establishing and formalizing the spirit of the movement, it becomes stale and loses its vitality.

This is what happened to King Solomon.

Solomon was King David's son. He grew up in the light of his father David's success, and Solomon saw the glitter of power and wealth. He built a huge temple that was world-class; we can see a temple contemporary to Solomon in the excavations at Limassol, Cyprus, built by the same architects. Solomon built a palace, expanded the army, built huge defense walls with six-chambered gates for Jerusalem, Hazor, Gezer, and Megiddo, and expanded the kingdom from Egypt to Syria. He was perhaps something of an international sex symbol with the Queen of Sheba, and obviously he had organized a vast underclass of builders to construct his buildings and empire.

The success of Solomon and its effect on Israel, along with the spiritual shift brought about by the prophets, is chronicled in Walter

Brueggemann's book, *The Prophetic Imagination*.[96] Brueggemann dismisses the central agenda of the prophets as only focusing on the sin of the people in disregarding the Torah. Undoubtedly, there is truth in the prophet's calling attention to the religious failure of the Kingdom, but Brueggemann says the far-reaching prophetic agenda was to create a new consciousness, a consciousness that goes far beyond social injustice and moral decay.

The quote by Rumi about Moses at the heading of Chapter 5 recalled the need for a new consciousness:

> *What you showed Moses was not fire,*
> *but a shape of consciousness.*

The old consciousness experienced by the people of Israel in Egypt for generations concerned the established Egyptian religion, a religion that supported Egyptian culture. We see the power of this "good ole religion" when the Israelites created a Golden Calf to worship at the foot of Mt. Sinai in the absence of Moses (who was learning about the new consciousness in the clouds and smoke up on the mountain). The people reverted back to the established religion, even though they knew the gods were idols and seemingly powerless. Better to stay with the known, rather than the unknown.

Moses was working with a different God, not one that could be captured in images. Moses was dealing with a God who did not show his face, a God-on-the-Move, a God who did not just promise the fruits of the Promised Land. Moses was dealing with a God who proposed *Challal Panui*, a working out of principles of living and deciding things based not on set rules but on a dynamic, relative ethic arising anew out of every situation. Moses was encountering a dynamic God, not a static God ensconced in a lavish temple with meaningless rituals.

---

[96] Walter Brueggemann, *The Prophetic Imagination*, 40th Anniversary Edition, (Minneapolis: Fortress Press, 2018).

God Was Kidnapped by Managed Religion

Walter Brueggemann suggests that God had been kidnapped by religion, a God imprisoned in the Temple, a religion that denied the freedom of God.[97] Thus, Second Isaiah makes a bold pronouncement in the context of Babylon taking over the country and taking the people into the land of the Tigris and Euphrates, where God says:

> *And I will do all that I please,*
> *calling a bird of prey from the east,*
> *the man of My Purpose from a far country.*
> *What I have said, I tell you I will make it happen.*
> *I have planned it, surely I will do it.*
> *— Isaiah 46:10 – 11(adaptation by the author)*

This was a big stretch from the religious orthodoxy of the dominant religion, proclaimed four hundred years earlier on the steps of Solomon's Temple.

So Moses had the task of introducing a God beyond the Israelites' imagination, one they had never considered. Abraham had the same challenge as he left his family's kingdom, caught up in the business of fake God images. But he wasn't leading a suffering nation. Moses just needed to have the people see the truth about the present "immovable gods of order," and in Moses' ingenious way, he set about dismantling the state religion of Egypt, which had no power, and that change of people's perception could not have happened until they got to the shoreline of the Red Sea.

There were many bumps and regressions along the way, but with Higher Help, Moses was able to keep the people on the path to a dynamic God, no longer confined to a static temple but to a movable tabernacle and an Ark that went wherever the people went. A God-on-the-Move. How long this "movable feast" of spiritual people lasted, we can't say, but it lasted from the time of Moses into the Kingdom of David, somewhere between 150 and 400 years.

---

[97] Brueggemann, p. 22-23.

With Solomon, the pendulum swung in the opposite direction, to the establishment of a controlled religion not unlike the experience in Egypt, but now remote in people's memory. Building the First Temple, a grand piece of architecture seemed like a good idea, an honoring of Yahweh. They heard God saying, "Make a place for me," not "Make me into a captive of your ego."

The principle of *enantiodromia*, coined six hundred years later by Heraclitus, gained a foothold. *Enantiodromia* means things become their opposite. The God of the unknown (in Moses' day) became the God of the known. The King now mediates God to the people; the King has special access to God, not the people. As such, Solomon was idealized as being wise. The King as the agent of Wisdom gives answers to the people. There arises here in government/societally sanctioned religion, a false consciousness, a manufactured religion, a religion that says things are all right, a religion in service to the settled culture that wants things to stay the way they are.

The religion of King Solomon is predictable and managed religion. What is known has already been given. There is "nothing new under the sun." The steady state of this "royal religion" extended into the area of Wisdom, where wisdom has degenerated to practicality, morality, and commonplace advice for solving problems and getting along. There was no place for the higher and true Wisdom described in the ninth paradigm in the previous chapter where the reach of spirituality extended beyond the reaches of the limited mind. Solomonic wisdom had no place for transcendence.

Stale religion. Religion without soul. Leadership that was self-serving. Enter the prophets. Like Abraham, like Moses, they had to create a new consciousness, a consciousness that would free the people from what bound them. To preach sermons that would chastise them for their blindness, that would preach social justice on the street corners, that would release them from a culture of depression and helplessness… that wasn't enough.

Like Moses, the prophets had to open the doors to a new God, a different spiritual consciousness. They had to deconstruct mainstream religion, reveal its bankruptcy. That is one thing to do for other people's religion, but to do it for one's own religion, that was risky. Ecclesiastes states the problem:

All things are full of weariness;
A man cannot utter it;
The eye is not satisfied with seeing,
Nor the ear filled with hearing
What has been done is what will be.
— Eccl. 1:7-9

So the prophet First Isaiah (ca. 722 BCE) and Jeremiah (ca. 598 BCE) had to tell the truth bluntly: The Solomonic kingdom is done. The prosperity and security is over. Continuity has reached an end. Things die. We will see massive change. But when a culture experiences major change, the political and institutional level is the last of the four levels of change.

Change appears first at the artistic level. The good artists and poets are listening to the higher levels of transformation. Walter Brueggemann observes that, for the most part, the prophets spoke or communicated in poetic verse, while those of the management establishment tend to communicate in prose, the form of discourse for rationalization and justification. The prophets lift up the higher transcendent Wisdom that points to a higher level of reality beyond the levels of the brain and rational discourse, and these prophets or mystics speak in poetic form using symbol and metaphor.

The next level of change noted by cultural historians is the philosophical level of cultural analysts. These may be the voices of those who observe societal injustice: the creation of different classes from the elite, to the business people, to the treatment of foreigners, to the farmers and producers, to the lower class of servants and people enslaved. The political and religious system created a caste system.

Another group became part of the changes in the kingdom—the people who sought to capitalize on the changes. They positioned themselves in the changing economy, they brought certain technical skills, they made deals with the captors, and did what they could to preserve wealth and ensure survival. We could imagine many in this group were the leaders and entrepreneurs of the Solomonic kingdom, doing whatever they could to bargain for power.

A fourth group would be the helpless, the victims, the powerless who have no voice in change, the ones who have no homes or businesses to lose. They would be servants, women, widows, and victims of injustice.

The prophets see all the groups, and one of the first movements away from the Solomonic establishment is to dismantle the caste system of inequality. God-on-the-Move is for all people, and the cultural sociology returned to resemble life while wandering in the wilderness. God is no longer managed by the temple cult and their profitable systems of sacrifice and relieving sins in a system like medieval indulgences.

The prophets have to create a new dream, a vision of the future, a new form of "passion" (Brueggemann) along with introducing the idea of a future messiah without the Davidic and Solomonic overtones of grandiosity and permanence.

> *From now on I will tell you new things,*
> *things that are hidden, things which you have not known.*
> *They are created now, and not long ago.*
> *You have not heard of them before today.*
> *so you cannot say, 'Yes, I knew of them.'*
> — *Isaiah 48:3,5, 7-8, 6 (adapted by the author)*

The prophets were tasked with creating a new consciousness, a new spirituality, a new mythology, in the midst of religious and societal collapse. It required a new encounter and experience with death.

People hang on to their beliefs, which are the scaffolding for their reality. Letting go of old ways of thinking and accepting new possibilities is daunting. It doesn't happen by simply saying, "Here's a new way to look at things." Old belief has to die. The prophets, psalm-writers, and Wisdom-keepers all recognized the limits to belief and doctrines held so dearly by the Solomonic establishment. They spoke not only of a God of new beginnings, but also a God of endings, recognizing no forms are permanent. They recognized that what emerges as a new future does not come from a present imagination—we don't just think up a new God and a new future. This future comes from the unconscious (although that was not yet perceived as a psychic reality then), or another way to say this, the future comes from an unknown God, a God who has yet to be revealed.

Ezekiel's Chariot, a Moveable Temple

Ezekiel was a prophet who introduced a different way of looking at God in the time of the Temple orthodoxy, introducing a new approach in the form of a vision.

In the center of [the chariot] were also the figures of four creatures. And this was their appearance: They had the figures of human beings. However, each had four faces, … The four of them had their faces and their wings on their four sides. They did not turn when they moved; each could move in the direction of any of its faces. Each of them had a human face the front; each of the four had the face of a lion on the right; each of the four had the face of an ox on the left; and each of the four had the face of an eagle the back. Such were their faces. And each could move in the direction of any of its faces; they went wherever the spirit impelled them to go, without turning when they moved.
— Ezekiel 1:5-6, 10-12 (Tanakh version)

It is tough to develop a spiritual movement from a vision of the Exile in apocalyptic times, like the Christian Book of Revelation, also composed in apocalyptic times when the world was falling apart. One can only approach this from the understanding of archetypes—human in the front, lion on the right, ox on the left, eagle on the back. These four archetypes were common in Assyrian mythology. What was Ezekiel thinking? Why did this get into the Bible?

These four faces were the symbols of the tribes of Israel; the lion symbolized Judah to the east, the eagle symbolized the tribe of Dan to the north, the ox symbolized Ephraim to the west, and the man symbolized Reuben to the south. These four faces represent the four faces of Israel now in exile. These four faces are called a Tetramorph, similar to what we call a cross, i.e., a Quaternity. A whole.

The same Tetramorph appears in the Christian Bible. These four faces represent the four sides of the person of Jesus Christ. In the Gospel of Matthew, Jesus Christ is figuratively portrayed with the face of a lion. He is the Lion of Judah, the Messiah of Israel, and the King of kings. In Mark, Christ is figuratively portrayed with the face of an ox, that is, as a

Servant. In Luke, Christ is portrayed as a man, the "second" Adam. In John, Jesus is figuratively portrayed with the face of an eagle, the Son of God. Such symbolic associations have varied widely in Christianity. The Revelation of John echoes the vision of Ezekiel in its fourth chapter: "And the first beast was as a lion, the second beast as a calf, the third beast had the face of a man, and the fourth beast was like an eagle." Ezekiel's four animals become the four gospels.

Again, what was Ezekiel thinking, and how is this mystical? Why does mysticism rise in apocalyptic times? It is an error to think of mysticism as escapist or other-worldly. If anything, it is the opposite; its movement is to move from a split world (dualism) to Oneness (nondualism), to find God present in the midst of chaos. Ezekiel's chariot created a movable Temple (a flying Temple on wheels) which says God is everywhere, not just in Jerusalem. Is that a foretelling of the Jewish Diaspora, the dissipation of Judaism after Rome destroyed the Temple?

Lest one be tempted just to throw out the organized Temple religion and swing to the religious novelty of the prophets, the wisdom of the ages has been that the priests and the prophets each have their place in religious development, and they serve to bring balance to one another.

As much as the prophets told of endings, of destruction and bankruptcy of the present order, they also introduced the possibility of hope. Where does hope come from? It doesn't belong to the present consciousness of reality and despair. Hope belongs to the ancient promises embedded in creation and the ancient ones. There is the memory of hope kept for safekeeping in the caves of those who wandered in their lostness in ancient times. And at the same time, hope is always being born in new and unfamiliar developments, places "we've never been before," technologies that create new possibilities. The transcendent had been erased in Solomonic orthodoxy and in its love of certainty; the prophets' reintroduction of transcendence was reborn out of the uncertain.

I am an ordained Presbyterian clergy, I live in an Episcopalian-related facility, I often encounter Anglican liturgies, I experienced post-degree training in Roman Catholic churches—all these are characterized by elaborate liturgies, prayer books with beautiful words, every aspect of worship has words crafted and read repeatedly—is this manufactured religion similar to Solomonic practice?

Today many say, "I don't like organized religion, but I like spirituality." Is this what the prophets were addressing? Does the beauty and crafted liturgy of the high church tradition block the flow of the spirit and the passion of the heart? In the formal liturgies, is God still a prisoner of our thoughts? Following Carl Jung, it seems that there is value in organized religion for the first half of life, where we join a community of believers and learn about the categories of religious experience and how to think. These may be seen as "training wheels." However, according to Jung, at midlife one turns inward and away from the collective experience of the organized church. One turns to the question, "Who am I?" One recognizes the illusion of all the beliefs and answers, realizing there is a much deeper reality beyond that each person experiences on one's own. Is this the turn from religion to spirituality?

So what is the sacred healing story here in the midst of the prophetic movement? Some would say it lies in the story of the refiner's fire in the prophetic book of Malachi 3:2-3.

But who can endure the day when he comes? Who can stand when he appears? For he will be like a refiner's fire, like the soapmaker's lye. He will sit, refining and purifying the silver; he will purify the sons of Levi, refining them like gold and silver, so that they can bring offerings to God righteously.
— Complete Jewish Bible version

The prophet's message is compared to a metallurgical metaphor, where the task of the refiner heats metal ore until all the impurities are removed and the purified metal is fashioned for optimal use and beauty, a metaphor for our own spiritual work in discerning higher truth on our way to becoming one with God.

The shift in consciousness away from the affluence and social ego of the Solomonic era and going back to the clarity of the apophatic simplicity of the wilderness of the time of Moses felt like going back to basics. The metaphor was the metallurgist burning out impurities, where true spirituality awakened an awareness that sometimes religion can get in its own way. However, over the next five hundred years, leading to the rebuilding of the Herodian Temple, religion once again returned to the ways of the First Temple.

Lao Tzu, who lived in China during this same prophetic period, observed, "In the pursuit of knowledge, every day something is added. In the practice of the Tao [i.e., Kingdom of God], every day something is subtracted."[98] Wisdom is the result of not adding information and knowledge, but letting it go. I have heard it said more than once by spiritual persons in their eighties, "The older I get, the less I believe." The healing story here says that the more one goes inward to find their core Self and God within, the more they let go (and burn off the dross) of all the answers they once lived by.

---

[98] Lao Tzu, *Tao te Ching*, translated by Stephen Mitchell (New York: Harper and Row, 1988), chapter 88.

CHAPTER 8

GLIMPSES OF THE TRANSCENDENT

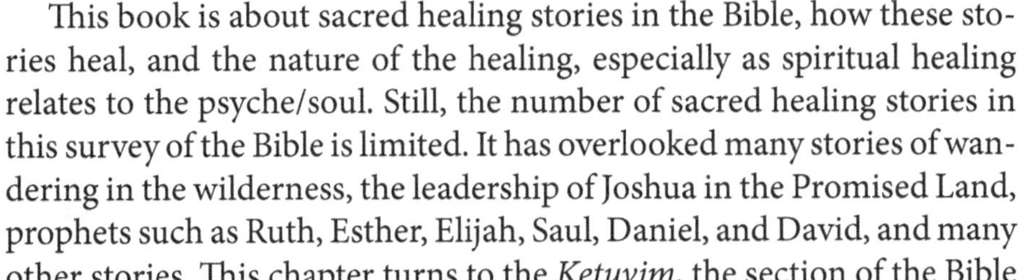

This book is about sacred healing stories in the Bible, how these stories heal, and the nature of the healing, especially as spiritual healing relates to the psyche/soul. Still, the number of sacred healing stories in this survey of the Bible is limited. It has overlooked many stories of wandering in the wilderness, the leadership of Joshua in the Promised Land, prophets such as Ruth, Esther, Elijah, Saul, Daniel, and David, and many other stories. This chapter turns to the *Ketuvim*, the section of the Bible also called Writings or Hagiographa. The Ketuvim includes 1 and 2 Chronicles and Ezra and Nehemiah, but we are looking at the poetic books: Psalms, Proverbs, and Job.

The books of Psalms, Proverbs, and Job particularly have to do with healing, but mostly healing at a concrete, physical, moral, and justice level. As a language, Hebrew has been referred to as *Lashon Hakodesh*, the tongue of holiness. The root of the word Hebrew means "beyond," or "the other side," but biblical Hebrew was not a mystical or transcendent language, for it often took things literally. For example, the Hebrew word for heart, *leb*, could be the organ in one's chest, or it could refer to emotions, but not much into the higher nature of God. One might see the phrase "the other side" as referring to the reality beyond physical existence, but that is not what most Semitic languages do.

For the most part, the healing stories of the Psalms and Proverbs are laments over loss of power, home, land, praise (singing songs is an antidote for depression), prayers for forgiveness and mercy and atonement, asking God for divine intervention, protection from enemies, and cries for justice. The importance of wisdom is acknowledged, but these themes are largely about understanding why things happen and moral rectitude. These stories should not be diminished in importance, but the perspective here is that deeper healing goes beyond these practical areas of everyday living.

Selections from Psalms, Proverbs, and Job speak to a higher level of spiritual experience and understanding, a level of soul-engagement and encounters with God above and beyond the themes of the psalms cited above. It is at this higher level that the healing of the psyche/soul occurs. The matter of narrative theory again rises, where one asks, do we take scripture at the level that the ancient Psalmist understood it, or do we see scripture as fluid and operating at the levels of understanding that later cultures bring? We may find the words of the Psalmist deeply significant, but we also bring other revelations and meanings beyond the reach of the Psalmist. We hold that this is how scripture works: it is always expanding in meaning with every generation.

In this chapter, we look at twenty-two selections from ancient writings, loosely grouped into nine themes related to higher healing of the psyche. The nine themes are: 1. Translating with a transcendent eye; 2. Sophia—meaning our true origin precedes Creation; 3. God is in *everything*, even the bad, meaning there is only God; 4. Walk in the ways of God: What ways?; 5. Experiencing difficulty in living is part of the plan; 6. The wish for higher seeing; 7. Beyond all words and thought; 8. All is one: cosmic intimacy; 9. Truth lies within the Self.

I. TRANSLATING WITH A TRANSCENDENT EYE

1. A mystic sees a slightly different meaning
Psalm 119: 25-37 (selected verses)

<table>
<tr><td>

TRADITIONAL TRANSLATION

[25] My soul cleaves to the dust; revive me according to thy word!

[27] Make me understand the way of Your precepts and I will meditate on Your wondrous works.

[29] Put false ways far from me and graciously teach me Your Law.

[32] I will run in the way of Your commandments when You enlarge my understanding.

[37] Turn my eyes from looking at vanities and give me life in Your Way.

</td><td>

ESOTERIC RENDERING (by the author)

My human nature is caught up in earthly things; bring me back to life in what is Real (i.e., eternal things)

Help me to understand the path of Your Way, and I will pursue the way sees as God sees.

Help me see what is illusion, and with your grace help me realize Torah (the divine Word, beyond all words).

I will "walk" [halakhah Heb] in the path of Your Mitzvoth [commandments], for you have opened wide the seeing of my heart. [different from "mind"]

Turn my eyes away from what deceives me (from what is not real), that I may be alive in your Truth.

</td></tr>
</table>

Figure 7: Traditional Translation Versus Esoteric Rendering of Psalm 119

Comment—The familiar translation above on the left calls the person encountering the Psalm to follow the commandments, and it asks for increased understanding related to the word of God. This tends to result in practicing religion as usual.

However, there is a much higher level of engagement beyond following the laws. The esoteric understanding of the Psalm sees the material things of the world as a gift from God to help one find the Way. But the physical, mental, and emotional things come and go, and thus they are temporary illusions (even though our senses tell us they are real). There is a higher world beyond all this that the Psalm calls us to embrace.

The path offered by God leads one from the present temporal world to the eternal divine world, while still living in the present body. The way to live in the divine world is to live in the heart, not the mind. This is a higher healing.

II. SOPHIA AND GOD CREATE TOGETHER

2. Our true origin precedes creation

The Lord (ADONAI) made me [Sophia] as the beginning of his way, the first of his ancient works. I was appointed before the world, before the start, before the earth's beginnings. When I was brought forth, there were no ocean depths, no springs brimming with water. I was with him as someone he could trust. For me, every day was pure delight, as I played in his presence all the time, playing everywhere, and delighting to be with humankind. For he who finds me finds life and obtains the favor of ADONAI.
— Proverbs 8:22-35 (selected verses, from the Complete Jewish Bible)

The Jewish book of Proverbs starts with just God for a moment, and then almost immediately, God has a companion, a female partner, called Wisdom, or, in Greek, *Sophia*. This same scene is repeated with first Adam, and then Adam and Eve. It is the same old "play"—first there was one, and then there were two, first nondualism, then dualism.

Proverbs sees her as existing before Creation, and she participates in every aspect of Creation. It is suggested that God thinks up what should exist, and Sophia brings it into form. What Sophia is doing is seen as play. Creating the universe is play. God is the aspect that is beyond all form, and Sophia is the aspect of the Divine that takes on form. Maybe we should play too.

Proverbs slips it in subtly: "She is playing everywhere and delighting to be with humankind." This suggests that human beings were there from the beginning, not as a secondary act of Creation. Elsewhere, the sages say we are God—we were there before the beginning, and we will be there at the end. We are eternal and timeless, but we don't know it.

One aspect of the divine is personal, relational, supporting us, comforting us, present in every birth and dying, God-with-Us. The other aspect is impersonal, the philosophical Ground of Being and behind all that is. One side is not superior to the other. One side is Father and the other side is Mother. Thank God for both.

III. GOD IS IN *EVERYTHING*, EVEN THE BAD

3. May I live with Presence! May I experience a sense of Ultimate Destiny in the little things I do. Pray to realize oneness with God.

Let the consequences of my life [mishpat in Hebrew]
come from Your Presence,
let your eyes see what is right.
— Psalm 17:2 (rendering by the author)

"Let the *mishpat* [the movement] of my life come from Highest Presence," the Psalmist begins. The Psalmist is seeking to expand the meaning of the *mishpat* from the level of being evaluated and judged by God to include God being involved in all we do, including our judgments. This is an aspect of the heart of God which is within each of us.

The word "consequences" brings the idea of karma into the picture. Every action and every thought has karma, i.e., the effects of action. Karma is the law of the universe. This is a new reality for the Psalmist. The Psalmist is asking to be aligned with God, to act as though God was doing the action: "Not my will, but Thy will be done."

What happens when we don't do the right thing? *Mishpat* here is expanded to include the ultimate play between both good and evil. The *mishpat* of God is about how love is known. The Psalmist is struggling to recognize the two sides of the same coin, one side being justice and the other being mercy. The Psalmist is trying to distance from the God of only wrath and judgment. It is a mistake to think of a God of *love* as different from a God of *not-love*, for this is the whole of *mishpat*.

"Let the *mishpat* of my life come from the Divine Presence," meaning there is only God, God is the only reality. May the sense of Presence serve as a mirror for all that I do and all that I think! May I live with Divine Presence! May I experience a sense of Ultimate Destiny in the little things I do! May I be mindful that the True Self, the Soul, is seeking realization as I meet other people, as I laugh and cry in my various encounters! May I feel the Macro with the Micro, may I feel the Full Life in juxtaposition with my lesser life!

In other words, when one lives with a sense of Divine Presence and acts and thinks accordingly, everyone benefits. The earth benefits.

4. Fear of the Lord is the beginning of Wisdom—meaning see God in everything

*The beginning of wisdom [hochma] is fear [yarat יִרְאַת] of the LORD,
and the beginning of understanding [binah בִּינָה].*
— Proverbs 9:10

*Fear of the Lord is divided into three categories. Two of the three have no source
or basis, and the third is the authentic foundation of fear. In the first category,
one may fear loss in life, that bad things will happen because of punishment.
The second category includes those who fear punishment in the next world. He
whose fear is based on the possibility of punishment lacks the fear of the Creator that leads to life. The only genuine fear of the LORD arises in reverence that
He governs over all and is the source and essence of all worlds. Fear [highest
awareness] of the Creator is the gateway to everything.*
— Zohar[99]

"Fear," as in "fear of the Lord," does not mean to be frightened and to
live with anxiety about punishment and bad consequences. The words
Hochma (Wisdom) and *Binah* (Understanding) are emphasized because they are words of such stature that they are the Highest of the
High. They are way beyond punishment and above what we think of as
fear. They point to a sense of God that is beyond all definition and
thought, beyond belief. We may be in over our heads in being with God,
but fear is totally out of place. We are just called to be aware that everything is one… God and everything one thinks and does.

The word fear, [*yara*], really suggests that when we approach God-
realization beyond all human understanding, when we grasp that
heaven and earth and all reality is One, then we become connected to
the Source of all Being and the source of Divine Mind beyond all human
understanding.

True Wisdom is always healing, for the individual and for the earth.

---

[99] *The Essential Zohar: The Source of Kabbalistic Wisdom*, Vol I, p. 188-189, by Rav
P.S. Berg New York: Three Rivers Press, 2002, p. 34-35.

IV. WALK IN THE WAYS OF GOD. WHAT WAYS?

5. We think we plan/control our spiritual life. No, God does.

The heart (mind) of man plans his way,
But Yahweh directs his steps (i.e., walking).
— Proverbs 16:9

How much spiritual free will do we have?

It seems that the course of our spiritual path arises from our developmental maturity. Most of us believe that we must choose our spiritual path. Of course, there is conscious intent in embracing these paths, but Meher Baba says that by and large the course of our lives is determined by the karmic consequences of our past lives and the sanskaric impressions created by our actions then and now.

Which path to follow depends on the spiritual disposition we have inherited from our previous birth. What we are currently doing arises from far more unconscious background than we can imagine, and this is far more than our illusion about self-determination. My life is a continuation of the previous life, whatever that was. We do have the freedom to take the larger path in a different direction.

This is not to dismiss the consequences of thoughts and actions that we bring on ourselves. Such karma is not punishment; rather, it is both justice and mercy—two divine qualities with exquisite balance that are always there.

The Proverb verse above is complicated. Like Joshua asking the people, "Whom will you serve?" we find ourselves making decisions about our path. But the answer we give goes far beyond our free will. The Hebrew word *leb* is translated here as both heart and mind; both are involved in human will and divine will.

To additionally say that God is involved with our "walking the walk" is interesting. It suggests that God is leading our path-walk into thickets, over rocky ground, and into the *mitzraim* (narrow places of risk and suffering) every day. Only God knows the individual experiences necessary to get us where we need to go.

6. How much of our life is already written?

My frame/bones were not hidden from you
when I was being made in secret,
intricately woven in the depths of the earth.
Your eyes could see me as an embryo,
but in your book all my days were already written;
my days had been shaped before any days existed.
How precious to me are your thoughts, O God!
How vast is the sum of them!
— Psalm 139:15-17

As in the previous Psalm, this Psalm also raises the question of our free will and the free will of God. The Psalmist here seems to speak of there being a "plan" for the unfolding of the universe, a plan that includes the life experience of every creature, every human lifetime. Does this mean things are fixed, or do we have any freedom? Can we shape our future?

I think we need to be careful about thinking everything is predestined and that our lives are "set." We have the freedom to live our lives, make mistakes, and experience the consequences of our actions and thoughts. I suppose the entire universe adjusts with every mistake we make. The Big Plan is that, one way or another, we eventually realize who we are and how everything goes to God.

The Psalmist begins with a Hebrew word "*aquila*" that is usually translated "frame," "He knows our frame," the structure that holds our living, the containment of parameters that shape what we are doing. It is an interesting concept, suggesting that we have a lot of movement within our frame of reference, but there are limits to how far we can get off the rails.

The Psalmist says God knows us before we were born, before we were even conceived, which is a way of saying God knows our Self before we were incarnated. We come from God, we return to God. And in-between, while we walk the earth, we are both the full presence of God, and we are the very fallible and stumbling creatures that we are. The larger message is that everything is One. When any realized master sees any of us, they see both the Divine Beauty we are and the broken piece of work that we are. "How precious are these thoughts!" This is a healing story.

7. Seven Paths, no path

To the one who becomes aware of the right Path
I shall show the salvation of God
— Psalm 50:23 (rendering by the author)

Traditional Jewish religion holds that one follows the *mitzvoth*, the religious laws and guidelines for righteousness. Obey the commandments. That's the right path. Right thinking, right action, as Buddha would say.

There seems to be, here in the Psalm, an invitation to dig deeper. The teaching suggests that we look into the heart of the Path itself, what it is, how it works, what it does to one's consciousness and way of being. If religion is simply doing the right thing, then we are lost, because then we have not ventured deep enough into ourselves.

Two phrases beg our deeper investigation. The first is "become aware of the right Path" (*dabaq aranoo* in Hebrew). What is the right Path for one? We could say in general that the right Path is the way that leads to God-realization, or realization of the Self, or realization of true Reality (all the same thing). There are many ways to do that, and the particular route is unique to each person. No one's spiritual path is identical to another's. No person can tell another what the path is. We must figure this out for ourselves.

There are seven classical archetypal paths common to all religions. There are seven corresponding yogas that parallel. One can follow the Path of Love, the Path of Knowledge, the Path of Sublimation, the Path of Beauty, the Path of Service, the Path of Evolutionary Action, and the Path of Integration. It takes decades to learn about these, and most of us follow aspects of a couple of these. They all lead to letting go of the self and realizing God.

If we are committed to a Path, it progressively opens up the way with every step we take. The Path is revealed as we travel.

There is a point where choosing a path for one's life is clarifying and exhilarating. But every "path" is just a thought-form of our own invention; it gives the illusion that we are more in charge of our journey to God. There is the more subtle realization that the true path is *no-path*. Our path is not under our intention and control. Just let go, and live life, and love God. God will do the rest.

8. A God who bends low to listen

Because he bends down low to listen,
I will pray as long as I have life (or days).
— Psalm 116:2

It takes a lot of living to come to the conclusion that God listens. Usually, we say we have a God who talks. What does listening and talking even mean? We read an anthropomorphic understanding into "a God who listens." Perhaps we can begin by saying that, from the perspective of modern physics, our emerging world says that *everything is interacting with everything*. Nothing is separate or alone.

We have this conversation with the "Transcendent," with Whom-we-do-not-Know. We are in this dialogue with the Beyond in ourselves, and we beautifully personify it, and feel a relationship with the divine. This is a powerful and risky move, and to do it with integrity is to engage with more than we know. There are those who call out to God as they encounter fear, anxiety, or their outer limits. There are those who make a habitual relationship with God at meals or at bedtime. There are those who make a connection with God in everything they do, and there are those who seldom fall to their knees or fold their hands.

The Psalmist teaches that we have a *listening-God*. In the tradition of universal spirituality, we understand that this also means we have a "listening-Self." Our core essence is always listening to every thought, every impulse, every move we make.

The simple phrase is striking: "because he bends down low." Most translations go in other directions, e.g., God "turns aside." But the Hebrew verb *nifh* does mean "bend down," as one would crouch down to listen to a child. It is a way to give God a human form. Genesis uses the same word in saying "he will bend his back to bear burdens" (49:15). The Greek version of this Psalm (earlier than the Hebrew phrase) uses the word *klino,* which also means "to bend," "bow." There is a humility in God here.

There is also the sense that God comes to us before we go to God. God always calls first, but we don't have the ears to listen. It is as if God prays to us to enable us to pray to God, which makes reality personal (and not impersonal). Healing in sacred stories always occurs within relationships.

V. DIFFICULTY IN LIVING IS PART OF THE PLAN

9. The more you seek God, the less you will find God

Be still, and know that I am God (Psalm 46:10)
Cease striving and know that I am God

The more you seek God, the less you will find God.
If you do not seek God, you will find God.
God does not ask anything else of you
except that you let yourself go
and let God be God in you.
—Meister Eckhart[100]

The main point related to spiritual healing here comes from Meister Eckhart, who offers a possible deeper meaning of the Psalms to understand our constant search for God. We try pilgrimages, meditations, rituals, yogic exercises, spiritual books—all on the hunt for God. It is good stuff, and we learn a lot and have mountain-top experiences, but generally… it doesn't work. The sages warn, "Be careful about collecting spiritual experiences."

Many of us have a "thing" about stillness… Zen gardens, meditation to quiet the mind, silence days, wilderness journeys. I think the deal is

---

[100] *Meditations with Meister Eckhart,* trans. and versions by Matthew Fox (Rochester, VT: Bear & Company, 1983, p. 52

that if we can shut out the noise and inner chatter, perhaps we can hear the voice of God. Or rather, the voice of the Self. It is true that if we can get the talk, images, beliefs, worries, and all other forms out of the way, we can behold the formless of the divine and the Self.

"Be still and know I am God" is the more familiar form of the Psalm. "Stop *striving* and know…" is more accurate. But with Eckhart's help, we can see the Psalmist is saying, as long as we are looking for some*thing*, for a voice, a word… we will have trouble finding the Divine. When one can let go, when one can surrender, release all… then the Infinite Truth is realized. The healing comes then.

10. Does God need to "break" us?

The sacrifice acceptable to God is a broken spirit,
a broken and contrite heart,
O God, thou will not despise.
— Psalm 51:17

Does God need to break us, as in breaking the wild spirit of a horse? The first line could read "the sacrifice acceptable *to* God," or it could read, "the sacrifices *of* God are a broken spirit." Two entirely different directions to go. Is God the one who sacrifices?

Does God want us to have a broken spirit? There is some free spirit within that we are born with, and surely God does not want us to be spiritually domesticated. The Spirit is not to be reigned in and limited.

But there is also the matter of being willful and caught up in our own desires and selfishness, and that egoism blocks us from seeing what is "Beyond." So religion counsels us to break this selfish spirit, but this "breaking" of the lesser blind self is like cracking the shell of a nut to get to the divine kernel. This understanding, it seems, is not best termed "a broken spirit."

Another problematic term here is "sacrifice." Rather than following the ritual act of giving one's things to God as if we were appeasing God, we seek the alternative meaning of *communion* or connection with God. In other words, when we come to God with a humility that means "true perspective," when we approach God without arrogance or a sense of deserving a reward for one's righteousness… then real connection with

God is possible. What we are reaching for is "an open heart." God does not want to break us.

Whatever sacrifice or breaking there is here is the letting go of attachments and holding on to what keeps us from God. The healing message here is to let go of whatever we want, whatever aspects of our lives that keep us from God.

11. Job: God wounds and then heals

Blessed is the person whom God corrects!

[Paraphrase] How fortunate is one whom God gives a hard time!
So don't despise Shaddai's chastening.
Don't argue your righteousness and protest your experience.
For He wounds, but he bandages the sore;
For God causes you anguish; and then binds the wound;
God ties up the trouble.
His hands may strike, but they also heal.
You may feel beaten to pieces,
but then you are restored to wholeness.
— Job 5:17 (Complete Jewish Bible)

The text tells us not to argue over whether our experience is just. God gives us what we need to work with our karma and our *sanskaras*, and to draw closer to God, even though it feels like God is pushing us away. God does not leave us alone but always stirs the pot to bring us to Him.

This passage begins with a Beatitude: Blessed are you when God gives you hardship and a difficult life! This is a hard saying to "sell." It takes extraordinary wisdom to see the underlying good in our being presented with great difficulties, including illness and death.

The bottom line of this teaching is that God may give one severe challenges, which may make us feel God is sadistic at times, but after we are broken, God also picks us up and makes us whole again. God is more loving than anything else, because love is the only way we can get to God.

"I have some tough questions," Job's friend continues. "Is anyone ever innocent? Oh, children are, but does anyone who lives a full life and dies, are they ever innocent? Never! Can humankind ever be just before

God? Can one be pure before the Maker? No! "(Job 4:17). Either life is rigged toward failure, or else suffering and impurity are part of the Plan.

Troubles are not imperfections. It is not because the gross world of physicality is bad. It isn't. Suffering is a fire where our losses burn up the things we cling to and incinerate the answers we hold. We are given blessings that awaken us to joy; we are given losses to make us realize we have not yet arrived at our destiny.

VI. THE WISH FOR HIGHER SEEING

12. We create the God we worship

Our God is in heaven; he does whatever pleases him.
[But the Gods of human perception], their idols are silver and gold,
made by human hands.
They have mouths, but cannot speak, eyes, but they can't see;
they have ears, but they can't hear; they have noses, but they can't smell; they
have hands, but cannot feel; [they have] feet, but they can't walk; with their
throats they can't make a sound.
The people who make them [Gods in their own image] will become like them,
along with everyone who trusts in them.
— Psalm 115:3-8 (Complete Jewish Bible)

The first verse is about transcendence, meaning God is beyond human perception and knowing. The true God is not made by the hands of men. The Psalmist is asserting that God is not created in "our own image," not a projection of human wants and needs, as Freud said. What is really Real lies beyond what any of us create or imagine.

We become what we behold. We do make up our perceptions of God, however. We do create our own idea of reality. We live in a world of our own imagination. We do create "images," "made by human hands and human minds." Still, these images in our minds—these projections of who we think the Holy One to be, these finite thoughts about the Infinite—are all idols, every one of them. All fictions. God is beyond all this.

So the Psalmist concludes with a sophisticated insight about the nature of projection (psychological and spiritual projection). Religion and all its forms by-and-large rests on such projection and imagination. It's not a bad thing as long as we are aware of what we are doing. This is another round in understanding the issue of idolatry. We become what we behold. The Psalmist poses the question: how can we get outside our own creations?

13. Grant me higher seeing with divine eyes
that I may see what is perishable before me and does not fill.

> *I will walk in the Divine Path*
> *when you give me the Divine understanding.*
> *Teach me the way*
> *that keeps me within the eternal.*
> *Give me true understanding [of Torah/Gospel]*
> *that comes into the heart.*
> *Lead me into universal Truth*
> *into what is divine delight (beyond my selfish interest).*
> *Grant me higher seeing with divine eyes*
> *that I may see what is perishable and does not fill.*
> *Turn my eyes from what is not real,*
> *and give me full-Life in your Way.*
> *— Psalm 119:32-37 (rendering by the author)*

The Perennial Wisdom is written in everyone's heart. It doesn't come from outside us. It is the higher seeing that we are born with. Still, it is difficult for us to realize the beauty of these words, much less grasp the reach of the Psalmist in realizing one's own Divinity and the infinite Self.

The true nature of what we think of as divine communication (even in the form of the Ten Commandments) is a Knowing from a perspective of universality and from a love that is far beyond anything we would ordinarily think of as a "law."

Jews often refer to the mystical path as "the Sacred Walk," and in Christianity it is called "the Way" (Acts 9:2). Sufis call the mystical path *al-Tasawwuf.* Hindus and Buddhists follow *dharma*, which is associated with path-work, and they speak of *marga* (a Hindu or Vedic term), which in the spiritual sense means path or way. In Taoism, the word *Tao* indicates path or way. This is why we used the words "the Way" and "the Path" above, and these are in the higher sense synonymous with Torah and Gospel in their true and unspoken sense.

Psalm 119, in the deeper meaning, prays for new eyes, i.e., Higher perception—the eyes of God, for that is what it takes to behold the Way of God.

14. I am the veil that keeps me from God

Lift the veil that covers my seeing
that I may see the wonder-full Truth
of the unheard-words of your Torah.
— Psalm 119:18 (rendering by the author)

"Listen to the *word of God…*" we say in church or synagogue as we read scripture, but we all have a seeing-problem. We see the outer form of the sacred words, but they are called *klifot* in Hebrew, meaning the outer shell with the kernel hidden within. But the words are only a form. Look closer. Look beyond. There's more… far more.

What we are seeing is our own perception… and perception is something we make up. The Psalmist realizes that he wants to see beyond his own limited perceptions. He wants to see beyond the words. The true scripture is not the words; the words are the outer dressing for the Truth, and we must remove the dress.

The Zohar, which is a major work of Jewish mysticism, says, "The narratives (or words) of the Law are the garment of the Law. Woe unto him who takes this garment for the Law itself!" The Torah (often translated as Law, but it is the word that organizes the religion)—the Torah has a *body*—the body is the words. The body is also the people. The words (and the people) are just an outer covering, the part we experience with our senses. If we can look behind the words to the "unheard-of words," we will behold infinitely more wondrous divine truth. Just as the written scripture is the outer, manifest form of the Word-less, so we in our physical bodies are the outer, manifest form of the image-less-Soul.

So David prays to have the illusions of his perceptions lifted so he could see the Truth beyond. We all pray that. Meanwhile, our spiritual practice is to continue to see our perceptions, to enjoy them, but continually see them simply for what they are, and know the Truth lies beyond. To do so opens the High possibility of getting "sacred glimpses."

15. We use the wrong eyes to see God

All my life I have looked for you.
Could you let these eyes fail
before they have rested on your form?
Could you forsake me in that way?

Oh, Lord, be kind to your servant—
show yourself to me.
This is my truth, this is my life.
This is what I want more
than the world has to offer.

— Psalm 119:6

Psalmist: All my life I have been looking for you. Why do you make it so hard to find you?

God: Because you use the wrong eyes to look for me.

Psalmist: What do you mean? I use the eyes you gave me.

God: I gave you outer eyes and inner eyes. Your outer eyes look for form. I am beyond form.

Psalmist: Well, so far the eyes you have given me have failed. Again, why is finding you so difficult? Are you going to let me die without seeing your form?

God: There you did it again. When you look for me you are looking for some "thing," an object for your subject. Any form you perceive and call it God is something you just made up. Do you think I should let you get away with that?

Psalmist: Sometimes you seem cruel in your hiddenness and inaccessibility. Don't you see most people become skeptics and give up. Like, what's the point of life?

God: The point of life is to realize me.

Psalmist: Well, I have loved you all my life. Can't you give me a little help? Just please give me a little glimpse of you.

God: If I gave you a glimpse of my essence, it would blow all your circuits. And you would not be able to speak of it. You would stop writing Psalms. I think it would be better for you to remain in your gift of writing poetry.

Psalmist: Well, what's the point for me to seek you, but if I were to really find you, I couldn't handle it, and I would be psychotic.

God: It doesn't work that way. It takes more than a lifetime to really find me. You can't see me until you see yourself. I am always helping you. You have to give up all your ideas about me, go beyond all the songs, and learn about the eyes of your heart, rather than the eyes of your mind.

VII. BEYOND WORDS AND THOUGHTS

16. Silence, non-silence, nothingness

My God! My God! Why have you forsaken me?
Why so far from helping me?
[why are you] so far from my anguished cries?
My God, by day I call to you, but you don't answer;
And at night there is nonsilence [dormiah] for me.
— Psalm 22:2-3 (and Aviva Gottlieb Zornberg)

The first line of this Psalm is familiar to Christians and Jews alike, but for different reasons. "My God, my God, why hast Thou forsaken me?" was uttered by Jesus as he was dying on the cross. It is a desperate opening for a spiritual cry, in which the Psalmist feels abandoned by God and all his efforts to reach God, day and night, are futile. Harsh as it is, who hasn't felt this anguish at one time or another?

The Hebrew of verse 3 (verse 2 in the English Bible) is generally translated "At night I get no relief." The Hebrew word *dormiah*, translated in English Bibles as "rest," is translated as in the Greek Septuagint (200 years earlier than the Hebrew Bible) as *anoia* (from which we get the word "annoying") which has two meanings: foolishness or a lack of understanding, and the more intense irrational anger, fury, and rage. The Greek word carries the nuance of deep irrationality when it comes to reaching out to God. This creates a lot of room for differing interpretations.

The Hebrew *dormiah* was translated *non-silence*, which means a silence more silent than silence. Zornberg says the word intentionally takes one into the deeper stratum of nothingness. This kind of liminal existence is beyond language and absence. The Psalmist (and possibly Jesus) has used a word that goes back to the beginning of Genesis, when "the earth was emptiness and void." That is a state that precedes form, which is way more than nothing. The absence of form before creation and before our life is our true state.

When the Psalmist calls to God in the day, he calls through the medium of form and ordinary communication, but the effort at night is beyond form and there are no words, and any response from God at this primal level is beyond thought, perception, comprehension, and experience. Psalm 42:8 says, "Deep calls unto deep." That's what's happening here. That's deep!

There is something going on here that is beyond words and our construct of reality. In crying to God, we are reaching beyond all form and beyond what we know, and our cries are heard beyond what we know.

17. The voice of silence. The true voice is never heard but is received.

> *The universe tells of God's abundance,*
> *The sky declares his infinite expansiveness.*
> *Day to day breathes "words"*
> *Night to night reveals Knowledge*
> *[Yet] there is no speech, there are no words*
> *The [True] voice is never heard*
> *Throughout all the earth the [divine] voice goes out,*
> *[divine] words to the world's very edge.*
> *— Psalm 19:2-4 (rendering by the author)*

If God is bigger than the universe, if God has a voice that big, why is it so difficult to hear God? God's "word" is everywhere. There is no "where" where it is not. Apparently, there are places or dimensions where we are hard of hearing.

Avatar Meher Baba said that enough words have been spoken, and the time has come to awaken. He did not speak a single word for the last

44 years of his life on earth. Meher Baba said, "What is real can only be given and received in silence."

The Psalmist here has a day-to-day" and "night-to-night" theme going, where daytime is about "breathing utterances" (speech that is beyond all words) and nighttime is about "imparting Knowledge" (in Hebrew, *data*, which is God-consciousness beyond all thought). It is interesting that here Wisdom comes from darkness and silence, rather than from the light.

But the infinite has no words. Words limit what has no limit. Lao Tzu says, "The Tao that can be spoken is not the true Tao." We are always being lured to see beyond form, to go through "the gateless gate," to hear the wordless word. There is no place where the Word isn't. It doesn't need missionaries to spread it.

We just need better hearing aids, ones that filter out all the interference.

VIII. ALL IS ONE: COSMIC INTIMACY

18. God knows us better than we do ourselves. Why pray?

Before I speak even a word, ADONAI,
you know all about it already.
You see all that's going on
both behind me [my past]
and before me [where I am headed]
and You have laid your hand on me.
Such wonderful knowledge is beyond me,
far too high for me to reach.
— Psalm 139:4-6 (rendering by the author)

The Psalmist is proclaiming that God knows more about us than we do. In Creation, God spoke and the world came into being. Sometimes we often reverse this, action first, speaking later. We pray, God listens. We act, God reacts. But not here. And of course, it follows that if God knows what we are thinking before we do, then why pray?

In the middle verse, the Hebrew word *tzur* is translated as "hems one in" or "encloses" one front and back. These translations seem to suggest that God "fences us in," limits us, and controls us. It is probably more accurate to say there is no restricting of us here, but that *we are met at every angle*. We can make a bad decision and God is right there, present in the consequences of what we think and do. This is why *tzur* was translated as "you see what is going on."

There is predestination or anticipatory action implied here. God is one step (or more) ahead of us, knowing what we will think or say before we do and what action we will take. As a result, the karmic possibilities are always laid out before us. We are always taking detours from the straight road, and don't know it, but even then, just like Google maps recalculates when we miss our turn, we are constantly rerouted.

19. Moving from impersonal to personal/intimate universe

ADONAI determines how many stars there are
and calls them all by name.
He veils the sky with clouds;
He provides the earth with rain;
He gives food to the animals;
He gives snow like wool,
and scatters hoarfrost like ashes;
He makes the winds blow, and the water flows.
— Psalm 147, selected verses

There are more than two trillion galaxies in the observable universe. The stars made our minds, now our minds look back. For the first time, we see the universe as one living being with a single soul.[101]

The following several paragraphs are observations by consciousness experts and physicists.[102] There is no separation between us and the universe. Nothing happens in the universe independent of us. We live in a participatory universe where we create the present and the past. The

---

[101] © Big Think, 548 Market Street, PMB 72296, San Francisco, CA 94104.

[102] Robert Lanza and Matej Pavsic, *The Grand Biocentric Design: How Life Creates Reality* (Dallas, TX: Ben Bella Books, Inc., 2020), p. 18. 20, 61, 78, 120, 121.

universe is always talking with us. The universe is always inviting us into the infinite.

The structure of the universe is explainable only through understanding this participatory aspect of the observer, because the universe is fine-tuned for life. The universe is simply the complete spatiotemporal logic of the Self. The universe supports human consciousness because it must. Our individual separateness is an illusion.

We need to see God's transcendence to see our own. ADONAI even calls the stars by their name. The "universe" is shifting from an impersonal concept to a personal one, allowing the possibility for relationship.

We are beginning to learn that all is one.

IX. TRUTH IS WITHIN THE SELF

20. The true Blessing (*berakah*) from God is not longevity, not wealth, not the good life, but the Blessing is the miracle of realizing one's own true nature.

Who may ascend the mountain of the LORD? Who may stand in his holy place?	"*ascending the mountain*" is climbing Jacob's Ladder, the way to God, to becoming God. The mountain-top is not only **being in God's "place,"** it is standing as God, for no one can behold God except that one become God. God is One. There is no one but God, says the Scriptures and sages.
He who has clean hands and a pure heart, who does not lift up his soul to an idol or swear by what is false.	"*clean hands*" — means innocent like a child, our original and true nature, untainted and no longer pulled by desire and lesser things "*pure heart*" is one who has *realized the inner being of the Self* "*idol*" — Does not invest in the temporal, does not fall for the illusion of "Maya," but rests in what is eternal.
He will receive blessing from the LORD And righteousness from the God of his salvation.	"*swear*" — not cursing, but binding oneself to what is impermanent and illusory "*blessing*" – a berakah — where God gives full knowing and seeing, and this blessing means the grace to realize one is God-like, i.e., righteous. The Hebrew suggests God will make you perfect, God who liberates will free you from all binding.
Such is the generation of those who seek him, those who seek Your face — even Jacob. — Psalm 24:3 -6	"*generation*" — This is the destiny of all seekers, even those who have really messed up their lives, like Jacob. There is hope for everyone. "Seek and you shall find."

Figure 8: Berakah (The True Blessing)

The commentary on the right carries the nuanced perspective of the mystical… a move that the Qabalists (mystical Jews) often made.

The true Blessing (*berakah*) from God is not longevity, not wealth, not the good life, but the Blessing is the miracle of realizing one's own true nature. This is what Jesus meant by the Kingdom within. The Hebrew word for "salvation" carries the sense of liberation, untying one from all that binds (attachments bind, beliefs bind, fear binds, even religion can bind)—a very Eastern idea. God helps us become like God.

21. God wants us to realize our true essence

Psalm 139:14-18 (RSV)	Rendition from Hebrew by the author
I praise you, for I am fearfully and wonderfully made. Wonderful are your works; and my soul knows it very well.	I will give thanks to You, for I am awed that I am a creation with highest possibility, i.e., becoming God-realized; your works are beyond what can be comprehended, and my soul knows it to the highest degree.
My frame was not hidden from you, when I was being made in secret, intricately woven in the depths of the earth. Your eyes beheld my unformed substance.	You see my innermost essence (divine), I am not hidden from you. As there was woven the outer garment of a body (hiding my essence) fashioned from the dust and depths of the earth you see who I am beyond my body.
All the days ordained for me were written in Your Book before one of them came to be.	In your book were written all the days that were formed for me, when none of them as yet existed. You made me You from the start.
How weighty to me are your thoughts, O God! How vast is the sum of them! I try to count them-- they are more than the sand; I come to the end-- I am still with You	How precious also are your life-intentions for me, O God! If I add them up, they are more than all the grains of sand. May I always be conscious of You, as You are of me. — *Psalms 139:14-18*

Figure 9: Our True Essence (Psalm 139)

You desire truth in the inward being, and you teach me wisdom in the secret heart.
— Psalm 51:8

The movement from the outer and more literal meaning (above left) to the inner meaning (above right) seems to heighten the spiritual reach of the poet. The "weight of the thoughts of God" comes when the Psalmist realizes God has made him to become God. It is beyond saying, this miracle and gravity of what each of us is *really doing*. And so he says that the core Self is beyond the brain's capacity to understand; it is the soul's knowing, the God-part of one that knows.

We can tell the Psalmist has moved beyond ordinary experience, because he gets into a discussion about the core part of a person that is beyond the body. Just as the rabbis describe the Torah (the scriptures) as being the outer "dress" that covers the Truth, the Psalmist uses the same words, "garment" and "weaving," to refer to the physical body that covers one's true essence. And he recognizes that God sees his core essence, his soul essence. No wonder he is in an ecstatic state!

The core Self within is the Soul, and experienced in the heart. The Psalmist expresses this unfolding as the intentions of God. God has infinite plans for us to bring us to Him. May we be conscious of this magnificent unfolding!

22. Divine truth is found in the Self

Pay attention! You seek divine truth in your innermost core
(i.e., the mystery of the unknowable Self)
There, divine unknowable Knowledge is realized.
—Psalm 51:6 (rendering by the author)

After reviewing eight translations, the Greek Septuagint and the Hebrew text, the following is the best rendering I found: "Behold you desire truth in the innermost being, and in the hidden part You will make me know wisdom" (Psalm 51:6, New American Standard Bible). I added the phrase "the mystery of the unknowable Self" (with a capital "S").

Hebrew is generally seen as a more concrete language that does not lend itself to talking about the subtle, non-physical realm. It is inadequate in being explicit about the psyche, soul, the infinite, and the divine, and thus the Qabalah was developed to address these subtle ideas after the biblical period.

In Hebrew, however, it really suggests that there is a hidden part within us that is beyond our regular conscious knowing. Often in spiritual literature, this is thought of as the thought of the heart (*enthymia*), rather than the brain, where the heart is an organ of infinite knowing, and the brain is an organ of finite knowing. In the same sense in which

God is known in the "voice of nothing," i.e., beyond form, the Psalmist is saying that the mystery of the divine is not accessible through rational effort, although highly developed consciousness takes one to the outer limits of the finite intellect.

Such thoughts are not usually expressed in the Bible. One feels like joining Job in saying, "Do you know about the layers of the thick clouds [the clouds of our unknowing], the wonders of one perfect in knowledge?" (Job 37:16).

Jesus seems to have picked up on this core part within that is a doorway to God, the point of entry to the realm of heaven, and that which lies beyond time and space. He usually called it the Kingdom of Heaven. Contemporary spirituality and transpersonal psychology calls it the Self.

This chapter has explored several passages from Proverbs, Job, and, mostly, Psalms, at times pushing the Hebrew text beyond its familiar use to introduce a more subtly esoteric and spiritual interpretation. Healing is usually visualized as the restoration of the physical body and functioning in the physical world—illness, physical injury, mental illness, emotional disturbance, protection from one's enemies, reviving one from death—sometimes healing extends to control over the material world and the environment. In this book, we are looking at a deeper level of healing found in esoteric areas that would be termed as salvation, wholeness, higher consciousness, realization of God, soul-awareness, realization of the core Self—that what happens at these levels is true healing, and connects one to the purpose of life.

The more physical suffering, the more healing we can consider in the material world, within the domain of **ex**oteric or outer spirituality. This includes energy healing. The healing that comes from inner work, the contact with the soul, the gradual encounter and eventual realization of the core Self falls into the category of **es**oteric or inner spirituality.

Summaries of the Esoteric Understandings in the Psalms

1. A mystic sees a slightly different meaning. (Psalm 119)
The Psalmist asks for help to see beyond the physical, phenomenal world. He asks for help to see beyond the illusion of his own thoughts, for help to realize the deeper Torah beyond words. He realizes deeper healing means seeing with the heart, that is, beyond the mind.

2. Our true origin precedes creation. (Proverbs 8)
Proverbs draws a contrast between the original nondualism in Creation and the dualistic consciousness resulting from the Fall. He asks what the point of life is, and the answer is given: it is the play of God. While it is often said that our human creation in Genesis was part of the world's creation, this story of Sophia says we existed in God before Creation began.

3. May I live with Presence! May I experience a sense of Ultimate Destiny in the little things I do. Pray for congruence between me and God. (Psalm 17)
This Psalm prays for the realization of oneness with God. Every thought and every action comes from God. God is more than an evaluator and a Judge, God is the doer. Karma is the consequence that connects us with God, for Karma is one of the ways God is known. Whenever one person realizes God, the entire earth benefits.

4. The fear of the Lord is the beginning of Wisdom—this means see God in everything. (Proverbs 9 and Zohar)
The fear of the Lord does not mean fearing what will happen; it means God is connected with us in everything we do. We are connected beyond all human understanding. The transcendent and the immanent are always present, opposite sides of the same coin. Realizing this is the basis for true Wisdom.

5. We think we plan/control our spiritual life. No, God does. (Proverbs 16)

Do we have free will in choosing our spiritual path? Only partly. Our path is determined by karma and past spiritual experience, by sanskaras (impressions of our thoughts and actions). These bring us into contact with spiritual teachers and influences that shape our path. Karma is not punishment; it is both justice and mercy.

6. How much of our life is already written? (Psalm 139)

We have the freedom to make mistakes. God knows the "frame" or larger structure of our living. God knows our love and our failure and brokenness. Everyone has the opportunity to rewrite the "givens" of karma and create a new path. Everyone ultimately ends up with God; there is no other possible way of ending, for this maintains the oneness of all.

7. Seven Paths, no path. (Psalm 50)

What is the right path? In truth, every path takes one to God, even atheism. Some paths take longer than others. Every person's path is unique to that person. A path is a map of one's own imagination and making. Eventually, one moves outside one's own strategies to find God, and in such surrender, the path becomes "no-path."

8. A God who bends low to listen. (Psalm 116)

We have a listening God, meaning we have a listening Self. It means that we listen to what we do not know, or we hear more than we know. We are porous. The phrase "a God who bends low to listen" means true Reality is personal, and all experience is intimate.

9. The more you seek God, the less you will find God. (Psalm 46, Eckhart)

In searching for God, our desire itself keeps us from God, because our hunger is about us. Spiritual narcissism (the love of one's spiritual journey) is a problem, causing people to practice rituals, meditation, and prayers. The true search involves surrender, a simple letting go of oneself.

10. Does God need to "break" us? (Psalm 51)
First, who does the sacrifice? Philippians says, "God emptied himself" in becoming a limited human being. Is this God being broken? Scripture asks, does God break our spirit as one breaks a wild horse? Generally, we say no. Still, another metaphor is more apt: the shell around a kernel must be broken to get to the fruit within.

11. God wounds and then heals. (Job)
Don't argue whether your experience in the world is just. Don't worry why good things happen to bad people, or why some have more than others. God gives every person exactly what they need to come to God. Living is not about abundance; it is about connection to God. God gives every challenge and difficulty to accomplish just that.

12. We create the God we worship. (Psalm 115)
The Psalmist begins by asserting the freedom of God, not bound by human limitations. Human beings create a God in their own image, a God they want to save them, a God that meets their own desire. God is always at work, releasing us from our own perceptions.

13. Grant me higher seeing with divine eyes that I may see what is perishable and does not fill. (Psalm 119)
The Psalmist prays to be let into the universal Truth beyond the limited mind of this world. The material world of things, feelings, desires, comforts comes and then it goes, it perishes. It is not real. Reality lies beyond the material, and it never dies. Wisdom teaches that the Truth of the divine is written on the heart of every person. We already have what we want. Give us the divine eyes to see the Truth we already are.

14. I am the veil that keeps me from God. (Psalm 119)
When we encounter the Word of God, we realize that what we see is our own perception. We see ourselves. We are ourselves the veil that keeps us from God. The journey to God involves our seeing the veil, that which is between God and us.

15. We use the wrong eyes to see God. (Psalm 119)
We want more than the world has to offer, or else we fail to see fully what it offers. Is our failure to see God by divine intent? It was said to Moses, "No one can see God and live." Can a mortal human being see God, that is, can one be God-realized? Only God can see God, but when one lets go of the limited self and becomes realized, they are given divine eyes of true seeing.

16. Silence, non-silence, nothingness. (Psalm 22)
It is often said that the voice of God is silence, as Elijah experienced on Mt Horeb. But the silence in this Psalm is *dormie*, a silence beyond silence, recalling the original silence at creation, the silence of emptiness and void. We call to God through the medium of form, and God responds at a level beyond words and form. We are always having to deal with the problem of form.

17. The voice of silence. The true voice is never heard. (Psalm 19)
God is metaphorically bigger than the entire universe, but if God has a voice universe-sized, why is it so difficult to hear God? Alternatively, we can say God's voice is never heard, but it is received. Avatar Meher Baba, who did not speak a single word for the last forty-four years of his life in the body, said, "What is real is only given and received in silence."

18. God knows us better than we do ourselves. Why pray? (Psalm 139)
Mohammed said, "God is closer to us than our jugular vein." This is a kind of intimacy beyond our understanding. This omnipotence doesn't limit us; it just means that we are met at every angle. The Universal Wisdom holds that we have the Mind of God if we can just get out of our way. Meher Baba described the divine open mind as follows: "My universal mind is the central station to which every individual mind is linked. So, wherever a person may be, I know what he is thinking and doing every moment. At every moment I know the thought of every person and the thoughts of the whole world simultaneously. Not only this, but I also know what you will think tomorrow or after a thousand years, and I also know what you

thought thousands of years before. This is knowledge—infinite and indivisible—and it is beyond your imagination."

19. Moving from the impersonal to personal/intimate universe. (Psalm 147)

To see God as beyond and separate from Creation is to see an impersonal God. Like the Psalmists, many physicists now see every aspect of creation as personal. Everything in the universe has a consciousness and is working together in a oneness. Everything creates everything, and everything is involved with everything. The universe is a single soul. We create the universe, and it creates us.

20. The true Blessing (*berakah*) from God is not longevity, not wealth, not the good life, but the Blessing is the miracle of realizing one's own true nature. (Psalm 24)

How does one reach God? There is no Tower of Babel, no Jacob's Ladder, no climbing of Mount Sinai. Becoming God-realized is the realization of one's own true nature. This comes from letting go of attachments, letting go of the illusion of things, letting go of personal righteousness. This comes from a knowing of the heart. It takes a God-realized spiritual master to help one with this.

21. God wants us to realize our true essence. (Psalm 139)

Of all the esoteric teachings in the Jewish bible, this may be the most profound. The core Soul within, which is also known as the Self, is God-within-us. This is beyond the mind's grasp, meaning we cannot think our way into understanding this. God has programmed us to be God.

22. Divine truth is found in the Self. (Psalm 51)

It is the core Self (not the ego-self) where divine Truth is realized. The Self is universal, not individual, meaning one doesn't possess the Self. The Self is the same as Soul, the same as God, the Same as Christ, the same as "the Kingdom."

CHAPTER 9

THE CHRIST PRESENCE BEYOND ALL KNOWING

The Ancient One (Jesus in Other Forms)

But you, Bethlehem, least among the clans of Judah, from you shall come forth for me one who is to be ruler in Israel; whose origin is from of old, from ancient days.
— Micah 5-1

"Who do you say I am?"[103] Jesus asked his disciples. It was not a simple question. We are still trying to find an answer to the question. He brushed off the theories—are you the Messiah, the son of David, Elijah, Moses come again, John the Baptist reincarnated? Jesus never really answered his question, suggesting every answer was at best only partial. He has been a Rorschach test for all our projections.

Again the question of Jesus's identity arose with prominent and knowledgeable Jews.

25 At this, they said to him, "You? Who are you?"23 Jesus said to them, "You are from below, I am from above; you are of this world, I am not of this world. 42 I came out from God; and now I have arrived here. I did not come on my own; he sent me.53 [They asked Jesus] "Abraham our Father died; you aren't greater than he, are you?"56 [Jesus answered,] Abraham, your father, was glad that he would see my day; then he saw it and was overjoyed." 57 [They responded,]

---

¹⁰³ Matthew 16:13-20

"Why, you're not yet fifty years old," the Judeans replied, "and you have seen Abraham?" [58] *Jesus said to them, "Yes, indeed! Before Abraham came into being, I AM!"*[104]

Jesus is making a very rare claim about his identity, a claim critical for us today. Jesus almost never explained who he was, and in some ways, we still don't know. Where do you get your authority? Jesus implies that he is The Ancient One.

The Ancient One is the name given to the recurring human form that the one-and-only God takes whenever God takes human form. It is one God and the same Divine-Human Presence, just dressed differently according to the culture and the times. The same God comes again and again innumerable times.

"Before Abraham I am." (The verb "am" is in the present tense, just as Jesus used it ["I am"] eight times in the Gospel of John.) Accordingly, we can conclude that there were many other times the "God-Man" we call "Jesus" came as the Ancient One prior to Abraham. He came as Krishna [ca., 3200 BCE].[105] Then he came as Abraham himself [ca., 1800 BCE], then Buddha [ca., between 563-480 BCE],[106] and a number of times since. And in the Book of Revelation, "I am the Alpha and the Omega, the First and the Last, the Beginning and the End," surely includes all his other forms.

Was Meher Baba the latest coming of the Avatar-Christ? That is a "big bite" for many to take, but a deep reading into what Meher Baba said and did suggests it could be none other. Meher Baba, acclaimed by many to be the "Avatar of Our Age," said, "I was Rama, I was Krishna, [I am the Christ], I was this One, I was that One, and now I am Meher

---

[104] John 8: 25-58, selected verses

[105] Krishna, *Bhagavad Gita*, 4:5-10 (Translated by Swami Shivananda, copyright The Divine Life Trust Society. Similarly, Krishna [ca., 3200 BCE] said, "When goodness grows weak, when evil increases, I make myself a body. In every age I come back to deliver the holy, to establish righteousness, ...I manifest Myself thus from age to age."

[106] Gautama Buddha, *Mahaparinirvana Sutra*, Chapter V, Verses 1-14. Again, in the Ancient One tradition, Buddha said, "I am not the first Buddha who has come upon the earth, nor shall I be the last. In the right time, another Buddha will arise in the world."

Baba. In this form of flesh and blood, I am that same Ancient One who is eternally worshipped and ignored, ever remembered and forgotten, and whose future (Advent) is anticipated with great fervor and longing."[107]

Meher Baba continues, "Every religion belongs to Me. My own personal religion is of My being the Ancient Infinite One and the religion I teach to all is of love for God."[108]

Many believe that the Ancient One has come again in our own time. Sri Ramakrishna, a Hindu Perfect Master, said, "It is one and the same Avatar [Christ] that, having plunged into the ocean of life, rises up in one place and is known as Krishna, and diving down again rises in another place and is known as Christ. The avatars [viz. Rama, Krishna, Buddha, Christ] stand in relation to the Absolute Brahman [the One God] as the waves of the ocean are to the ocean."[109]

The major religions all have teachings about the reincarnation of the Avatar-Christ, not just a Second Coming but an Infinite Coming. This has happened innumerable times, most of which we have no record. Age after age, when the wick of Righteousness burns low, the Avatar comes yet once again to rekindle the torch of Love and Truth. There are innumerable names for the human person in whom God takes redemptive form. It does not matter what particular name a person chooses. They are all the Sacred Chosen Ideal.

Jesus the Christ did not come to found a religion. If anything he sought to rescue us from the idolatry and bindings of religion. The same is true for the eight major avatars in our current cycle of avataric events—Zoroaster, Rama, Krishna, Abraham, Buddha, Jesus, Mohammed, and Meher Baba. True enough, religious movements have grown up around each of these, but the avatar is infinitely more than any associated religion.

---

[107] *Meher Baba: The Ancient One*, edited by Naosherwan Anzar, © Meher Nazar Publications Meherabad, Meher Baba Calling No. 77, Jamshed B. Mistry & J. Flagg Kris, ed.

[108] Meher Baba, *When He Takes Over: Avatar Meher Baba*; compiled by Bal Natu, Copyright 1988 AMBPPCT, p. 3.

[109] Sri Ramakrishna, *Sayings of Sri Ramakrishna*. http://1stholistic.com/prayer/Hindu/hol_Hindu-ramakrishnas-teachings.htm

Why was Jesus so vague? Why did he not clarify who he was and what was happening? Why did he teach in parables with many levels of meanings? Why is God and the truth always behind a veil? The nature of sacred healing stories and how they heal is embedded in this question.

One answer is we are hidden from ourselves. We want answers. We want to think we know ourselves. We want certainty to build truth around. We know our essence is called the "Self," but it is beyond our conscious reach. It is beyond our control. It is beyond our mind and knowing. It is this aspect that is core to the nature of true healing.

So far, as we approach Jesus, we have considered that he is the Ancient One. This means the re-emergence of the ancient and original spiritual religion beyond all religions. An ancient Way. It means a spiritual experience that is beyond all religions, a way that is beyond all beliefs, a way that is accessible to everyone, a way that is given to every person before birth. A universal religion.

The way of the Ancient One raises yet another possible name for the question we ask Jesus, "Who are you?" In recent years there has been interest in The Universal Christ.[110] This universality does not refer to the evangelical confession that Jesus is one "before whom every knee shall bow and every voice confess him as Lord and Savior."[111]

The Universal Christ is beyond Christianity and beyond belief. This figure has innumerable names (all to which He/She responds) and is the Ancient One as the source for all. The Universal Christ is a universal religion of oneness, leading every person beyond the idolatry and dualism of their beliefs, and into the nondual way of not only becoming one with God, but letting go of all personal identity so that one becomes God. One becomes the ocean of all reality. As noted, Sri Ramakrishna used the image of the avatars being the waves of the ocean, but we all go beyond the waves to become the formless ocean of everything and nonthing.

---

[110] E.g. Richard Rohr, *The Universal Christ: How a Forgotten Reality Can Change Everything We See, Hope For, and Believe* (Convergent Books, 2019.)
[111] Philippians 2:10-11.

So how are we to approach the healing story of Jesus? Most of the thousands of books about Jesus tell about his life, even though we don't have access to 98% of who Jesus was, and if we did, we wouldn't really understand the rest. The books seek to understand his mission, and this book has little to add to his miracles, his death, the mystery of resurrection, his ethics, his teachings, his mission, his goal, and the mystery of the Kingdom. This book has little to add to the tens of thousands of commentaries written about all of that.

We can differentiate between the name of Jesus (Yehosua, Joshua, "one who delivers," "who saves"), the boy from Nazareth, apparently the second to the fourth of five sons and at least three daughters whose fathering is unknown. Jesus was a *mamzer* in Jewish society, without a legitimate father who could make him a Jewish blue-blood. No wonder he made so much of *Abba*, our Father! We can differentiate between Jesus, the unique human being unlike anyone else, and the Christ, the *Christos*, who is a universal archetype of the avatar, the one with the full and conscious mind of God.

The Gospel of Philip further differentiates between Jesus and Christ, stating that "Jesus" is a personal name, while "Christ" (the anointed) is a public name, or impersonal name.[112] The Gospel of Philip says Jesus is a hidden name, Christ is a revealed name, and the goal is to move from being a Christian to becoming a Christ.[113] In other words, we realize the Christ within ourselves, and as we ultimately become Him, we become universal and cosmic, moving beyond our doctrines and beliefs.

To understand the nature of the healing Christ, we must approach him, not as a Palestinian outcast, not as a reforming Jew, but as the Ancient One, the Universal Christ. The intent here in this chapter is to *place him alongside all the other Avatar-Christs*, each who played a key role in leading humanity into divinity, each who knew of all the other Ancient Ones and taught and awakened similar realities in every advent. Most of us approach Jesus by asking who he was as a man. A much broader understanding is possible in approaching Jesus from the perspective of all the other Avatar-Christs before Him and after Him.

---

[112] Gospel of Philip, Saying 17

[113] *The Gospel of Thomas, The Nag Hammadi Library*, James M. Robinson, ed, E. J. Brill, (1988), Gospel of Thomas, 56: 4, 67:25.

I Have Sheep in Other Folds
— John 10:16

There are lots of non-canonical stories of the child Jesus doing little miracles, being precocious in school, even being a bad boy at times.[114] We wonder, when did Jesus realize he was God?

We don't know exactly when Jesus was born. There are conflicting accounts of where and when he was born. Many of the details of his birth are shaped to match the story of Moses. We like to imagine Jesus as the firstborn of Mary, but Mark's narrative reports that Jesus was one of five brothers[115] and at least two sisters. There is the story in Luke where twelve-year-old Jesus stayed behind his parents' departure from Jerusalem, discussing Torah with the rabbis in the temple, astonishing them with his insight. Professor Elaine Pagels suggests this story is unlikely.[116] So, how do we account for Jesus during the first 30 years of his life, prior to his emergence in Judea and his baptism?

In 1887, a Russian journalist, Nicolas Notovitch, was traveling in Ladakh, in northern India north of the Himalayas, when he fell off his horse and broke his leg. While he was recuperating at the Buddhist monastery at Hemis, a monk read to him from Tibetan scrolls of the presence of Issa (Jesus) among the Buddhists. Notovitch wrote them down and tried for a decade to have them published, in spite of the fact that the Roman Church desperately sought to purchase these and destroy them to keep the church's accounts of Jesus unchanged. Notovitch's accounts were recently published in English, and they parallel a number of other books on the silent years of Jesus by Levi Dowling

---

[114] Jesus' childhood is described in the Infancy Gospel of Thomas, the Gospel of Pseudo-Matthew, the Syriac Infancy Gospel, and the Book of James among other sources.

[115] Jesus had four brothers—James, Joseph, Simon, and Judas—recorded in Matthew 13:55.

[116] Elaine Pagels, *Miracles and Wonder: The Historical Mystery of Jesus* (New York: Doubleday, 2025), p. 49. In her book *Why Religion*, p. 206, she says, "I think it is extremely unlikely that Jesus spent his 'lost years' in India as some people like to speculate."

and Nicholas Roerich. Respected scholars John Dominic Crossan, Marcus Borg, Robert Van Voorst, Paula Fredrickson, Leslie Houlden, Bart Ehrman, and Elaine Pagels have all called these reports into question, saying there is not enough evidence to substantiate Jesus' visit to India and Nepal during the silent years.

However, Professor Fida Hassnain has conducted an exhaustive study from apocryphal, Islamic, and Sanskrit sources on Jesus' travels and teaching in Persia, India, and Nepal during the silent years. As Director of Museums and Antiquities for the state of Jammu and Kashmir, Dr. Hassnain, a Muslim and a Sufi, has compiled a possible narrative of Jesus' ministry for the decades preceding our biblical narrative, which begins with Jesus' ministry among Jews.

From the Tibetan scrolls that Roerich found in 1925, Jesus departed for India when he was thirteen years old.[117] The Gospel of the Hebrews[118] informs us that Jesus journeyed to India via Assyria and Mesopotamia with a train of merchants, then proceeded to Sindh by ship or by road through Persia, but there is no definite proof. Jesus' first destination was Sindh, where he would have come into contact with the followers of Jainism. But Jesus journeyed on to the Temple of Jagannath, south of Calcutta in Eastern India.

Jagannath (dedicated to Vishnu) is a major religious center. Evidence suggests Jesus stayed here six years, also visiting Varanasi (Benares)[119] where he was introduced to the Vedas by the priests. It is reported that Jesus gave his first sermon there, saying in part, "God the Father establishes no differences between his children, who are equally dear to him."[120] The Brahmin priests resented the ideas of Jesus, which undermined their status and privilege; they asked him to abandon the company of the untouchables and threatened his life.

According to Hassnain, Jesus left Jagannath and journeyed to the birthplace of Buddha at Kapilavastu in Nepal. The Buddhists received

---

[117] *Natha Namavali Sutra,* quoted in Hassnain, p. 61.

[118] Quoted in Hassnain, p. 61.

[119] Meher Baba commented, "What there is about Benares, or Kashi as it was earlier called, is the atmosphere of great souls. Rama, Krishna, Buddha, Christ, Shankara, all were here for a period of their lives. Ivy Deuce, *How a Master Works,* (Hartsdale, New York, 1952), p. 709.

[120] Quoted in Hassnain, p. 64

him, and he lived with the monks in a monastery. In time, he embraced the teachings of Buddha, and he began to give sermons like the Arhats, the spiritual masters. They even accepted him as a Bodhisattva. The chief monk declared, "This Hebrew prophet is a rising star of wisdom. He brings to us a knowledge of God. All the world will hear his words, will heed his words, and glorify his name."[121] Jesus lived among the Buddhists for six years.

On his return journey, Jesus passed through Punjab, again joining a caravan of merchants. When they heard him speaking like a prophet and performing miracles, they became followers. When he came to Persia, the priests asked many questions about Zoroaster. Jesus answered, "I preach no new God but our celestial Father, who existed before the beginning and will exist after the end." Jesus journeyed westward and arrived back in the land of Israel about 22 CE.[122]

It was also reported that Jesus journeyed to Egypt to see his Essene friends in Egypt and inform them of his experiences in the East. Meher Baba also went to Egypt and recalled visiting the temples there when he was Jesus.[123] Jesus also went to Tyre and Sidon in Lebanon and healed the sick.

I have learned more about Jesus from Meher Baba than from all other sources. Between 1925-1926, Meher Baba wrote a book-length manuscript that has never been published nor seen by the public, and its whereabouts have been unknown since 1958. Ivy Deuce, a disciple, asked, "'Baba, are we ever going to know more about Jesus' life? We have no knowledge of what happened between the time he was twelve and when he was thirty.' Baba smiled brightly and said, 'Yes, it is in the book.' 'Are we ever going to get a chance to read it?' I asked. Baba nodded assent."[124]

---

[121] Quoted in Hassnain, p. 67

[122] Quoted in Hassnain, p. 68-69

[123] On August 24, 1932, in Cairo, Egypt, Baba told Kaka and Chanji, "The Coptic Church contains a cave where Mary and Joseph stayed after fleeing Herod. The reason why I came to Egypt is to visit this church." They visited the Coptic Church the next day. Baba's face was radiant with joy as he walked through the church. He said, "This is my dear old place," and explained that Jesus had come and stayed there with his apostles. Bal Kalchuri, *Lord Meher*, Vol. 5, p. 1705.

[124] Ivy Deuce, *How a Master Works*, p. 130-131.

While Professor Hassnain shows familiarity with many biblical and nonbiblical sources throughout middle Asia, some sources which are solid and others less so, it cannot be ascertained whether the above narratives have scholarly merit. But the recounting of the teaching and actions of Jesus in India, Nepal, and Persia are consistent with what is seen in the canonical gospels.

The accounts above by Notovitch, Roerich, and Hassnain can be dismissed by scholars as unreliable or fictional. Nonetheless, their accounts of what Jesus said and did in his journeys eastward, and his interactions with Zoroastrians, Buddhists, and Hindus, do support his character and message. They raise the uncomfortable matter of whether all our stories about Jesus and his teaching, some canonical and some not, may be partial, subjective, and to some extent fiction (i.e., we made it up or constructed what we thought he said and meant). The stories about Jesus are more about us than about him. The truth is, Jesus is beyond all telling, and we live with a partial picture of this man of God.

The "Way of Jesus" Versus "Normative Christianity"

Jesus said, "Whoever drinks from my mouth will become like me; I myself shall become that person, and the hidden things will be revealed to him."
He said to them, "What you are looking forward to has come, but you don't know it."
— The Gospel of Thomas, Saying 108[125]

"Now as the church submits to Christ, so also wives should submit to their husbands in everything."
— Ephesians 5:24)

---

[125] *Gospel of Thomas,* trans. by Lambdin, http://www.gnosis.org/naghamm/gth-lamb.html

Note: This submission is not one of compulsion, but of willing alignment with Christ's will and purpose. The Church is to reflect Christ's character, uphold His teaching, be his obedient servant, and carry out His mission in the world, empowered by His authority and presence.

And he is the head of the body, the church; he is the beginning and the firstborn from among the dead, so that in everything he might have the supremacy.
– Colossians 1:18

Many evangelical churches say they want to be as close as possible in belief and structure to the church in the first century, thinking they could be closer to Jesus if they made themselves into a first-century church. Meher Baba says that when the Christ (in any form) leaves his physical body on earth, when he leaves his physical presence with whom so many people felt a deep connection, what he called the "outer links" of connection begin to fade in intensity, but the "inner links" of the divine presence of the Christ strengthen and intensify.[126]

The point is, I think we know far more about Jesus today; he is closer to the world than he was in the company of his disciples.

We can imagine living in the time of Jesus and having the gift of being a direct witness to Jesus must have been exciting, inspiring, and powerful. We imagine that the disciples believed they had a deep and clear sense of who Jesus was. They had heard him preach, teach, and perform miracles. They heard him pray and connect to God. What an exciting time to be alive!

It was just the opposite. Except for a few letters from the Apostle Paul, who had never physically met Jesus in the body, few understood what had happened. No one could say for sure what the Kingdom of God was. For a hundred years, no one understood what his death by crucifixion meant and what had happened after that. The movement collapsed, and the followers went back home to Galilee. No one was writing any gospels. A generation passed largely in silence.

A dozen years later, the Apostle Paul began writing, but he was not talking about the life of Jesus, his teachings, or his ministry. He did not tell stories of Jesus. If Jesus had been crucified around 30 CE, some

---

[126] *Lord Meher*, p. 3651.

twelve to fifteen years later Paul began talking about what he thought it all meant. After forty years, two generations later, the Gospel of Mark appears (now thought to be after Rome sacked Jerusalem in 70 CE), the first narrative to portray the life of Jesus, particularly his death and resurrection. Somewhere in the 9th decade of the first century, Matthew and Luke wrote their versions, copying parts from Mark, and adding nativity stories, although very different ones. Around the end of the first century CE, the Gospel of John took a different tack, a more esoteric approach. John's version had no baptism, no birth story, no parables, no transfiguration, no wilderness experience, no Last Supper, and the miracles he reported are different from the other gospels.

And then late in the first century, other gospels and accounts about Jesus popped up all over the place. Some guess there were a hundred gospels; we have fragments of at least twenty-eight gospels. The thing is, everyone had their own opinion about who Jesus was. None of the gospels fully agreed with one another. Each has a subjective point of view and a different understanding of Jesus.

Figure 10 below depicts a partial picture of the divergent views in the first century of the ministry and work of Jesus. Peter and Paul fought one another. Each of the canonical gospels had its own perspective and audience it was writing to. There was anything but peace and unanimity in the early effort to make sense of Jesus. Matthew was writing for a Jewish audience, connecting the story of Jesus to Isaiah and Moses. Luke, a non-Jew, told the story of Jesus from the perspective of a Greek historian. Mark's gospel emphasizes the passion of Christ, and emphasizes his actions over his teaching. He emphasizes the fulfillment of the coming of the Kingdom. Mark offers the most human portrait of Jesus. He has no genealogies, no birth story, no Beatitudes, no Lord's Prayer, no resurrection appearances. John's gospel emphasized the divine nature of Christ. John incorporates elements of Greek philosophy, such as Logos and Word, dualistic images such as light and darkness. He emphasized belief and unbelief and eternal life.

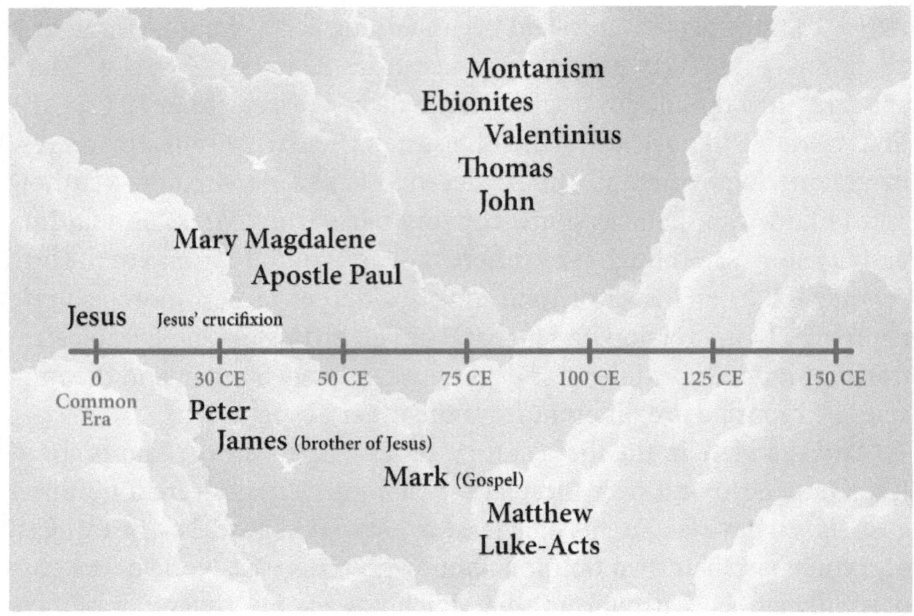

Figure 10: Partial Picture of the Diversity of Christianity at the End of the First Century

The gospels of Matthew, Mark, Luke, and John came into existence in the latter part of the first century, after the Roman destruction of the Temple in Jerusalem in 70 CE, although it is believed there were earlier versions or proto-gospels, and they borrowed material from one another. Coupled with the Book of Acts, seven letters of Paul, fourteen other epistles, and the book of Revelation, they were made official as the canon in the fourth century. The New Testament became known as "Normative Christianity."

Normative Christianity, which we see as "orthodoxy," the straight and official perspective of Christ, holds that the church is the body of Christ, a body with a hierarchical leadership structure, including lay people, priests, bishops, and apostles, all subservient to Christ. Believing that the end time was possibly near, followers felt they had one life to live, one chance to surrender to Christ. The new emerging religion emphasized the importance of belief and surrender. Its view of salvation centered on the atonement of the cross, that Jesus took on our sins and erased their power in his death on the cross, which came to be called the expiation of our sins. The early church saw its mission summarized by the great commission in Matthew to convert everyone everywhere to follow Christ, that every knee should bow and confess that Jesus Christ is Lord.

It took the early church a century to somewhat formulate the understanding we call Normative Christianity. The Christian movement remained in a fluid state, with different perspectives and movements emerging and some fading. By the fourth and fifth centuries, the church welcomed all sorts of people with divergent beliefs, while at the same time, the councils narrowed official Christian orthodoxy. With over 325,000 Christian denominations today, there is still a lot of fluidity even with the canonized writings of the New Testament. The canon of the New Testament has never been closed.

Before the canonical gospels reached their present state, there was another Jesus movement that seemed to arise, a movement very different from the orthodoxy described here. The sources for this movement have only come to light in our lifetime. By the fourth century, there was a major "book burning" to eradicate views of Jesus and Christianity to make room for the canonical gospels. The erasing of other gospels was effective, but in 1945, in a cave near Nag Hammadi (about 50 miles north of Luxor, Egypt), 52 manuscripts, leather-bound in 13 codices, were sealed in a jar and were discovered by shepherds. They change the way we look at early Christianity. These Nag Hammadi texts have been labeled "gnostic" and largely dismissed as heretical and divergent from Normative Christianity until recently. A growing number of scholars see the term "gnostic" as a twentieth-century label, and only partly true.

While these papyrus manuscripts are seen as dating from the second to the fourth century, it is likely that there are earlier versions of some of these, which could even be contemporary or predate the canonical gospels, and reflect an earlier version of understanding Jesus. These include The Gospel of Thomas, The Gospel of Philip, The Gospel of Mary Magdalene, The Gospel of Truth, The Tripartite Tractate, The Dialogue of the Savior, and Thunder Perfect Mind. Other sources include the "Q" source (from the German *Quelle*, meaning "source"), a contemporary collection of sayings that uses common material found in Matthew and Luke, but not in Mark. It is believed that Q, along with earlier versions of Matthew, Mark, and Luke, was part of the oral gospel tradition.

These sources reflect a different Jesus whose teachings were similar to Buddha, Krishna, and later to Meher Baba, teachings about how to become God-realized. These teachings are called "The Way of Jesus," to differentiate them from the church's canonical gospels, Normative Christianity. Instead of positing Jesus as the head of the church with all powers of authority and different from all other human beings, the Way of Jesus sees Jesus as the one who shows us to ourselves. As seen in the Gospel of Thomas, Jesus seeks to have us realize our true nature:

Jesus said, "Whoever drinks from my mouth will become like me; I myself shall become that person, and the hidden things will be revealed to him."

He said to them, "What you are looking forward to has come, but you don't know it."

In this approach, Jesus is saying, "I am like you, you are like me. You are God, but you don't know it yet. That is the only difference between us. My work is to be the Teacher within you, to introduce you to your Divine Self, and in doing that you enter the Kingdom of God."[127] He is saying, "To say we drink from the same cup is to say I am not above you, I am the same as you. You do not have to die to realize this, for you already have it. And when you become me and allow me to become you, you will no longer need me externally." As the Gospel of Philip says, "Become a Christ," and when you realize this, you will be eternal.[128] And Jesus added, "In becoming a Christ, you will also do the things that I do; and [you] will do even greater things than these."[129]

In effect, in the Way of Jesus, Jesus says, "You can't know God unless you become God, you can't know Me unless you become Me...." The only ones who get this are those who have gotten rid of their theories and who are open enough to allow them to truly see. This is a radically

---

[127] "Rather, the (Father's) kingdom is within you and it is outside you," Gospel of Thomas, Saying 3.

[128] And he said, "Whoever discovers the interpretation of these sayings will not taste death." From The Gospel of Thomas, Saying 1.

[129] John 14:12

different message from Normative Christianity. Rather than seeing Jesus as the "savior," one sees him as the Wisdom Jesus.[130]

Another core teaching of the Way of Jesus was the idea that everything is one, the original state in the Garden of Eden, the state called nondualism. When we mythically left the Garden, everything became two, or dualistic. Jesus taught the Shema[131] and his work was to restore oneness—one with God, one with the Kingdom, one with the world—thus, in the Gospel of Thomas, he says, "When you make the two into one, and when you make the inner like the outer and the outer like the inner, and the upper like the lower, …then you will enter [the Kingdom]."[132] And again, Jesus said, "When you make the two into one, you will become children of Adam, and when you say, 'Mountain, move from here!' it will move."[133]

As we compare the Way of Jesus to Normative Christianity, in a sense the Church kidnapped Jesus for its own needs. In the Book of Acts, Jesus is likened to the cornerstone: "Jesus said, 'Have you never read in the Scriptures: the stone the builders rejected has become the cornerstone; the Lord has done this.'"[134] What was the cornerstone that was rejected? Often the church has taken this to refer to Jesus and his crucifixion. When Jesus spoke of the cornerstone being rejected, what was he referring to? When I look at the earlier Jesus before the church remade him into an atoning savior figure, I see a Jesus who wanted to open the door to realizing one's core Self; Jesus' metaphor for this was the Kingdom was within, and all is ultimately one. Isn't this the cornerstone from which all else builds?

The earlier Ancient One, Krishna, said, "Nothing in this life purifies like wisdom."[135] What we bring to the party from our journey, our study, our books, our worship, our teachers—all this "knowledge" is tainted

---

[130] Cynthia Bourgeault, *Wisdom Jesus: Transforming Heart and Mind: A New Perspective on Christ and His Message Transforming Heart and Mind—A New Perspective on Christ and His Message* (Shambhala, 2008).

[131] Deuteronomy 6:4. "Hear O Israel, the Lord your God is one." Matthew 22:37-40, the Shema is implied as the most important aspect of religion.

[132] Gospel of Thomas, Saying 22.

[133] Gospel of Thomas, Saying 106.

[134] Acts 4:11

[135] Bhagavad Gita 4.38

through and through with illusion and stuff we contrived on our own. But when one experiences something from above or beyond (as did the Apostle Paul on the Damascus Road), this creates a new consciousness that is not conditional on the old and familiar. The "nothing in this life" aspect of Wisdom cauterizes, burns out, and purifies the old knowledge we had.

The New Testament Letter of James speaks of two kinds of wisdom. There is worldly wisdom dictating moral behavior, but there is also a "*wisdom from above*, pure, peaceful, kind, open to reason, full of mercy and good fruits, without partiality and without hypocrisy." This is a wisdom above and beyond reason.[136] I believe the *wisdom from above* is different from the everyday wisdom of compassion, the love your enemy, do good to those who persecute you, kind of moral behavior—again, not to disparage these gospel encouragements to love others. The canonical Normative Christianity sees the Kingdom of God as something we enter into after death, and the best we can do is be selfless, loving people who follow Jesus' saying, "Love one another."

The Way of Jesus, which seems to reflect the teaching of Jesus before the Christian movement got hold of it, says that the wisdom from above is the universal perspective of God-realization, or becoming a Christ, not just following Christ.

---

[136] Letter of James 3:13-18. "*Who among you is wise and understanding? Let him demonstrate it by his good way of life, by actions done in the humility that grows out of wisdom. But if you harbor in your hearts bitter jealousy and selfish ambition, don't boast and attack the truth with lies! This wisdom is not the kind that comes down from above; on the contrary, it is worldly, unspiritual, demonic. For where there are jealousy and selfish ambition, there will be disharmony and every foul practice. But the wisdom from above is, first of all, pure, then peaceful, kind, open to reason, full of mercy and good fruits, without partiality and without hypocrisy.*"

Way of Jesus	Normative Christianity
Wisdom Jesus	Savior Jesus
The way of nondual realization	The way of dualistic consciousness
We become Jesus	We follow and obey Jesus
One can be "saved" *(realize God)* in this life	Salvation happens at death
Jesus introduces one to the Teacher within	Jesus is the external Teacher above
Jesus is an experience of the inner Self	Jesus is an object of belief
Leave all, die to the ego self	Surrender to the Christ
Coming to God has to do with letting go of oneself	Christ is above all human attainment
To be saved, one must conquer the Mind	Conquer lower nature, become the higher mind
Jesus is beyond all doctrines and beliefs	Saved by accepting theological beliefs and creeds

Figure 11: Comparison of the Way of Jesus and Normative Christianity

Figure 11 contrasts these two early Christian movements, but this goes beyond what is said in the biblical and extra-canonical texts (Nag Hammadi manuscripts and proto-gospels). Figure 11 is more reflective of the esoteric and exoteric approaches in spirituality. Meher Baba said that Buddha only taught up to the Fifth Inner Plane, because no one would understand what lay beyond. That Jesus went beyond Buddha is not clear, but Meher Baba has made clear the reach of the esoteric, mystical way.

It is misleading to look at the early church and judge that it presented a watered-down version of Jesus in the form of Normative Christianity. It is doubtful whether the early church would have survived politically if it had opted for the Way of Jesus, which located the spiritual path in the inner journey into each person, an approach that had no centralized control and authority. Mysticism can't be codified. The early church needed to become an institutionalized movement with bishops and a pope, in opposition to the Holy Roman Empire.

Rather than looking at the Way of Jesus and Normative Christianity as requiring a choice between them, it makes more sense to see them as related to personal development and maturity. Normative Christianity represents a more concrete religious approach to Christ, a kind of "training wheels," until one is mature enough to make the inner journey to see the illusions of the ego self, and approach the universal core Self that is beyond all form and thought. The journey into the Self, the Way of Jesus, is a journey into a life where there is no egoism, opening the door to being the Highest Self.

This book is about sacred healing, with the point that true healing comes from this journey into the Self, into the Way of Jesus. The stories of the Jewish Bible (Old Testament) explored here support this higher healing.

CHAPTER 10

SIX FACES OF JESUS

Can We Become God?

The Roman myth of Eros and Psyche (I will use the Greek name Cupid rather than Eros) is a story of divine-human love. Psyche was the youngest of three sisters, so beautiful that men were intimidated by her. The goddess Aphrodite was jealous of her beauty and hatched a plan to get her out of the way. She sent her son, Cupid, to shoot an arrow into Psyche that would make her fall in love with the first creature she saw—in this case, hopefully a horrendous monster. When Cupid saw her, he was so rattled by her beauty that he shot himself in the foot; he himself fell in love with Psyche. He took her to a divine palace where they could be lovers at night, forbidding her from seeing him and from realizing he was divine, and he would be away doing godly business during the day. It was blissful, but Psyche had never seen her lover and didn't know he was a god. Lighting a lamp at night, against his admonition, she saw Cupid, and this created a crisis. How could the divine and human be together? How they could marry?

The second half of the story concerned how to either make Cupid human or make Psyche divine. Aphrodite made a plan for Psyche to earn divinity by undertaking three impossible tasks, ensuring that the couple would be doomed, forever separate. Psyche, however, used exceptional resources beyond ordinary human capability and succeeded, thereby becoming divine.

Is this the story we play out with Jesus: that we undertake what seems impossible, only to realize in the end that we are divine? How does this happen?

We approach this question by telling the story of Jesus. But it isn't a straight story. It has what seems to be a historical account of his life, what he did, and where he went. But the gospels are not really biography; they are part preaching, part teaching, part political action, part miracles, part spiritual devotion, and loaded with stuff that begs for interpretation. The story has more mystery than fact.

One approach is to look at the modes or faces that Jesus seems to show us, ways that Jesus shows up, knowing we are not getting the whole picture. It is a little like looking at the Trinity, where we see faces of God, or different aspects of God—the ancient Creator, the God who takes on human form—but it is ambiguous, and we see the God who keeps showing up inside and outside of time. This same Creator is also a Destroyer. The Trinity is only a small mythic model. And we remind ourselves that these "faces" or modes of being present are aspects we make up for the sake of our understanding. They are both true and not-true.

One of the things we realize is that each face is an archetype, that is, an aspect of the human psyche. Each face applies to the other Avatar-Christs, the Ancient Ones. Each Face attracts aspects that were present every time God has shown Himself in form.

The Six Faces of Jesus we will consider are:

1. **Rabbi/ Teacher** (teacher of spirituality and the Way)
2. **Chassid** (healer, exorcist, shaman, miracle-worker)
3. **Ritual Priest** (Kingdom as a Sacred Meal, and ways to experience the holy)
4. **Political Iconoclast/*Jalali* nature** (Kenotic Iconoclast—breakdown images of religion, power, separateness, righteousness, ego)
5. **Qabalist/Mystic** (the way to become a Christ, God Realized)
6. **Universal Christ** (Avatar-Christ giving an evolutionary boost for all creation)

1. Rabbi/ Teacher
Teacher of Spirituality and the Way

One of the Torah-teachers came up and heard them engaged in this discussion. Seeing that Jesus answered them well, he asked him, "Which is the most important mitzvah of them all?" Yeshua [Jesus] answered, "The most important is, 'Sh'ma Yisra'el, ADONAI Eloheinu, ADONAI echad [Hear, O Isra'el, the LORD our God, the LORD is one] and you are to love ADONAI your God with all your heart, with all your soul, with all your understanding and with all your strength.' The second is this: 'You are to love your neighbor as yourself.' There is no other mitzvah greater than these." The Torah-teacher said to him, "Well said, Rabbi; you speak the truth when you say that he is one, and that there is no other besides him."
— Gospel of Mark 12: 28-32 (Complete Jewish Bible)

Jesus is called "Rabbi," but there is no record of whether he had formal training or went to rabbinic school. The people were amazed by his teaching and asked, "How is it this man has learning when he has never studied?"[137] Apparently, while he spoke the common vernacular of Aramaic and probably Greek, he could also read the Hebrew scriptures, as he read from the Book of Isaiah in Nazareth. There is evidence that realized spiritual masters known as Perfect Masters can read and function with any language.[138] And of course there is the story of Jesus at the age of twelve consulting with the learned chief rabbis in the Jerusalem Temple.

In the passage from Mark at the head of this section, the top Jewish scholars of the day asked Jesus the provocative test question, "What is the one thing to know about religion?" Jesus answered by reciting the Shema,[139] which we considered earlier with Moses offering the Torah. The Shema is the key mantra of Judaism, recited at nearly every occasion of worship. Translator Stephen Mitchell said, "Everything Jesus

---

[137] John 7:14

[138] Meher Baba's Father, Sheriar, was not educated but after the point where it was revealed to him that he would be the "Father" of God, he worked in advising scholars of many languages, including Jewish rabbis in understanding the scriptures in their respective languages.

[139] Deuteronomy 6:4-6

said was a commentary on Deuteronomy 6:4-5 ('Love God with all your heart') and everything that Jesus *did* was a commentary on Leviticus 19:18 ('Love your neighbor as yourself.')[140]

As was said in Chapter 5, the Shema is not about monotheism, i.e., it is not saying there is only one God (even though that is true), but it is about every aspect of reality, including what we think is good and bad, is all one. There is no such thing as a good side and a bad side. This oneness was the original state of Creation in the Garden. The "oneness" has nothing to do with number, as in 1, 2, 3. And the effort to divide and separate things is an illusion and false. This includes our picture of heaven and hell, which is a dualistic idea. Heaven and hell are not true reality. There is no reality but God. That's oneness. This is the ultimate message of religion. It is the ultimate healing.

Most would agree that the central theme of Jesus' teaching was the kingdom, usually stated as the Kingdom of Heaven or the Kingdom of God. In many ways, Jesus was apolitical ("render to Caesar what belongs to Caesar, to God what belongs to God" (Matt. 12:17)) in an extremely politically volatile environment, severely antagonistic toward Rome, and looking for a messianic liberator. Why did he use such a charged word as "kingdom," evoking the connection to King David? To be sure, that word kingdom got everybody's attention.

What did Jesus mean by the kingdom, when he said the kingdom is here, the kingdom is coming? Scholars have debated this to the present. In Luke 17:21, Jesus says the kingdom is within or among you. In the Gospel of Thomas, Jesus said, "The kingdom is inside of you and outside of you," and he adds militant images.[141] Was Jesus talking about an external kingdom that would mean political independence and success? Was the kingdom an earthly kingdom or a state experienced in the afterlife? Or was the kingdom an inner state of faith, an internalization and deepening of Torah? Or was the Kingdom of God an ultimate state

---

[140] Stephen Mitchell, *The Gospel According to Jesus: A New Translation and Guide to His Essential Teachings for Believers and Unbelievers* (New York: Harper-Collins, 1991), p. 134.

[141] Gospel of Thomas, 3 (Lambden). Also (10) Jesus said, "I have cast fire upon the world, and see, I am guarding it until it blazes (16). Jesus said, "Men think, perhaps, that it is peace which I have come to cast upon the world. They do not know that it is dissension which I have come to cast upon the earth: fire, sword, and war."

of spiritual awareness beyond the mind, a letting go of the ego self and experience of oneself as divine, a state that can be experienced in this life? In this latter understanding, the Kingdom of God is the same as the Self, the Soul, the Christ. This means to enter the Kingdom is to become God-realized.

We just don't know what Jesus was saying, or perhaps he was saying all of the above, with the understanding resting on the spiritual maturity of those who received his words. This raises the matter of Jesus' style of teaching (or preaching or communicating). Jesus spoke ambiguously, in parables, in words that carried many levels of meaning.

Judaism differentiates between two forms of Torah teaching, *haggadah* and *halakah*. *Halakah* refers to the laws of the Torah, the mitzvot and commandments, as well as the rituals and traditions. *Haggadah* comes from a root that refers to telling stories. It involves narratives, explanations, illustrations, ethical conclusions, and the nuances of law and practice. Some scholars ask, did the Apostle Paul teach *halakah*, teaching doctrine and law as he had been trained, and did Jesus speak *haggadah*, telling stories and making observations that expand on experience? It may be too simplistic to conclude such a generalization, but Paul was didactic, and Jesus was experiential.

It may be that the understanding of the Kingdom of God was literal and a present expectation for Jesus and the disciples, or that it was a future state in this world or the next, or that it was the ultimate state of spiritual experience of God when one let go of themselves—it may be that all three are true, and Jesus intentionally spoke in parables and metaphors, intentionally departing from the literal, requiring people to let go of their own desires and expectations. To understand Jesus, one had to let go and make a leap.

It is interesting that, while Buddha lived four centuries before Jesus, and there was a center of Buddhists not far from Sepphoris where Jesus grew up, and many scholars believe Jesus had some encounter with the Buddhists, and over a millennium later, Buddhism also began to use the *haggadah* or a parable-like format to teach Buddha's way, a form that was called the koan. Koans are antithetical to normal understanding; they shock one out of the logic of ordinary thinking, allowing a higher state of enlightenment.[142] They were used by the Rinzai school of Zen Buddhism and to a lesser extent by Soto Zen.

I taught a class that explored seven teachings of Jesus, treating them as though they were koans.

1. The Kingdom is within
2. God is One so [we must] become one
3. Do not worry
4. Leave all and come to me
5. All is as it should be
6. Death comes before life
7. Be perfect, be God

Each of these sayings is something of a puzzle or a challenge to the logic of the mind, so one concludes that Jesus asked impossible things of his hearers, or that he is pushing people to rethink the limits of consciousness, a requirement for entering the Kingdom of God.

After a lifetime of living with Jesus the Christ, and having the gift of the insight from Meher Baba, whom I see as an incarnation of Jesus, I made a short, incomplete list of what I understand to be the major teachings of Jesus.

Jesus—Major Teachings

- There is a personal and an impersonal way to find God. I will show you the personal.
- To find fuller life, you must let go of the lesser life. It involves dying and rising, over and over. You can do that.
- Religion, ritual, righteousness, piety, prayers, commandments—these can block you from God. Organized religion can be a good thing, but there is more.

---

[142] Several examples of Buddhist koans are: "Two hands clap and there is a sound. What is the sound of one hand?" And, "If you meet the Buddha, kill him." A third well-known koan is, "Without thinking of good or evil, show me your original face before your mother and father were born."

- There is much more here than meets the eye. You need to develop special eyes.
- There are many paths to God (mind, service, power, beauty, suffering, love). Choose the one that fits you. The path of the heart generally works the best.
- Beliefs and the need to know everything will stump you. I can show you a knowing that rises far beyond your best Mind. So close your books… and keep thinking until your brain shuts down, then we can talk.
- Worse than disobeying the Ten Commandments or any other sins you do, what God hates most is being hypocritical. God hates pretending to be more religious than you are. God hates false piety. Thou shalt not fake it with God. Thou shalt not fake it with your Self. These are the same thing.
- My presence is more important than my teaching. You want to be one with God? Come to me. Come here! I will help you.
- Being with God is not a risk-free zone. God-realized persons see everything and can suffer a lot around the little stuff and the big stuff (that you mostly don't know about).
- Repentance and forgiveness is not so much about moral behavior. It is more about releasing the things that block you and hold you back.
- Learn the ultimate name of God and you will learn your own true name. (I just thought I would throw one in there to remind you this isn't simple.)

What is the gospel according to Jesus? Simply this: that the love we all long for in the innermost heart is already present, beyond longing. …Like all the spiritual Masters, Jesus taught one thing only: presence. Ultimate reality, the luminous, compassionate intelligence of the universe, is not somewhere else, in some heaven light-years away. It did not manifest itself any more fully to Abraham or Moses than to us, nor will it be any more present to some Messiah at the far end of time (credit here to Stephen Mitchell). The full love we long for in our innermost heart is, in the words of Kabir, "the breath inside the breath."[143]

Jesus is beyond all saying. It is awkward at times when people want to know about Jesus and what he taught. He himself is the teaching, but it can't be reduced to explanation or even the church's creeds. At several points, we have considered that Jesus was offering the opportunity and the healing to reach beyond ordinary consciousness and logic, beyond the mind. Just as we have observed with Abraham, Moses, the Prophets, Wisdom, and Jesus pointed beyond our everyday understandings to a reach of experience beyond all knowing. No wonder he chose multi-leveled parables, metaphors, and actions that challenged the deepest ways that we see the world and see ourselves. As he quoted Psalm 82, "You are gods," so his teachings sought to loosen up our present world comprehension and lift us up into unimagined levels of who we are.

2. Chassid (Healer Who Has Higher Powers)
Healer, Exorcist, Shaman, Miracle-Worker

Only the Gospel of John ventured to say that Jesus was God, and the early church struggled for over two hundred years over whether this was true. What is it about the divine that makes us want to see the supernatural, to see manifestations that go beyond the perceived operating rules of the natural world as we know it? We want proof. For some reason, we see God as being outside our physical and natural world.

As long as we maintain a dualistic consciousness, in which God is "up there" and we are "down here," we will have difficulty with the Word becoming flesh. Perhaps it is because we see the world as corrupt and a sinful place where we can't put God and God's Creation together as one. Emmanuel, God-with-us, is too much to believe, and so we look for miracles and the supernatural. We look for signs of the unlikely, if not the impossible. We want to be shaken out of ourselves and awakened to another reality.

---

[143] https://wordsfortheyear.com/2015/12/05/breath-by-kabir/, (as translated by Robert Bly, *Kabir: Ecstatic Poems*)

Maybe the problem is that we view reality as physical, a perspective on how the world's physics operates that is too low, too diminished. We are locked into a materialistic worldview, a science that says atoms, molecules, and the physical properties of the world are what is real, which is severely limiting and delusional. We are caught up in cause and effect, but more and more we are becoming aware of *acausality*, referring to the things that are connected and happen synchronistically, and it just seems miraculous, and we don't know why. A lot of miracles happen because our understanding of the world and of ourselves is too undeveloped.

This is not to argue that Jesus did not do miraculous things, things that violate the laws of nature, like walking on water. Our view of healing is also severely limited by the illusions of our view of reality.

The miracle of miracles is Jesus himself. He did more for humanity, and is still doing it, more than we can ever know. His teaching and his healing are only the tip, the tiny tip, of the iceberg.

Those who encounter Jesus for the first time want to see evidence that he is not like us. It does appear that performing miracles attracted attention to the Jesus movement; it drew large crowds, and it brought a lot of selfish neediness… heal me, heal me, heal me. Jesus himself did not promote himself as a healer, and he increasingly needed to escape the crowds.

Coincidentally, a lot of people experienced miracles while they were around Meher Baba, although Meher Baba almost always said he did not do anything. He said, "All miracles are child's play, whereas spirituality is far above them. Miracles in themselves have no spiritual value or significance. But they are necessary, and at times are performed by the Master as a means to convince people of Truth and spirituality. Jesus performed miracles, not for his own gain, but to make people recognize the Truth and to create faith in them. Yet when he was crucified, he who could raise the dead did not stop it."[144]

---

[144] *Lord Meher*, Vol. 6, p. 2130. Baba said this in an interview with a Catholic priest on March 13, 1937.

Both Jesus and Meher Baba often deflected the perception that they were miracle workers. They turned it around to the ones receiving the miracles, saying, "Their faith made them well."

As Jesus went, with the crowds on every side virtually choking him, a woman who had had a hemorrhage for twelve years, and could not be healed by anyone, came up behind him and touched the *tzitzit* (fringe/edge) on his robe; instantly her hemorrhaging stopped.

Jesus asked, "Who touched me?" When they all denied doing it, Peter said, "Rabbi! The crowds are hemming you in and jostling you!" But Jesus said, "Someone did touch me, because I felt power go out of me." Seeing she could not escape notice, the woman, quaking with fear, threw herself down before him and confessed in front of everyone why she had touched him and how she had been instantly healed. He said to her, "My daughter, your trust has saved you; go in peace" (Luke 8:42-48).

Comment—An imagined conversation

Jesus: Who touched me? Who reached into my Life-Force?

Woman: Oh, I didn't want to bother you. I didn't want you to know. I have given up on doctors. And I didn't want to be like the others, looking for a miracle. But I am at the end of my rope.

Jesus: But you didn't give up on me. Why?

Woman: You are different from the others. I can see that performing miracles obscures your real work. I can see that the healing you offer is deeper than healing illness and curing psychotics.

Jesus: Yes, I can see you, and I can see how you see me. Your seeing is what is possible only when one is at the end of their rope, only when there are no more options.

Woman: I do not feel worthy of your seeing me.

Jesus: It is your letting go of your needs, releasing your expectations, your humility, that allows you to see. Only when you let go of yourself can you see me.

Woman: I came to you wanting my affliction to end. But when I saw you I wanted nothing for myself. The others cry, "Heal me! Give me a cure! Take away my suffering." To me, that seems insignificant.

Jesus: And, my daughter, you asked for nothing.

Woman: I am not used to a man speaking to me with respect.

Jesus: God sees everyone with respect. You are His Holy One, the delight of His heart.

Woman: My bleeding has made me a Jewish outcast. I now feel a higher healing beyond what I know. I am grateful to you, Lord Jesus, for making me well.

Jesus: No, I did not make you well, you made yourself well. The true Healer lies within. The full presence of God lies within. That is what you realized when you touched me. You touched me because you can touch the Infinite. That is what has made you well. Your faith has made you well.

And so the faith itself of those who trusted Jesus seemed to play a key role in the healing. The faith precedes rather than follows the miracle. Other examples include the blind man from Jericho, Bartimaeus, son of Timaeus, who recognized who Jesus was: "'Jesu's, Son of David, have mercy on me!' So Jesus answered and said to him, 'What do you want Me to do for you?' The blind man said to Him, 'Rabboni, that I may receive my sight.' Then Jesus said to him, 'Go your way; your faith has made you well.' And immediately he received his sight and followed Jesus on the road."[145]

And similarly, "'This woman has anointed My feet with fragrant oil. Therefore I say to you, her sins, which are many, are forgiven'.... Then He said to the woman, 'Your faith has saved you. Go in peace.'" When asked about miraculous healings or making it rain in a drought, Meher Baba often said the faith of the people made it happen.

In considering the faces of Jesus, or the aspects of how he presented himself, it is not the intent here to explain all the miracles, and certainly not to diminish their significance. But the unusual phenomena around Jesus does not make the case for his divinity. Much of what amazes people is due to their own impoverishment in experiencing the full human life with its remarkable possibilities.

In approaching the deeper understanding of our bodies, the esoteric sages speak of three bodies: the physical body, the subtle or energy body,

---

[145] Mark 10:46-52

and the mental body. We usually think of illness as involving the physical and emotional bodies, and our practice of medicine focuses on this.

But both what is higher health and negative health enter us first in
the mental body, then the subtle/energy body, and finally in the physical
body. The mental body is where the molecules of emotion[146] and spirit
first take form, and then they enter into the chakra system of the subtle
body, and finally in the organs of the physical body. The growing field
of energy medicine sees that illness and psychic disturbance always
shows up in the subtle body before the physical body. Shamans, Reiki
Healers, Pranic Healers, and Healing Touch specialists all can detect
disturbance in the Subtle Body or higher, and can remove the physical
and emotional seeds of illness before it shows up in the physical body,
or lessen and resolve the illness at the energy level in the Subtle Body,
and bring the body back into a state of balance and energy flow. I have
been trained in all of these modalities; my teachers have effectively repeatedly caused cancer and other illnesses to go into full remission, with
Board Certified physician certification.

These healing modalities are ancient. Did Jesus utilize these healing
modalities? Princeton professor Elaine Pagels says that hostile reports
in early Jewish sources say that Jesus had learned magic in Egypt, that
he had tattoos suggesting he had undergone *magical* initiations and
knew spells.[147]

More interestingly, Mark says his disciples invoked Jesus' "power
word" to exorcise demons. In Mark 9:34, Jesus uses the Aramaic or Syriac word *Ethphathah* to heal a deaf-mute. This word means "Be open.
Be opened." It is often paired with a similar word, *Shamayah*, which
means to allow God's wholeness to flow and take over." These secret
power words have been incorporated into the healing of advanced Reiki
healers today. The words are not magic; they are words to awaken the
higher knowing of the body, words the body already knows.

---

[146] Candace Pert, *Molecules of Emotion* (Simon and Shuster), 1999.

[147] Mark 9:38-41. "Teacher," said John, "we saw someone driving out demons in
your name and we told him to stop, because he was not one of us." "Do not stop him,"
Jesus said. "For no one who does a miracle in my name can in the next moment say
anything bad about me."

Again, the effort here is not to rationalize Jesus's healing work, but to place it proportionally within the more significant work he was committed to. This "face" of Jesus is being called a "Chassid," which refers to a person who is on a superior and advanced spiritual level. A Chassid lives and acts beyond the line of the law, and is a person who is selfless and beyond the limitations of the ego. A Chassid does not judge others, but lifts up other people to love God. A Chassid is a mystic, meaning one who lives in the Oneness with God as said in the Shema, one who sees the sacred in everything, one who relates to the soul of a thing rather than its body, one whose life is full of joy and passion. This level of being active and alive is far above the miraculous, but does not exclude it.

Another facet of the work of Jesus' miracles has to do with his encounter with demons, exorcisms, the occult, and Satan. Was the world of demons and principalities and powers the world of Jesus? There is no question that demons belonged to the world of the New Testament writers, including the Apostle Paul. The problem is to see the world of Jesus as being Jesus versus Satan, Heaven versus Hell, and demons being personifications of people's fears, … all these concepts are dualistic. Jesus' deeper message was to rise above all dualism and realize the Oneness of God makes all those opposites go away. There is no such thing as eternal hell, for ultimately everyone returns to God where they began. Hell is an interim state in between lifetimes.

This would mean that after his baptism, Jesus was not tempted by Satan; this was a creation of Matthew. Luke 8:2 and Mark 16:9 mention that Mary Magdalene had seven demons; again, this was a creation of Mark, and later Luke who borrowed from Mark. In Nag Hammadi's The Gospel of Mary Magdalene, Mary cites seven areas or breakthroughs that led to her being able to be one with the Christ. Are these the seven "demons?" I think so. Here they are: her literal gospel words are bold-faced.

These are the seven powers:

- **Darkness**: Darkness is original ignorance
- **Desire**: Desire is being self-centered, egotistic, wanting, looking for security, getting one's needs met

- **Ignorance:** This is the awakening of consciousness of mind, in Judaism, the movement from Knowledge to Wisdom
- **Zeal for death**: One has to understand what death is, and how it is necessary to understand its working in having us let go of everything but love for God
- **The realm of the flesh**: One comes to see what the world is, why we have a body, the role the body plays in realization, why Jesus had a body
- **The foolish wisdom of the flesh**: Foolish wisdom of the flesh is the illusion of thinking that our bodies and the physical world is real, the illusion of Maya in Hindu terms, what Jesus means when he says "Leave all and come to me.
- **The wisdom of the wrathful person**: One must come to terms with anger, and become a master over anger, able to let it go… which is necessary to overcome the ego

It is powerful that Mary cites this as her last hurdle to overcome, considering all the anger and resistance and horrific accusations projected on to her all during her adult life. This is the clearest description of the path to God anywhere in Christianity.

Around Jesus, the miraculous did happen; things occurred that went beyond the rational understanding of nature. For example, the feeding of the five thousand people with five loaves and two fish. The exact thing happened with Meher Baba when there was not enough food to feed everybody, but to the astonishment of the cooks, the food kept coming. Defying all explanation, God seems to see to it that people's needs are met.

In conclusion, Meher Baba said, "The ability to perform miracles does not necessarily connote high spirituality. Anyone who has reached the Christ Consciousness can perform them. People must not come to me merely for help in their physical infirmities or for material purposes. I shall perform miracles when the time and situation demand and not to satisfy mere idle curiosity. Spiritual healing is by far the greatest healing, and this is what I intend to give. The highest is latent in everyone, but has to be manifested."[148]

---

[148] Bhau Kalchuri, *Lord Meher*, p. 1618.

3. Ritual Rabbi/Priest
Kingdom as a Sacred Meal, and Ways to Experience the Holy

*For I received from the Lord what I also delivered to you, that the
Lord Jesus on the night when he was betrayed took bread, and when he had
given thanks, he broke it, and said, "This is my body which is for you. Do this
in remembrance of me." In the same way also he took the cup, after supper, saying, "This cup is the new covenant in my blood. Do this, as often as you drink
it, in remembrance of me."*
— 1 Corinthians 11:23-25 (ESV)

If one were looking at Rabbi Jeshua (Jesus), we don't see him reforming formal worship in the temple, and only once do we see him in the
pulpit of the synagogue at the beginning of his ministry in Nazareth,
and that didn't turn out very well. Otherwise, there are several instances
in which Jesus violates the strict Sabbath laws by healing and picking
grain, saying, "The Sabbath was made for man, not man for the Sabbath,
and the Son of Man was Lord of the Sabbath."[149] While there is evidence
that Jesus participated in Passover events, Jesus was not particularly a
ritualist upholding organized religion.

While the Gospel of John positions the Last Supper as a Passover
Meal, the other gospel writers do not. It is tempting to link the ritual of
the "Passover lamb" with the sacrifice of "the Lamb of God" on the
cross.[150] With Matthew, Mark, and Luke, Passover had already begun,
and most scholars agree that the Lord's Supper was not a Passover Seder.

The ritual above, known as the Last Supper, the Lord's Supper, Communion, or the Eucharist, is the most ubiquitous ritual attributed to Jesus in the role of a "Priest" (to Christianize the role). The passage above
from 1 Corinthians is almost always quoted as the "Words of Institution" as people come forward to eat bread and drink wine or grape juice
in this sacred meal. It is interesting to ask where these words come from,

---

[149] Mark 2:27-28

[150] John 1:29, where John the Baptist sees Jesus and says, "Behold the Lamb of
God who takes away the sin of the world."

because the Apostle Paul was not there at the Lord's Supper and he rarely quotes sayings of Jesus.

It is also interesting to note that the bread is not unleavened bread, and that it was an anathema for Jews to consider eating flesh and drinking blood; such symbolism would most certainly arise from a non-Jewish environment, most likely from Hellenistic mystery cult mythology.

The familiar Words of Institution have long been subject to misunderstanding. The Greek text is significant. **"For I received from the Lord** [Εγὼ γὰρ παρέλαβον ἀπὸ τοῦ κυρίου] **what I also delivered to you** [ὃ καὶ παρέδωκα ὑμῖν], **that the Lord Jesus on the night when he was betrayed** [ὅτι ὁ κύριος ᾗ παρεδίδοτο] **he took the bread** [ἔλαβεν ἄρτον [**"bread"** here "is accusative masculine singular] **and after giving thanks**, [καὶ εὐχαριστήσας—this word is eucharistos "thanks" from which we get the name Eucharist] **he broke it and said**, [ἔκλασεν, καὶ εἶπεν], **"Take. Eat.** [Λάβετε φάγετε], **"This is my body"** *broken for you*. [Τοῦτό, the word "this," is Nominative neuter], μού ἐστιν τὸ σῶμα— which is the word "body," nominative neuter singular] **this do in remembrance of me** [ὑπὲρ ὑμῶν κλώμενον·[τοῦτο i.e., the word "this here" is Nominative neuter singular], **which is given for you** [ποιεῖτε εἰς τὴν ἐμὴν ἀνάμνησιν].

The point is to highlight the problematic phrase "broken for you." Often spoken as the priest tears the loaf of bread in half, breaking bread as the symbol for the shared meal. The symbolic gesture misses the point of what Jesus was apparently doing. The problem is that when Jesus uses the pronoun "this," we think he is referring to the bread. The pronoun "this" is neuter, and "bread" is masculine in gender. Jesus is *not* saying, "This bread is my body." The phrase "broken for you" was mistakenly added later in the fifth century, where translators were thinking that Christ's body was broken on the cross, and the breaking of bread enhances the symbolic meaning.

What does the masculine "this" refer to? The best guess by scholars is the Greek word "*deipnos*," a word that's not there in the text, but it is a neuter noun meaning "supper." Imagine Jesus picking up the bread, and with his hands gesturing to all those gathered around the table, "This group, this meal, this community is my body. This is for you. 'Whenever two or three are gathered, I am there.' This gathering around this bread, this community of soul and Presence, this body of visionary people who love…this is for you!"

This usual interpretation of the Last Supper recalling the breaking of Jesus' body is tied to the view of atonement that Christ died for our sins, in 1 Corinthians 15:1, Romans 5:6-8, 1 John 2:1-2, Hebrews 2:9. There are other ways to understand the significance of the cross and how we experience how the cross saves in the Way of Christ. The sacrament of the Lord's Supper, along with the interpretation that Jesus was calling attention to his bodily sacrifice for us, is a limited way to understand the universal Christ.

There are other "eating events" in the life of Jesus that are not sacraments, but they are significant and revelatory. There is the feeding of the five thousand (or four thousand[151]), where a simple lunch was expanded to feed a multitude. The very same experience of supplying food to feed many more people happened several times with Meher Baba. Other eating events happened with the woman anointing Jesus feet with her hair, the meal with Mary and Martha, and the post-resurrection story of eating at Emmaus where Jesus was made known to them in the breaking of bread. Neither Jesus nor the church made them into repeatable sacramental rituals.

Baptism is another major sacramental ritual that most Christians see as an act of remembrance to be followed by all. Sacraments are rites believed to have been initiated by Jesus. Protestants recognize two sacraments: the Eucharist/Last Supper and Baptism. Roman Catholics recognize seven sacraments—Baptism, Confirmation, Holy Communion, Confession, Marriage, Holy Orders, and the Anointing of the Sick. As the Roman church sees it, the first three sacraments—Baptism, Confirmation, and Holy Communion—are known as the sacraments of initiation because the rest of our life as Christians depends on them.

The Abrahamic religions each have sacramental rituals to mark a person's entrance into the religious community. Christians have Baptism, Jews have *Brit Milah* (circumcision), and *Bar/Bat Mitzvah*, and Islam has *Adhan* and *Aqiqah*. These rituals of initiation connect one with previous generations and often serve as a rite to set one apart from the general population with purpose and intent. Baptism carries the

---

[151] Feeding 4000 is found in Matthew 15:299-39 and Mark 8:1-10.

symbolic gesture of washing away original sin (which we debunked earlier). Sometimes Baptism and the other initiation rituals mark the transition from childhood to adulthood, or when performed with children signifies that God chooses everyone, and that all people of all ages benefit from the grace of God. This latter practice places everyone under the care and responsibility of everyone else. There is no issue of who is "in" or "out" or discrimination in Baptism as a sacrament, but it is a ritual of community, inclusion, and love.

The Gospel of Philip, part of the Nag Hammadi manuscripts, addresses the matter of whether Baptism is a magical rite. "If one goes down into the water and comes up without having received anything and says, 'I am a Christian,' he has borrowed the name at interest. But if he receives the Holy Spirit, he has the name as a gift. He who has borrowed it at interest, payment is demanded. This is what happens when one experiences a mystery."[152]

Is baptism something that mattered to Jesus, after the death of John the Baptist? Jesus did not baptize others; only his disciples did baptisms.[153] Jesus did not identify a community of those who were followers or faithful. As with every Ancient One, none who founded a religion, Jesus did not found the church. For all people—sinners, tax collectors, Roman soldiers, non-Jews such as the Samaritan woman, children, old and sick people, lepers, thieves, prostitutes, rich and poor, Jewish leaders—they were all equally children of God. Jesus didn't ask whether they were baptized. He didn't ask what they believed.

Jesus' washing the disciples' feet before the Last Supper has many characteristics that resemble a sacrament, as it reversed the perception of who is the servant and who should be served. As the early church was establishing lines of authority, reverence, and respect, it was a complicated idea to elevate every person and have the Lord of the Universe be the servant of all in washing their feet (a dirty job).

Another command of Jesus, "Let him deny himself and take up his cross and follow me,"[154] has taken on ritualistic and even sacramental

---

[152] *Gospel of Philip* 64:24-29, in *The Nag Hammadi Library*, ed. by James M. Robinson (HarperCollins, 1990), p.148.

[153] John 3:2

[154] Matthew 25:24

dimensions. For that matter, the holy days of the church also resemble the sacraments as reminders of the Christ. Holy Week in particular often becomes a drama of re-enactment of the last week of Jesus' life, suggesting that we do what he did, we suffer with him, we experience what he did, but this is not what Jesus wants us to do… wave palm branches, re-enact the trials, literally create our own crosses. Even the Lord's Supper is far more than a re-enactment; its reach extends to the Heavenly Banquet with overtones of being in Paradise.

Biblical scholar Bruce Chilton said that Jesus wanted his meal to replace the Temple sacrifice, announcing the presence of the Kingdom everywhere (and not just in the afterlife). This symbolic body and blood bring one into union with God. It left the disciples with a challenging question: "Do I choose the Temple and my traditional faith, or do I choose Jesus and his new symbol of the meal with God?"[155]

We are considering the Faces of Jesus, in particular whether he intended to create forms of religious practice and whether these are healing for the psyche. The Lectionary is a list of suggested scripture readings from the Old Testament, the Gospels, and the Letters that are to be read each week in worship over a period of three years. Their intention is also to expose people in worship to almost every aspect of the Bible. When one takes all the lectionary readings for Advent, Christmas, Epiphany, Lent, Easter, and Pentecost, and examines the archetypes within the suggested readings, they serve as a primer in human development from infancy, to childhood, to all phases of adulthood, to old age and death.

Does the Lectionary serve as another healing connection to the biblical story? As unconscious as the structure of the Lectionary is for most people, it makes a contribution to healing in the journey to wholeness.

At stake in this aspect of Jesus as a priest, is the matter of whether the disciplines and forms of organized religion are enhancements or impediments to healing. Both. There are some who are so caught up in the forms and practices that the forms become the religion itself, rather than the vehicle that leads them beyond themselves to the Christ-in-

---

[155] Bruce Chilton, *Rabbi Jesus: An Intimate Biography* (PRH Christian Publishing, 2002), p. 257.

form and beyond-all-form. When people become attached to creeds and prayer, to hymns and orders of worship, to prayer books, they have made religion itself into an idol that blocks them from God.

Meher Baba said, "The diverse rituals and ceremonies of religions and cults are intended to release divine love, but they mostly bind the soul to the repetitive mechanism of expressive forms. Attachment to the rigid forms of external expressions of love to God, limits the love itself, binding the soul to ignorance and becoming an obstacle to real illumination. The true spiritual aspirant is therefore more keen about the inner life. Inner life is based on love for God, and it is this love that annihilates all desires."[156]

It is what we bring to the ritual forms and disciplines that make it holy. The ritual itself, the ecclesiastical trappings, the sacred cups, the meal elements, the special words really have nothing to do with it. We take these common elements and endow them with special power. We confess to the priest or the rabbi and we grant them the power to release us into forgiveness, or offer last rites. But the true power of holiness comes from the Self within.

Rumi gives an example of how the inner Self seizes forms and rituals and turns this into a healing experience.

A Christian goes to his priest and tells a year's worth of sin—
fornication, meanness, hypocrisy.
He wants to be forgiven and he hears the priests absolving as grace.
The priest himself may have no experience of that mercy,
but the Christian's imagination gives it to him.
Love and imagination do many things.
Let your teacher be love itself,
not someone with a white beard.
When a Christian longs to be forgiven,
the priest disappears in that longing.
These forms we're in are like bowls.
They acquire value from what pours through

---

[156] *Lord Meher*, Vol. 11, p. 3998-3999.

to serve as nourishment.[157]

Yunis Emre, a thirteenth-century Sufi dervish in Turkey, explained how our forms of worship may not take us as far as we need.

Reality is an ocean; the Religion is a ship.
Many have never left the ship,
never jumped into the sea.
They might have come to Worship
but they stopped at rituals.
They never knew or entered the Inside.
Those who think the Four Books [Gospels]
were meant to be talked about,
who have only read explanations
and never entered meaning.[158]

As can be seen in Jesus' interaction with the non-Jewish woman at the well, he was offering her "living water," which allowed her to transcend herself. The effect of this priestly interaction was to help her release her perceived self ("Why are you, a Jew talking to me, a Samaritan?") and the effect is the shattering of the old self. This should be the effect of the sacraments and religious rituals.

Rabbi Jesus performed priestly gestures, such as when he said, "Pray like this, 'Our Father who art in heaven...'" and when he said pray in private, be modest, and don't parade your piety before others, don't judge other people, love your neighbor, God loves what comes from the heart as this woman expresses with perfume.

There were other times when the priestly or devotional/religious side of Jesus' words at first seemed difficult, if not impossible.

---

[157] Rumi, *The Soul of Rumi*, trans. by Coleman Barks (HarperSanFrancisco, 2001), p. 226.

[158] Yunus Emre, from *The Drop That Became the Sea: Lyric Poems of Yunus Emre*, Translated by Kabir Helminski and Refik Algan. http://www.poetry-chaikhana.com/E/EmreYunus/Thosewhobeca.htm

- I say to you who hear, Love your enemies
- do good to those who hate you
- bless those who curse you
- pray for those who abuse you
- to one who strikes you on the cheek, offer the other cheek also,
- from one who takes your cloak, do not withhold your tunic either
- give to everyone who begs from you
- judge not, and you will not be judged
- condemn not, and you will not be condemned
- forgive, and you will be forgiven[159]

What is Jesus doing with these difficult sayings? The essential message of Jesus is, "Leave all and come to me." Leave your parents, leave your work identity, leave your religious practices, leave your beliefs, leave your self! Only when one leaves their own identity, their religious plan, their view of righteousness, the need for control, only when one lets go of their ego self, only then can one come to God. These sayings have to do with "let go of yourself."

How does one let go of oneself? This can be a way to madness, or to the true life. All these difficult sayings, beginning with loving one's enemies, are ways to move beyond self-interest and personal agenda and self-interested ego. This makes Jesus a spiritual teacher who takes one beyond personal religion and belief to the eternal life beyond all form and beyond the mind. Letting go of oneself is the primary healing strategy of the biblical story.

This "Face" of Jesus as "Ritual Priest," who creates possibilities for renewal, begins with the awareness that organized religion, be it Pharisaic Judaism with its 613 laws or Christianity with its emphasis on creeds and beliefs, can only lead the seeker to the threshold of the true way to God. Meher Baba said the intent of religion is to release divine love, a different consciousness than what is usually expressed in our word-dominated sacred rituals.

What Jesus seemed to be doing with religion was to create a bridge into what is higher, even though others saw him violating Sabbath laws.

---

[159] Luke 6:27-37

What God wants is not ceremonies, not yogas, not prayers. God wants love, the love that makes one forget themselves in Him.

4. Political Iconoclast/ *Jalali* Nature
Kenotic Iconoclast—Breakdown Images of Religion, Power, Separateness, Righteousness, Ego

I came to cast fire upon the earth; and would it were already kindled. I have a baptism to be baptized with; how am I to be constrained until it is accomplished? Do you think I have come to give peace on earth? No, I tell you, rather division.
— Luke 12: 49-51

Was Jesus always nice, kind, loving, and gentle to people? No! Jesus had a harsh side. There is a side of Jesus that we can archetypally see as the Warrior Jesus. We can say the same thing about God. In ways, it helps that Jesus was like us, for we all have anger and lose it at times. The issue, however, turns on what Jesus got angry about, and whether his anger had a higher purpose.

This fierce Jesus does not sound like the one who said we should "turn the other cheek." What is the relationship between the warrior and the pacifist? The pacifist must move beyond indiscriminate reverence for all life. The warrior knows where the battle is, and what is required is impeccable clarity, direction, and action.

To want to lump all the spiritually advanced into lovely saintly people is just not possible. Some of them are very difficult to live with. Moslems speak of two different personalities of saints. There are the *jamali* types, who are gentle, loving, kind, inspiring, compassionate, and friendly, who often enjoy human company. There are the *jalali* types, who are easily angered, fierce, crude, antisocial, harsh, angry, and fearsome. There are some spiritually advanced ones who have both qualities.

Whenever the Ancient One comes, according to Meher Baba, there are always the highest God-Realized Masters who awaken the Ancient One into his true God-identity. It is likely that John the Baptist played this role for Jesus. Of the Perfect Masters who attended to Meher Baba, most of them were *jalali* types. They would be mean, harsh, throw rocks, and slap the devotee. Even early in his twenties, as Meher Baba assumed his role as an avatar, he could be *jalali*-like, slapping or hurting devotees. He was a little man, but had super-human strength; he once challenged all the disciples to a tug-of-war. Even 40 of the men, using all their strength, could not budge him an inch in a tug of war pulling on a rope.

The question here is whether Jesus was a *Jalali* type. We think of him throwing out the money changers for making a profitable business out of the temple… turning over tables, spilling money on the floor, striking people, being furious… was this *jalali* behavior?

There was the time when Jesus turned and cursed those around him who ignored people in need. "You who are accursed, depart from me into the eternal fire prepared for the devil and his angels" (In short, "Go to hell!").[160] There was another point where Jesus healed a man with a withered hand on the Sabbath, and the religious leaders were upset. The text says, "And he looked at them in anger, grieved at their hardness of heart."[161] And as anger creates anger, the Pharisees went out with the same anger, counseling how to destroy Jesus. Is this *jalali?*

There is no commandment, "Thou shalt not be angry!" It is how we act on our anger that matters.

Christians have the Trinity—Father, Son, Spirit. There is a more universal trinitarian form common to all religions—Creator, Sustainer, Destroyer. The Destroyer archetype is the aspect we have difficulty with. We may over-revere the Creator side. But we cannot really create something unless we can uncreate it. Getting rid of forms is a way of recognizing illusion and our attachment to forms. Nothing is permanent, and we need to remind ourselves of this. The Destroyer side of God appeared at the Tower of Babel and with Noah. As we address the Destroyer side of the universal Trinity, we realize we are accessing the Hindu Goddess Kali, who brings an end to illusion and attachment. So we approach the Face of Jesus the Destroyer, who is just as important as Jesus the Creator.

To connect with the Holy Spirit aspect of the Trinity, Spirit is often symbolized with fire, as with the tongues of fire at Pentecost. The best

---

[160] Matthew 25:40-41
[161] Mark 3:4

word to describe the *jalali* side of Jesus is "fiery." This has the properties of destruction, purification, and inspiration.

And behold, a man came up to him, saying, "Teacher, what good deed must I do to have eternal life?" And he said to him, "Why do you ask me about what is good? There is only one who is good. If you would enter life, keep the commandments." He said to him, "Which ones?" And Jesus said, "You shall not murder, You shall not commit adultery, You shall not steal, You shall not bear false witness, Honor your father and mother, and You shall love your neighbor as yourself." The young man said to him, "All these I have kept. What do I still lack?" Jesus said to him, "If you would be perfect, go, sell what you possess and give to the poor, and you will have treasure in heaven; and come, follow me." When the young man heard this he went away sorrowful, for he had great possessions.
— Matthew 19:16-22 (ESV)

Further conversation between Jesus and the young man

Young man: Master Yeshua (Jesus), I would like to better understand what you are saying. I am trying to be a good Jew. I believe in the Torah and all Moses taught. But you have really been hard on our spiritual teachers. You have been mean even. Isn't being judgmental and harsh against the Law?

Jesus: What do you mean?

Young man: You have called our spiritual teachers "snakes." You have said their guidance is false, that they have been "straining gnats but swallowing camels," which is kind of funny, but harsh.

Jesus: I am saying that the teachers are focusing on the inconsequential and missing the true point of the faith. But so far, you are doing a good job. You understand what I have been saying.

Young man: Sometimes I worry that you are poisoning the well. You say we clean the outside of the cup and make religion look good, but the inside is full of greed, selfishness, hypocrisy, uncleanliness, and lawlessness. That sounds ugly and anti-religious. You told the spiritual leaders of the temple that they are going to hell. This doesn't sound like a wise and deep appreciation of our tradition.

Jesus: Yes, I understand what you are saying. I began my work trying to be very caring of people, healing some, demonstrating that what God wants from us is love. When the spiritual leaders saw I was preaching a message counter to their message of righteousness, they became vicious and ugly toward what I was saying, so, in a sense, I guess you could say I began to fight fire with fire.

Young man: Are you trying to destroy the Jewish way?

Jesus: Yes and no. I am a Jew like you. I believe in the Torah of Moses, just like you. And at the same time, I am above all religion. I have not come to destroy what Moses taught us, but I have come to fulfill the law. There is a sense in which I have been deconstructing our current religious practice. Maybe the word "reorient it" is a better phrase, to point spirituality in a different direction.

Young man: Isn't trying to be righteous a good thing?

Jesus: Being righteous and perfect is a discipline of the spiritual way, but it is not the goal. The goal is loving God, loving God to the extent that you let go of all else and there is nothing but God. Sometimes people focus on the means and not the goal. Being righteous is a means to the end, not the end.

Young man: I am not sure what to do. I have devoted my life to keeping the *mitzvot* (commandments), and I seek to be a *tzaddik* (a righteous person). I respect others. I have not been guilty of violence, murder, stealing, lying. I honor my mother and father.

Jesus: How is that working for you?

Young man: Well, I think it is going pretty well. I am hoping that I am a really faithful Jew. When I asked you what I should do, in addition to following the commandments, you said I should "enter into life." What does that mean?

Jesus: Many think the way to God requires that they be saints, do good deeds, practice disciplines such as fasting, meditation, and obedience to the law. These spiritual disciplines have two edges like a sword. They can help or harm. The fastest way to God is to enter into life itself. Live your life. God gives you exactly what you need to come to him. Trusting your life is for the higher good rather than obeying the commandments.

Young man: Why do you say spiritual disciplines can do harm?

Jesus: The danger of your spiritual ambition is having spiritual pride. Your spiritual discipline in keeping the *mitzvot* feeds your personal ego and self-importance. This distances you from God. That is what I was getting at when I criticized teachers who display their piety in public to be seen by others.

Young man: I am still reacting to your anger about our saintly temple teachers. I have been listening to you criticizing our spiritual teachers for doing what I have been doing, and it has got me thinking, concerned, even. Are you saying that the way of being a good Jew is wrong?

Jesus: Unless your righteousness exceeds that of the scribes and Pharisees, you will never enter the Kingdom of God.[162] They know neither the scriptures nor the power of God.[163]

Young man: What do you mean when you say, "They don't know the Torah or the power of God?"

Jesus: It is good to practice the disciplines of religion, but it is important to know you worship what you do not know.[164] The Kingdom lies beyond your imagination. To occupy yourself with moral laws that you think you have mastered is to labor with food that perishes, rather than to partake of the food that endures to eternal life.[165]

Young man: I have a different question now. They say you are a healer. How are your sharp attacks healing?

Jesus: The Father sent me to heal his children from their practices that prevent true healing, healing of their souls.

Young man: Master Yeshua, what am I supposed to do?

Jesus: I know that you follow the laws and disciplines. I know that you are a loving person. Your question about what to do suggests you recognize that your religious practice alone is not enough.

Young man: This is why I came to see you. I just have the sense there is more. More to being spiritual.

Jesus: Your longing for this "moreness" is what will save you. I am not sure you will like what I am going to tell you. You have prospered

---

[162] Matthew 5:20
[163] Matthew 22:29
[164] John 2:22
[165] John 6:27

and been successful. Sell all your goods and treasures, and give to those who have nothing.

Young man: Ouch! Why? That is impossible! That frightens me!

Jesus: What I am asking you to do is to let go of all your attachments, what you hold on to. A moment ago, we talked about letting go of the beliefs and spiritual practices that make you proud to be a spiritual being. Now we are talking about letting go of your material belongings. You could retain them if you had no attachment to them. Empty yourself of yourself. The spiritual way is not obeying the laws, although they point to good practice. The spiritual way is letting go of everything temporary, and what remains is eternal. Leave all and come to me, and you will enter the Kingdom.

Another aspect of this Fourth Face is Jesus the Iconoclast, the destroyer of images. He destroyed images of the prevailing religion and images of himself. The first half of the word iconoclast is "icon," which traditionally means a picture to be revered. The Eastern Orthodox Church celebrated painted images or icons of Jesus and the disciples in their worship and homes. The second half of the word is "clast," meaning one who destroys or opposes images. An Iconoclast is someone who attacks or opposes settled beliefs or institutions, or who destroys religious images. There was a major clash between the Eastern Orthodox churches and the Western Roman Church from the 6th-8th centuries over whether icons should be objects of worship in themselves or whether they lead one beyond the image to what lies beyond all images.

Jesus was a significant iconoclast, blasting the Pharisaic Jewish religion for its over-obsession with following the 613 *mitzvot* of the Torah, which were seen as the object of religious faith. They were seen as idols of belief around which religious people had to serve, and severe judgments were levied. Jesus violating the Sabbath laws was a primary example of smashing the icon of the Sabbath, so Jesus challenged them by healing on the Sabbath, saying the Sabbath was made for man, not man for the Sabbath. Jesus challenged the laws around purity, handwashing, who one could associate with, especially not fraternizing with non-Jews such as gentiles or Samaritans, tax collectors, pro-Roman folk, criminals, prostitutes, and lepers. He told the story of the Good Samaritan, who was beaten and left lying on the road, and the priest and Levite walked by on the other side without helping, and only the non-Jewish Samaritan helped. Jesus was a severe iconoclast when it came to Jewish isolationism and elitism.

He attacked the iconic character of Jewish privilege, of being chosen people, of thinking they were holier and better than others, of thinking they were spiritually superior (seen in the woman at the well story). Jesus said to the Torah scholars, you know neither the scriptures nor God.

The major issue in this aspect of Jesus' issue with the Jewish elite was their spiritual arrogance, thinking they were closer to God. This is an issue in every religion, which claims it knows the Truth and the way to God. The point of Jesus' iconoclasm is that every human mind, every religious idea, every religious practice, every spiritual action, every belief, every physical aspect is limited, partial. It may have value, but it is only a small part of the Higher Truth and the life of God. We human beings live in the world of our own making; we make up what we see and what we believe, for it all falls short of God. As lovely as devotion is, it is an illusion. That is what Jesus means when he says, "Leave all and follow me."

Although Jewish scholar Martin Buber was not speaking about Jesus, he made the same point. "The historical religions have the tendency to become ends in themselves and, as it were, to put themselves in God's place, and, in fact, there is nothing that is so apt to obscure the face of God as a religion."[166]

In a sense, Judaism in the world of Jesus had devolved into a cult of following religious laws, and people failed to see the transcendent reality Jesus was pointing to. Somewhat similarly, many Christians have also fallen into a cult of belief, hearing only "believe in me and you will be saved." Over the century, religion has focused on the limited and the illusory, while missing the infinite, transcendent beyond all knowing that Jesus called the Kingdom of God. The Kingdom is beyond all words, all knowing, all definition, all imagination… and Jesus-the-Iconoclast said, in effect, when you let go of yourself and the world of your

---

[166] Martin Buber, in Donald J. Moore, *Martin Buber: Prophet of Religious Secularism* (New York: Fordham University Press; revised edition, 1996), p. 234.

own making, you will be able to see the world of God's making, the only world that is real. We have a religion that is tied to the ineffable. Come to me, and I will help you do that.

Jesus broke the icons of who people thought God was. He broke the icon of the Torah, he broke the icon of belief, he broke the icon of purity, he broke the icons of Abraham, Moses, and the Prophets. The one icon he did not break was the icon of love, because that was the one infinite icon. He left his own physical body in its power.

5. Qabalist/Mystic
The Way to Become Christ, God Realized

Jesus said to them, "You are from below; I am from above. You are of this world; I am not of this world. So they said to him, "Who are you?" Jesus said to them, "Just what I have been telling you from the beginning. Jesus said to them, "When you have lifted up the Son of Man, then you will know that I am he, and that I do nothing on my own authority, but speak just as the Father taught me.
— John 8:23-24, 2

Was Jesus a mystic? What did he mean when he said, "I am not of this world? What did he mean [in the context of this Face], "I am the Son of Man?"

There are many misconceptions about mysticism, such as Jesus saying, "I am not of this world." Mysticism does not mean otherworldly. It does not mean "up in the clouds" and "woo-woo," where one is in an alternative reality disconnected from this world. Mysticism is often separated from mainstream, orthodox religion, which involves normal spiritual disciplines, worship, and practical works of service to others and the community. It is seen as different from "Normative Christianity."

This could not be farther from the truth. The mystic sees the world as one, in the sense found in the *Shema*. The mystic sees that we are not separate from God except as we make God separate. God is not separate from the world. All of Creation is God-in-form, where the God-without-form is called the Beyond-Beyond, but the God-above and the God-below (God in form) are different sides of the same coin. The world of atoms and all physical matter is the world of form. We talk about the creation of the Universe (the World of Form) as having a beginning and an end. The "world" beyond all form has no beginning and end, but it is an extended aspect of every physical and mental form.

Mystics are completely involved in the physical world and the universe, but they also see the world-beyond-form in everything. Sometimes mystics say that the physical world, which is temporary and comes and goes, is an illusion, and the formless world is reality. But it is all one and the same. When Jesus says, "I am not of this world," he is not saying, "I am not part of the world." He is saying to the Pharisees, "The world you see is limited and partial. If that is all you see, then your seeing is false. The world I am in sees everything, seen and unseen, and the world I am in sees God everywhere." In this sense, Jesus would say, "If you call me a mystic, that is true."

Throughout the Bronze Age and Iron Age (3000 – 500 BCE), cognitive perception was concrete, specific, and physical. Mathematics had to do with how many cows or sheep (or wives) one had. With some help from the Egyptians, the Persian Zoroastrians, and more from the Greeks, the world began to think more abstractly and theoretically. In biblical history, the Babylonian and later Persian "Captivity" of the Jewish people introduced them to an entirely different perception of the world. The physical world was not the only world people could think of. Reality became multi-leveled. This epochal change introduced a new spirituality, with traditional conservatives liking the familiar biblical story, and the new "liberal" visionary thinkers creating a different way to see the world and envision the future.

The prophets Ezekiel and Isaiah were among these revolutionaries, preparing the way for a future man from Nazareth. After Assyria had taken over northern Israel in the seventh century, in 598 BCE (and again in 587), Babylon swept through southern Israel (Judea), including Jerusalem, and marched the people of the land to the land of the rivers Tigris and Euphrates, effectively ending the nation of Israel. What was left of the Temple and religious cult ended. Accordingly, it was in this scene that the Prophet Ezekiel, at the beginning of the sixth century, received a vision he thought from Heaven about how the religion of the people of the Bible could continue.

It was Doomsday for the children of Israel. A crisis of belief in God. How could God allow this, the destruction of the Temple and the Holy of Holies, and the deportation of the people from the Promised Land? What sin was committed that warranted this? Or was it that God was not as powerful as the other gods? Or was God the cause of this holocaust? (These were the same questions that Jews faced with Nazi Germany in World War II.)

Ezekiel foresaw the destruction of the Temple by Babylon, and he saw something higher. He realized that in whatever happened, God would go with them. God would be with them in the resettlement camps. The vision that "came to him" (he insisted that he did not make it up) was a chariot that flew in the air. Along with the four wheels were four human-like creatures, each with four wings and four faces. The face in front was a man, a lion on the right, an ox on the left, and an eagle at the back. They could move in any direction, and their moving had the sound like many waters and the thunder of the Almighty. And above the chariot was what looked like a throne and a celestial figure, "the appearance of the likeness of the glory of the Lord."

Interestingly, Ezekiel's chariot took the form of the most advanced transportation of the day, the fearsome war machine that crushed Israel. The story of the chariot of God is loaded with symbolism. The sound of the rushing waters is reminiscent of the original creation, and the crystal rainbow is reminiscent of the new peace God made with humanity after the destruction of the Flood. The animals—man, lion, ox, eagle—represent the mightiest of animals, the grounding of human labor, and the transcendence of the eagle that takes one to God. The quaternio of the four directions (which later the cross represents) is the symbol of wholeness.

These are remarkable images for a culture that had trouble with abstract thinking. The chariot was a vehicle outside the gross world (a new idea), an image that was primeval, transcendent, beyond space and time, and even somewhat timeless and eternal. Elijah had been transported to God by a divine fiery chariot (2 Kings 2:11-12). Later, Isaiah also saw the Chariot/Throne (Isaiah 6). A new spirituality was being born; this was the beginning of Jewish mysticism, something that Jesus tapped into.

In the fifth century BCE, the word "rabbi" appeared, and rabbinic academies were established. The Pharisaic rabbinical sect gradually secured its position of dominance and orthodox authority over Judaism during the Hasmonean period from 140 to its end with King Herod in 37 BCE. The Jewish Mystical Kabbalah took form during this period.

The Pharisaic movement also began in this period. The word "Pharisee" comes from *parush*, meaning one separated for special learning. Perhaps as a reaction against the transcendent movement precipitated by Ezekiel, the Pharisees sought to preserve the traditional religion, establishing schools that taught special knowledge and carrying the sense of being spiritually elite and exclusive by the time of Jesus. Additionally, after the Roman destruction of the Temple in 70 CE and the dispersion of the Jews, the Pharisaic obsession with being righteous increased. The Kabbalah within Judaism gave the effort to be righteous a cosmic dimension. As Daniel Matt noted, the Kabbalah was the mending of all the worlds. It was not the "world that is coming," but the "world that is constantly coming."

There are two types of spirituality, **ex**oteric spirituality (outer spirituality) and **es**oteric spirituality (inner spirituality). Pharisaic Judaism was an exoteric spirituality that emphasized outer, organized religion, going to the Temple, performing sacrifices, and following the *mitzvot* (commandments). Jesus emphasized esoteric spirituality, which involved going inward to the core of one's being, to the thought of the heart. Jesus said that adultery was more than having physical sex, but if one lusted after another, that was also adultery. The Fifth Commandment said honor your mother and father, but Jesus said, leave your mother and father and come to me. By this he didn't mean to violate the Commandment, but do your work with your father issues and mother issues, and rise above your attachments in this way, for your attachments keep you from God. This is esoteric spirituality. It leads one to a mystical approach of seeing the divine in all aspects of living.

This brings us to the question of whether Jesus was a Qabalist rather than a Kabbalist. Jewish spirituality has two major mystical movements. The first is the movement that arose from Ezekiel's vision of transcendence and immanence. This can be called the Way of the Chariot

(*Merkabah*). The second form of Jewish mysticism emerged in the Hasidic movement following the Baal Shem Tov (1700 – 1760 CE) in eastern Europe, specifically Poland.

The word Kabbalah is given two distinctive spellings; Kabbalah is uniquely within Judaism. The Mystical Qabalah (spelled with a "Q") refers to "an ancient mystical transmission that preceded and supersedes any of the religious vessels through which it has subsequently filtered and adapted."[167] The mysticism behind the mystical movements cannot be reduced to a writing, a system of beliefs, or a person. For example, Sufism has taken many forms, from the first-century Essene Communities of Qumran and the integrated Essene sect of Mt. Carmel near modern Haifa, to the Sufi movement (derived from Qabalistic spirituality), which later attached itself to Islam. The mystical Qabalah, the incipient Jewish Kabbalah, Mystical Christianity, and Sufism all seem to be successive fresh versions of the same underlying tradition.

Recognizing that Jesus was not contained by the Pharisaic movement, not even Judaism, we will explore his mysticism in the more universal Qabalah. As will be seen in the sixth Face, the Universal Christ, Jesus had infinite awareness, and while he connected to the Chariot mysticism of Judaism, the mystical aspect of the Essenes, the mystical elements of Buddhism, of Advaita Vedanta of Hinduism, and the Zoroastrian mysticism, he was far above all these "downloadings" of universal mystical Qabalah beyond all names and definition.

Qabalah (and Kabbalah) means receiving, or what has been received. *Qabal* means "to grasp the vision," and it also means "Welcoming of God," alluding to direct communication and union with God. It is synonymous with the Sanskrit word "Yoga," which comes from the Sanskrit *yug* or oneness with God. Qabalah is the technique of altering one's consciousness to enter the Kingdom/ become a *yordai Merkavah*.[168]

As Jesus contemplated the challenge of awakening the Jewish people to the higher spirituality that would invite people to enter the Kingdom of God, we are not in a position to fully see the intention of his mission. He seized upon the image of the Prophet Ezekiel's Chariot as a kind of

---

[167] Daniel Hale Feldman, *Qabalah: The Mystical Heritage of the Children of Abraham*, (Santa Cruz, CA: Work of the Chariot, 2001), p. 14.

[168] Feldman, p. 23.

esoteric spirituality that was beyond the literal and fundamentalist organized religious approach of the Pharisees. The Chariot image said God was everywhere, including within every person.

Drawing on scriptural stories that people knew, Jesus also seized on another vision from the prophetic tradition, one from the book of Daniel. Admittedly, this was an even more bizarre vision than Ezekiel's. Daniel's witness was apocalyptic, like the New Testament book of Revelation with its bizarre images. Again, it was a time of great political uncertainty, and Daniel had a vision of some vehicle (? ?) lifted off the ground. Like Ezekiel's chariot, the sea was stirred (reminiscent of creation), and there were four animals with wings: a lion with eagle's wings, a bear, a leopard, and a fourth beast. The lion was put on the ground and given a mind like a man. There was a fiery throne above, and the Ancient of Days sat on it, and "one like a human being was present to the Ancient of Days on the throne.[169]

The symbolism was striking: although it was written almost entirely in Aramaic in the second century, the book of Daniel reflects the same conditions that the sixth-century BCE Ezekiel described. The lion with eagle's wings, the leopard, the man, and the beast are often thought to be the empires threatening Israel—Assyria, Babylon, Persia, and the Seleucids (Syria).

These four figures—man, ox, lion, eagle—are mystical archetypes to this day. They are often found in an order beginning in the north or forward-facing, i.e., the face of a man in Ezekiel's case. This archetype is the North, the Source, the primordial, the transcendent, the unknown from which we emerge. The ox represents the West, a gross physical animal, representing the herd, the community of belonging, the family, or

---

[169] Daniel 1:1-48. The vision is abbreviated as follows: Daniel saw a dream and a vision of his mind in bed; afterward he wrote down the dream. "I saw the four winds of heaven stirring up the great sea, four mighty beasts different from each other emerged from the sea. The first was like a lion but had eagles' wings. …it was lifted off the ground and set on its feet like a man and given the mind of a man. I saw a second, different beast, which was like a bear; as I looked on, there was another one, like a leopard, there was a fourth beast. As I looked on, thrones were set in place, and the Ancient of Days took His seat. Its wheels were blazing fire. A river of fire streamed forth before Him. As I looked on, one like a human being came with the clouds of heaven; He reached the Ancient of Days And was presented to Him.

the land. This is what gives life grounding, order, tradition, covenant, and it is the place of ending and death. The South archetypically carries what is personal, individual (in contrast to the ox energy). It gives identity, ego development, beliefs, and the unwinding of illusions. In Ezekiel's vision, the eagle occupies this position. The East has the lion archetype, which is what brings everything into one—the group and the individual, body-mind, yin-yang. It is the place of beginning, the place of realizing the Self.

Daniel's vision has roughly the same archetypes in a different order, and he adds the "four winds of heaven," the four cardinal directions, also reported in Isaiah 11:2, suggesting the four corners of the earth, and the story of the birth of creation.

The Kabbalists/Qabalists claim that the mystical beginnings were with Adam and Eve in the Garden. What they are referring to is that we live in a nondual world, a world where everything is one, as it was originally in the Garden. When "we" left the Garden, the Garden went with us. The Garden is not past, it is everywhere. This is the underlying Reality.

The Chariot with these archetypal figures, at the four corners, or four faces at each corner, moving in the four directions, with the four winds of creation, is a "map" of the human possibilities and the journey to God, a journey of traveling through the four levels (referred to in Chapter 2). Sitting within or above the Chariot is the throne of the Almighty. The four aspects of every human and the four worlds carry Almighty God.

The archetypal power of Ezekiel's and Daniel's visions continued into the days of the New Testament. These images were given zoomorphic expression in Christian art, with each of the four gospels designated. Matthew is associated with the winged man because his gospel focuses on Christ's humanity. The lion is related to St. Mark because his gospel emphasizes the majesty of Christ and his royal dignity. The ox represents Luke, because his gospel focuses on the sacrificial character of Christ's death. John, finally, is associated with the eagle because his gospel describes the Incarnation of the divine Logos, and the eagle is a symbol of that which comes from above. The Book of Revelation in Chapter 4 also depicts these four archetypal figures.

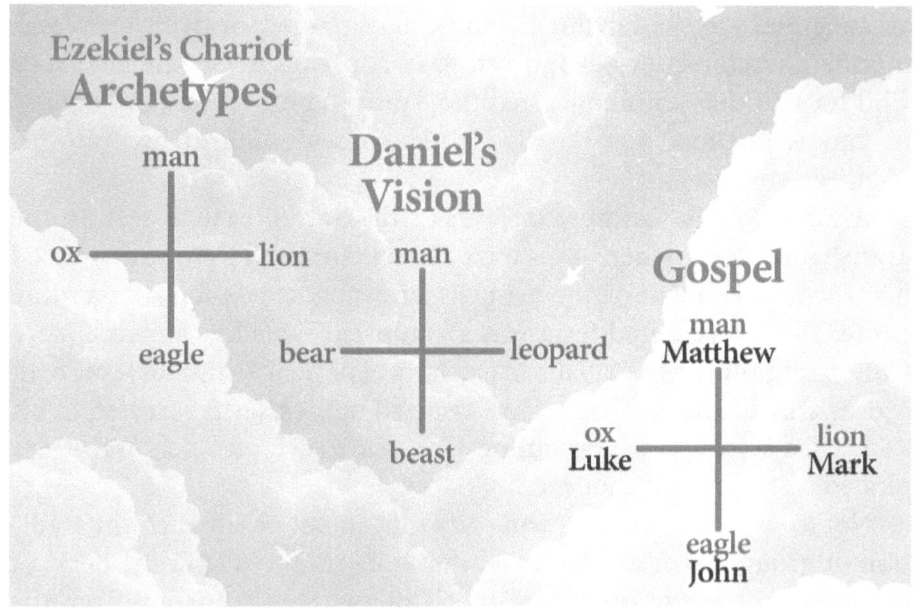

Figure 12: Ezekiel Chariot Archetypes compared to Daniel and Gospel Archetypes

The power of these images and archetypes was not lost to Jesus and his audience, although they may not have understood the symbolic meaning of the animals. Jesus used the image of the chariot itself to help the people see that experiencing God was not limited to Temple worship and was beyond the geographical place of Jerusalem—the experience of God was within everyone. God was beyond time and space, and a few may have received the message that so are all of us human beings. Jesus used the Qabalah message to support his invitation for people to see the Kingdom, the emerging transcendent reality in the midst of every one of us. The *mystery* of the Chariot moves from the Holy of Holies and the fire-and-cloud of the Ark to the mystical *cloud of unknowing* related to the Holy Spirit. Now, everywhere one could access the Chariot, a moving Throne of God, a portable Temple, and a new kind of religion. It was a new approach to God, in which riding the chariot represented a higher consciousness.

From what can be interpolated, Jesus didn't stop there. He seems to have grasped the phrase "one like a man" from Daniel's vision. It seems that he used the image of "one like a man" to mean a person who was an angel next to the Divine Throne/Chariot, a person with universal, infinite consciousness beyond ordinary consciousness. Scholar Bruce Chilton said that Jesus converted the Aramaic phrase "one like a man" to the designation "Son of Man."[170] He is beginning to step into his identity as a Christ.

A rather unique glimpse of Jesus as the Son of Man is seen in the Transfiguration,[171] where Jesus took Peter, James, and John and revealed his true transcendent divine being as far as that is possible, in dazzling white. The Transfigured Jesus was a glimpse of "one like a man." Bruce Chiton said this was a Qabalistic teaching experience, linking Jesus with Moses, Elijah, and two other God-realized figures. Jesus revealed to his selected disciples what becoming God-realized looks like, and it exploded into their consciousness.[172]

Not to say Jesus was following any movement or ritual of any tradition or group, but it can be noted that holy meals were at the heart of the mystical/Chariot practice. Bruce Chilton cited a portion from the Jewish Talmud (*Chagigah* 14b) that speaks of rabbis' disciples joining angels in the banquet halls of heaven. The holy meals were at the heart of the mystical/Chariot practice. One of the classic texts on the Chariot (in the Talmud) speaks of rabbis' disciples joining the angels in the banquet halls of heaven.[173] The Last Supper may have been related to Chariot mysticism.

All this brings us to the question of whether Jesus was a Qabalist, that is, the ancient way of becoming one with God, as it was at the beginning of Creation. Many people heard this oneness as union with God, following the metaphor of the bride and bridegroom. This is lovely, but the wedding metaphor is still a state of "twoness" or dualism. As Jesus said in the Gospel of Thomas, if you drink the cup I drink, we will become one; you will be me, and I will be you. You will be God. That is nondualism, true oneness, where everything started at the beginning—our true state.

---

[170] Chilton, p. 132.
[171] Matthew 17:1-8, Mark 9:2-13, Luke 9:28-36, and Second Peter refers to it
[172] Chilton, p. 192.
[173] Chilton p. 257.

Entering the Kingdom of God was at the heart of Jesus' message throughout. It means that one moves *beyond* worship of God to *being* God and nothing else. The Gospels of Normative Christianity are dualistic throughout, and this is not a criticism of them or a dismissal of them. The teachings in the Way of Jesus, which are before, above, and after the canonical gospels, are largely a call to become nondualistic. Several of the Gospels tell of Jesus being asked in various ways what the one thing most important about religion is, and each time he says the *Shema*, "The Lord your God is One," meaning that any separateness, or the idea of "God-and-me," is an illusion. God is the only reality.

As the Qabalistic tradition has flourished from the beginning, the true Teachers have taught others very carefully, recognizing that the general population is often not spiritually mature enough to understand the high teachings about nonduality. With no intention to be elitist, the higher teachings are often called "closed door" teachings. This might explain why Jesus taught in parables and metaphors and so much mystery surrounded him.

There is a teaching that could be appropriately heard from the lips of Jesus:

> *To the people in the crowd who came to hear Jesus, he said,*
> *"God is here among us."*
> *To the disciples who were at his side he said, "I am God."*
> *To the few disciples closest to him and who understood his*
> *message, He said, "You are God."*[174]

6. Universal Christ
Avatar-Christ Giving an Evolutionary Boost for All Creation

---

[174] I believe Meher Baba said this, i.e., he had been Jesus before he was Meher Baba. I do not have this quote from a written source, but I believe it came from an acquaintance who was a disciple of Meher Baba and who had heard this with his own ears.

To link the term "Christ" with the Jewish hope for the Messiah is to not see the Christ. To see the Christ in the same category as the other "Faces" (as it is the Sixth Face of Jesus) frankly misses who Jesus was. This concept of the Christ is a different category from the other Faces, for it is not a Face. Even seeing Christ as a figure of Christianity is not even close. The "Christ" belongs to no religion. Even to use the term "Universal Christ" to say that Jesus belongs to the world, and that everyone should be a Christian, is still to miss the meaning of Universal Christ.

The Gospel of Philip is clear on this point. Jesus is a personal name, a family name, a Jewish name, like the name of Joshua, who followed Moses and led the people into the Promised Land. Jesus was named *Yeshua*, "one who saves."

Christ [*Christos* in Greek] is an impersonal name, meaning it connects with the abstract dimension of God beyond the level of personal intimacy. God is both personal and impersonal. *Christos* means that God is connected to all aspects of creation, from human beings, animals, plants, atoms, and air. The Christ does not belong to any religion or any particular people. When the word "universal" is added, it is to say in part that the Christ is for the universe throughout, the Cosmic Christ who has no beginning and no end, for the Christ is beyond time and space.

To attach the archetypal name "Christ" to Jesus is a bold move to make, and to do so with understanding beyond the expression of piety is to force every one of us to move beyond our highest capacity to understand. It calls us beyond ourselves, beyond all thought, beyond all rationality, and when we risk doing so, the unknowable term of Christ takes us into God's Country.

The Universal Christ is not exactly an historical figure, not even precisely a "man," (i.e., he is neither male nor female), but he shows up again and again in history in the midst of messy human affairs. There is another root name for *Christos* which covers all the bases—the Ancient One. The Ancient One comes again and again to lift up the world, both physically and spiritually, whenever needed, usually in intervals of 700 to 1500 years. With all the dark clouds looming in the present world, isn't it amazing that we are cared for in ways we can't even imagine! The Universal Christ comes again and again, and so we wisely don't speak of a Second Coming, but rather an "Infinite Coming," for God is always involved in human craziness, whenever we "fall off the wagon."

The Universal Christ has innumerable other names: Avatar, Prophet, Savior, Buddha, Allah, Rasool, Zoroaster, Rama, Krishna, Parvardigar [Sanskrit], and Kali. In our time, we often see the term "Avatar" used to refer to figures like Meher Baba (often called the Avatar of the Age) and Christ. Sometimes it helps to link them together as in Avatar-Christ, but they are all the same universal God-Presence. Just as the word "Qabalah" is the universal archetype, where "Kabbalah" is the local version of it in Judaism, "Christ" can refer to it all. In Judaism, all these Christ figures in history are called "Small Face" because we give them definition and history, while the divine that is beyond all names, all form, all time, is called "Vast Face."

From what we can tell, all of the Avatar-Christs knew of their previous and future incarnations. For example, Meher Baba said, "Christ attained that state of divine love. I am in the same state and I have its experience. I am always in the Christ state of everlasting bliss."[175] Jesus had Christ-consciousness. This means that Jesus was conscious of himself as Christ.[176]

Meher Baba went on to say, "Christ, Buddha, Krishna.... these are names for states of consciousness." One might say that we can follow any state-of-consciousness-path, for they all lead to the same place. Every Avatar-Christ has all the states of consciousness of all the religions, which is beyond the reach of the intellect. Furthermore, every state of consciousness leads to the experience of everlasting bliss.

When we consider the Universal Christ to be a "Face" of Jesus, we begin by admitting it is beyond all understanding and beyond all rational explanation. Yet, this is the most important Face of all, and it encompasses all the others. A veil hides the Christ, and as has been said before, one cannot know it until one becomes it. There is the image of Christ, and there is the reality of Christ vastly beyond the image. One state is false, and the other is true. If we are lucky, we dance between the two. Inwardly, this is not a mental dance, but an experiential encounter

---

[175] *Lord Meher*, p. 1440.

[176] Meher Baba, *The Everything and the Nothing* (Sheriar Foundation, 2015), p. 133.

with the absolute, with perfection, with the Self. It is not something to be seized. The disciples couldn't take hold of it, nor can we. It can only be given. But we can position ourselves and be awake to our consciousness.

The avatar lifts up and advances all of creation. "Whenever God manifests on earth as Avatar," Meher Baba explained, "his Godhood gives a universal push, and the result is universal, i.e., not only humanity reaps the benefit, but everything in the whole creation reaps the benefit of the universal push."[177] This eternally One-and-the-Same-Avatar repeats his manifestation from time to time, in different cycles, adopting different human forms and different names, in different places, to reveal Truth in different garbs and different languages, in order to raise and liberate humanity.[178]

When the Avatar-Christ appears, God becomes a human for all humankind; simultaneously God also becomes a sparrow for all sparrows in creation, an ant for all ants in creation, a pig for all pigs in creation, a particle of dust for all dust in creation, a particle of air for all air in creation, etc. for each and everything else that is in creation.

There is a Hindu way of speaking about Creation, saying not "God created the world" (as we in the West say), but "God *became* the world." God is not separate, and God is present in every aspect of creation, from the cosmos to the atom.

With full awareness of the push given to all aspects of creation, Meher Baba visited zoos all over the world, doing universal work with the animal species he encountered. Meher Baba kept many animals at Meherabad (India) during the late 1930s and 1940s, including cats, dogs, birds, a monkey, a goat, pigs, a rabbit, a lamb, a horse, and a gazelle. "Animals have always played a special role in our life with Baba, not only as His pets, receiving His personal touch and contact, but also, it seems, as a channel of His work, reaching out to all the animal world and the whole of creation."[179] This is a connection we could make with Jesus'

---

[177] Meher Baba, *God Speaks* (Walnut Creek: Sufism Reoriented, 1972), p. 68 and Ivy Deuce, *How a Master Works* (Walnut Creek: Sufism Reoriented, 1975), p. 444. Meher Baba said this before 1955.

[178] *Lord Meher*

[179] https://avatarmeherbabatrust.org/osg-10/

relationship with sheep, noting that shepherds were the first to recognize him.

Stories abound with the special attention spiritually advanced masters gave to animals in this present Avataric Age. Swami Gambhirananda (1899-1988) used to play music far into the night for his disciples and admirers. One night, while he was playing, a tiger appeared before him. The audience members began shouting and running out of the room. But the Master remained calm and said to the tiger, "Come, let us go. Let me put you back in your den. These people are afraid of you."[180] Sri Ramana Maharshi, a Perfect Master (who had the mind of Christ) and being the Self in all, drew wild animals, from vipers, to peacocks, to monkeys, to a cow, and a leopard who wanted to make their dens near him on Mt. Arunachala in southern India. All this has to do with the avatar's push throughout all Creation. With many of the avatars, whenever animals were in his presence, they seemed to recognize him.

Every Avatar-Christ brings a new release of power, a new awakening of consciousness, a new experience of life—not merely for a few, but for all. Qualities of energy and awareness, which only a few advanced souls had used, are made available for all humanity. Life as a whole is raised to a higher level of consciousness and is geared to a new rate of energy. This is happening yet again in our own time.

The avatar does universal work of "giving creation a push where spirituality has become mired in religion and illusion. The avatar descends on earth for his beloveds, his real lovers, and he works for them side by side with his working for the entire universe."[181] The general spiritual push that will be given to the whole world will automatically address problems such as politics, economics, and sex, though these are not directly connected to the original theme. New values and significance will be assigned to things that currently seem to baffle solutions.

All of this universal work is far beyond the limits of the rational mind. While we have been providing examples from Meher Baba's work, all indications are that Jesus did the same. Whenever the Avatar-

---

[180] https://avatarsandyogis.com/stories-about-gambhirananda/

[181] *Lord Meher*, Vol. 4, p. 1196. Meher Baba said this at Harvan, Kashmir, in 1929.

Christ would leave the crowds and even leave the group of disciples, it is usually stated that he would go off to pray or perhaps meditate (not exactly a biblical word). If Meher Baba is any indication, these would be times Jesus was doing "universal work" for all aspects of the world and perhaps the universe. Again, we do not have records of what this was and what happened. And once more, we may learn a little from Meher Baba.

As we will see, the Avatar-Christ has a mind that is not limited by space or by time, and this is true of the avatar's universal work. We will identify half a dozen areas where this work might lie, but this is only extrapolating from what we learn from Meher Baba. We already explored the first area, his work with animals: sheep, pigs, goats, donkeys, fish, birds, etc. This work was not on the radar of the gospel writers.

A second area of universal work lies in special contact with people from other lands. During World War II, Meher Baba would bring individuals into his circle of followers, people from England, Germany, France, the United States, Italy, and India. He would work with each of these on their connections to their homeland, without their conscious awareness, affecting what was happening during the War. Furthermore, Meher Baba often attended sporting events and movie theaters, engaging in deep collective work with everyone gathered rather than watching the game or movie. When he completed his specific work, he would abruptly leave without seeing the end of the movie or game.

Thirdly, in all likelihood, Jesus used similar ways of working with "sheep of different folds" following up on his travels and deep connections with the Hindus in India with the Brahmins and untouchables, the Buddhists in Nepal and in Galilee, the Zoroastrians in Persia, the followers of Egyptian religion and mysticism, the Greeks in Galilee and Lebanon, the settlers from the steppes of southern Russia who settled in northern Israel. One can't think otherwise than that he continued his work with all these nations and religions.

A fourth action of the Universal Christ was that he *prayed* for all these people. One has to ask, what does it mean that Jesus prayed to God, when he said he *was* God ("the Father and I are one")? Was he praying to himself? At other times, he separated himself from God

("Why do you call me good? Only God is good).[182] We can't explain this for sure, but there are times when the Master is in a nondual state (praying not to himself but praying on God's behalf), and times when he was in a dualistic state ("Father, remove this cup from me"). Sometimes Jesus modeled prayer for others to see, such as the Lord's Prayer. Sometimes he revealed the highest form of prayer: "It is not I who prays, but God who prays through me."

This being said, unquestionably he prayed God-Prayers for people all over the known world, and perhaps beyond that. This is the fourth form of universal work.

Similar to the third way of doing universal work (working with people in faraway places to impact their respective cultures and homelands), a fifth form of universal work involved Jesus deeply interacting with everyone around him in Jerusalem, Galilee, Lebanon, and Syria. Just as Meher Baba did universal work with the crowds, so Jesus also probably did the same in the marketplace, at festivals, or in the synagogue—for example, working not only with a Roman centurion but also with the Roman empire. Violating Jewish practice, he spent time with Samaritans, non-Jews, hated revenue agents for the Romans, the Pharisees, Sadducees, Zealot factions, the opposing Jewish schools of Shammai and Hillel, the lepers, prostitutes, criminals, the marginal group of Essenes, the homeless, and the mentally ill. They are all God's children.

A sixth form of universal work for Jesus was to introduce system changes in the structures and scaffolding of religious movements, particularly working to reform Judaism… and all other religions as well. Every Avatar-Christ before Jesus (Zoroaster, Rama, Krishna, Abraham, Buddha) had the same message: "Let your love for God be so great that you will let go of all else." Jesus addressed anything that stood in the way of this effort.

In challenging the Sabbath laws—"the Sabbath was made for man, not man for the Sabbath" (Mark 2:27)—Jesus addressed the religious obsession with the Fourth Commandment. Similarly, Jesus addressed the purification practices, bathing, the obsession with not touching people like lepers, and against ordinary practice, he washed the feet of

---

[182] Mark 10:18

others. His saying, "Render unto Caesar…," challenged the Jewish intent to have nothing to do with Rome. Similarly, Jesus interacted with political power and religious freedom, challenging the idolatry of being Jewish. He challenged the religious scholars with their inadequate understanding of scripture and their obsession with belief over practicing love.

In enumerating possible ways the Avatar-Christ operated, a seventh way involves being in many places at the same time, which we call bilocation. The gospels mention several instances where Jesus appeared in their midst when the doors were closed, and other instances in which he just appeared with them on the road or in Galilee. The Apostle Paul writes that after the resurrection, Jesus "appeared to more than five hundred brothers at once," most of whom remained alive at the time of his writing.[183]

Kitty Davy was part of the inner circle of disciples around Meher Baba. On one occasion, she was driving a car with Meher Baba sitting beside her in the front seat, and he put a towel over his head and became lifeless. For over thirty minutes, his form was motionless and unreactive. She was a very sober observer of reality, and she concluded he left and "went somewhere" without explaining, and eventually returned in his normal form.[184] We just don't know what to make of these possible instances of travel outside of time and space.

An eighth example of the Universal Christ is the transhistorical figure of Christ, the same figure who said, "before Abraham I was." When one becomes God-realized, meaning they no longer are limited by their body and identity, they become God, in the sense that Paul said, "It is not I who live but Christ who lives in me."[185] Similarly, Jesus taught that whoever is truly in him, even though he dies in his body, he will never die."[186] The point is, when one becomes God-realized, they do not return for another lifetime; they never die again. These realized figures have become the same as the Christ, and they are always available to be

---

[183] 1 Cor 15:6. Scholars don't know what to make of this assertion. Some say it was a formula or creedal statement about the resurrection.

[184] *Lord Meher*

[185] Galatians 2:20

[186] John 11:25-26. *"I am the resurrection and the life. Whoever believes in me, even though he dies, will live, and whoever lives and believes in me will never die."*

involved with anyone, at any time, any place. When Meher Baba went to Assisi in Italy in 1936, he met with St. Francis, who left his body in 1226. An individual who has become God is absolutely beyond all normal bounds; his every activity is outside the scope of one's human, limited vision. The Universal Christ is transhistorical, or outside of time and space.

When one surveys the thousands of books about Jesus, it is understandable that almost nothing has been written about the Universal Christ other than pietistic confessions of his divinity. We observe aspects of the avatar in Meher Baba and transfer them to Jesus because Meher Baba intentionally allowed us to do so. In a conversation in our home with Bill LePage, he described sitting in a circle with Meher Baba and Baba said (through his finger movements), "As I am talking with you, at this moment a man in Ethiopia has come to me, a woman in Austria has spoken of her love for me, an old man in India has died with my name on his lips… [and Baba continued to mention several additional experiences with other people in far away places], and all this in just the last minute or two." Bill said that Baba was just showing us the Avatar's omniscience.

The true mind is completely quiet at rest. The true mind is also without limits. When one surrenders and becomes God, their mind is also without limits. Meher Baba explains: "My universal mind is the central station to which every individual mind is linked. So, wherever a person may be, I know what he is thinking and doing every moment. At every moment, I know the thoughts of every person and the thoughts of the whole world simultaneously. Not only this, but I also know what you will think tomorrow or after a thousand years, and I also know what you thought thousands of years before. This is knowledge—infinite and indivisible— and it is beyond your imagination."[187] The gospels include several examples of Jesus' omniscient seeing, such as when he saw his disciple Nathaniel under a tree. This is the mind of Christ.[188]

---

[187] *Lord Meher*, revised online edition, p. 1354; http://www.lordmeher.org/rev/index.jsp? pageBase=page.jsp&nextPage=1354

[188] John 1:46-50

The Gifts of the Avatars

There is yet another aspect of the Ancient One's coming to lift up humanity and all of creation. Meher Baba explained that every time the Avatar-Christ came, he would bring a gift that would benefit humanity. Meher Baba said his Gift to humanity was the Gift of Intuition which many social psychologists and physicists are beginning to acknowledge as it shows up as "a-causal reality" (as opposed to causal reality, cause and effect) in the form of synchronicity, coincidence, where every aspect of reality is "talking" with every other aspect, nothing happens in the universe without human participation.[189]

Historically, referring to the Jungian archetypes, prior to about 1550 CE, humanity lived by the dominant "Sensate Brain," where the primary task was to have enough food and enough firewood to survive the winters, a very physical, sense-oriented existence. Rather abruptly, humanity moved to the Thinking Brain, which gave rise to science, literacy, rationality, individualism, objectivity, and materialism, which have dominated Western humanity for the last four hundred years. Apparently, we are moving toward the Intuitive Brain, which is driving us toward understanding the oneness of everything.

Figure 13 is a list of the Gifts of the Avatars, although this list has never been authoritatively spelled out. These Gifts are inferred by the teachings and actions of each Avatar-Christ, and each Gift is an aspect of the Avatar-Christ related to their unique incarnation.

---

[189] Robert Lanza, MD and Matej Pavsic, *The Grand Biocentric Design: How Life Creates Reality* (Dallas, TX: BenBella Books, Inc., 2020), p. 61. "No configuration of the cosmos's contents unfolds independently of us." "Material objects do not exist in themselves" (p. 64). "An interconnectedness across the universe is now established oneness" (p. 69). "Our individual separateness is an illusion" (p. 71).

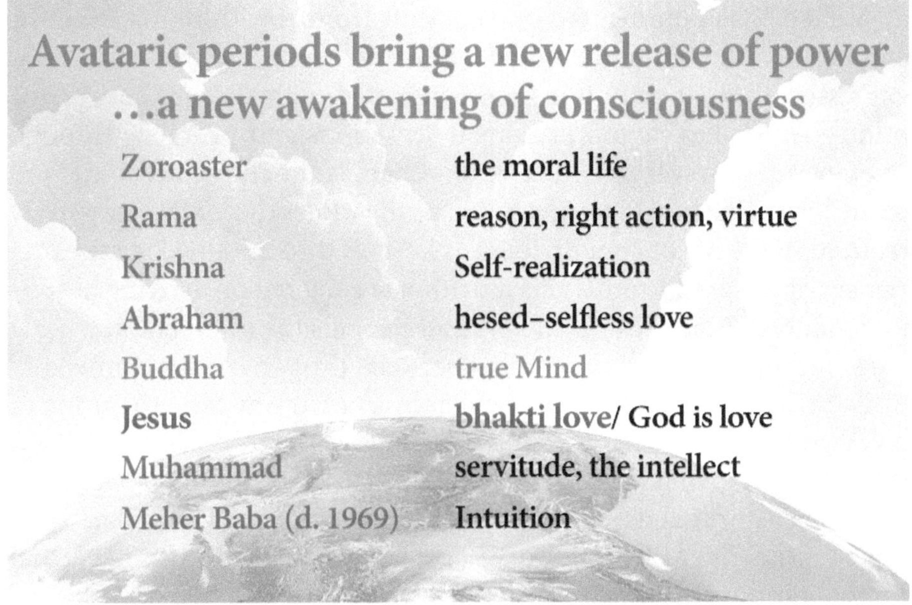

Figure 13: The Gifts of the Avatars

Of particular relevance is the Gift of Jesus the Christ, which is love. The Greek word *agapé,* meaning "love," is mentioned over 100 times in the New Testament. The Sanskrit *Bhakti* is sometimes linked to *agapé* to convey that this love is a deep, devotional, and emotional attachment to God. Interestingly, love was not really introduced as a major aspect of spirituality for four thousand years, although Abraham's selfless love in the Hebrew word *hesed* is close to *agape. Hesed* is usually translated as "steadfast love."

There is an aspect of the Gift of agapé that is often missed. It is not just our usual idea of love as deep care and perhaps attachment, as in "love your neighbor as yourself." Agapé is more than human love. It is a love that comes from God, originates in God, is conscious of God, acts as though God were doing the acting, and is not separate from God. Agapé is not a love that is ego-bound and has any self-interest. Agapé can be both personal and impersonal, the latter being love for the world and the environment.

Agapé is a significant aspect of the Universal Christ, a major boost to humankind. The agapé love of the Christ is still being given, and one could say this Gift is still in the infancy stage.

Meher Baba commented on this shift from the Thinking Brain or emphasis on the Mind to the "thought of the Heart," *enthymia* in Greek, expressed through Intuition. "As contrasted with the method of the mind—which has its foundation in sensations and proceeds through inference and proofs to conclusions—there is the more direct method of the heart. The heart intuitively grasps the values that are progressively realized in the life of an individual as he goes through the diverse experiences of the world, and as his attention is centered on arriving at spiritual understanding. In the life of most persons the mind and the heart are at loggerheads, and the conflict between the two creates confusion."

Baba continues: "The heart, which in its own way feels the unity of life, wants to fulfill itself through a life of love, sacrifice, and service. It is keen about giving instead of taking. It derives its driving power from the inmost spiritual urge, expressing itself through the immediate intuitions of the inner life. It does not care about the proofs or intellectual corroborations that the mind seeks while dealing with material objects.

"In its objective handling of the material world," Meher Baba continues, "mind is saturated with experiences of multiplicity and separateness and therefore feeds the egocentric tendencies that divide humanity and make it selfish and possessive. But the heart, feeling in its inner experiences the glow of love, has glimpses of the unity of the spirit and thus seeks expression through self-giving tendencies that unite humanity and make it selfless and generous. Therefore, there is necessarily a conflict between the inner voice and the deliverances of the intellect, which are based upon the apparent and superficial aspects of life."[190] This is the Gift of the Avatar to humanity of Jesus the Christ and Avatar Meher Baba.

I am very conscious that creating a parallel between Meher Baba and Jesus may not suit some readers. I have learned far more about Jesus from Meher Baba than from the hundred-plus books about Jesus in my library. There is no divided loyalty or choice one needs to make between these two Avatars. I cite a conversation between Kitty Davy's mother Helena Davy and Meher Baba:

---

[190] Meher Baba, *Discourses* (Myrtle Beach, SC: Sheriar Foundation, 7th revised edition, 1987), p. 95.

Helena Davy to Meher Baba: I always keep Christ's picture in front of me when I pray.

Baba: Continue gazing at his picture. It is one and the same. Christ's love is the most supreme ideal. I shall help you inwardly.[191]

We can only assume that in the first century, Jesus did not explain about his universal work because the people would not have understood it. God meets where we are.

It speaks to the advancement of spiritual evolution or to the urgency of our present global crisis and stage evolution that Meher Baba chose to reveal a small part of the universal work of the Avatar-Christ.

Figure 14: The Christ of Christianity and Meher Baba, the Christ above all Religion. They are the same.
(A drawing by Diana LePage, used with her permission. She had personal contact with Meher Baba through her husband Bill LePage. We do not know what Jesus looked like.)

---

[191] *Lord Meher*, Vol. 4, p. 1428, September 1931.

Meher Baba added, "Nothing can be imagined about this 'Universal work,' since its very nature is infinite and, consequently, it includes everyone and everything in all creation."[192]

"You will never be able to understand my Universal work." Meher Baba continues, "During this period of my Avatarhood, I have to cleanse the world completely. This overhauling will last a thousand years. During this Avatarhood of mine, the greatest work of mine will be achieved—the union of East and West."[193]

Jesus' basic work was not through the masses; he worked one person at a time, then and now. The universal work of the Christ sounds like it is creating mass change, and that may be partly true, but Meher Baba addressed this in his *Discourses*, explaining that bringing about change with religious groups and their entrenched belief systems is extremely complicated. Baba explained, "Thus with me, there are Hindus, Mohammedans, Parsis and Christians, Easterners and Westerners, each with certain tendencies, temperaments, inclinations, and fitness or fondness to do a certain type of work. Each has at times certain weaknesses and prejudices side-by-side with good qualities, and it is all these things I have to observe and consider if I want a particular person to fit in somewhere for certain work of mine."

This book is about sacred healing stories, not about a revisionist effort to explain Jesus, hinted at in the title for Chapter 9, "The Christ Presence Beyond all Knowing." In this chapter, we have examined six dimensions of the work on Jesus.

1. **Rabbi/ Teacher** (teacher of spirituality and the Way)
2. **Chassid** (healer, exorcist, shaman, miracle-worker)
3. **Ritual Priest** (Kingdom as a Sacred Meal, and ways to experience the holy)
4. **Political Iconoclast/*Jalali* Nature** (Kenotic Iconoclast—breakdown images of religion, power, separateness, righteousness, ego)
5. **Qabalist/Mystic** (the way to become a Christ, God Realized)

---

[192] *Lord Meher*, 6230.
[193] *Lord Meher*, 1535.

6. Universal Christ (Avatar-Christ giving an evolutionary boost for all creation)

Each one of these aspects brings a specific form of higher healing.

We tend to see the term "Christ" as an honorific title for Jesus, similar to the words Master, Lord, Saint, His Holiness. "Christ" is an archetype so vast and universal that it dwarfs all these terms of respect. Richard Rohr observes the following. "What if Christ is a name for the transcendent within everything in the universe? What if Christ is a name for the immense spaciousness of all true Love? What if Christ refers to an infinite horizon that pulls us from within and pulls us forward to? What if Christ is another name for everything in its fullness?"[194]

The Apostle Paul's driving mission was to demonstrate that Jesus was the Christ. I am not sure he or anybody could really accomplish this. The real Christ is yet to be revealed; our psyches are too small to contain such an experience. Rohr observes, "The Universal Christ was just too big an idea, too monumental a shift for most of us."[195] Sometimes Christians view the Old Testament as a preface to the New Testament, and this is a huge mistake. Each of the eight major religious paradigms has its own form of healing, important in its own right and embedded in the work of Jesus.

The higher healing is finding one's home in the life of God or in the Kingdom, a state in which one is freed from worry, loss, brokenness, judgment, and even religion. It is a state beyond heaven, beyond the New Jerusalem, beyond the Garden of Eden. Master Jalaluddin Rumi, in the thirteenth century, pointed out that every healing story is a "ladder" of escape from a lesser life to the ultimate life. He wrote:

> From the moment you entered
> Into this world of being
> A ladder was placed
> Before you for escaping.[196]

---

[194] Richard Rohr, *The Universal Christ* (New York: Convergent, 2019), p. 5.
[195] Rohr, p. 57.
[196] Rumi, *Rumi: Poems,* Translated by: Manavaz Alexandrian
https://caroun.com/Research/Literature-ClassicPoems/Rumi.html

CHAPTER 11

The Healing Mystery of "Who Am I?"

Apostle Paul—From "Giving Milk" to Spiritual Hardball

But brothers, I could not address you as spiritual people, but as people of the flesh, as infants in Christ. I fed you with milk, not solid food, for you were not ready for it. And even now you are not yet ready, for you are still of the flesh.
— 1 Corinthians 3:1-3 (ESV)

When it comes to the "sacred healing story" of the Apostle Paul, the story is almost more complicated than the story of Jesus the Christ. The Apostle Paul intellectually talks about religion, whereas Jesus demonstrates living in God, almost apart from religion. It seems offensive when the Apostle Paul talks about his audience as infantile babies, not ready for the real truth about the Christ. He says he is feeding them milk rather than solid food. That seems insulting. Why is this part of the New Testament canon? Shouldn't the canon be solid food?

An example of the solid food metaphor would be the claim that the Christ was present *before* the creation of the world, and for that matter, we were latently present then as well. And this metaphor is extended in the non-Pauline book of Colossians, where the Christ is referred to as the Cosmic Christ over the entire universe. These are very bold claims, impossible to understand, likely to make one think the Apostle is guilty of overreach, saying more than anyone can know.

While I was feeling unhappy with Paul's belittling of his audience, saying they were immature and "couldn't handle the truth," I realized I am in the same position when trying to talk about Meher Baba: I speak only about those teachings or actions that fit our contemporary field of plausibility. When it comes to Meher Baba, there is so much more that could be said. If this "more" was shared, it would either awaken awareness that a God-human is indeed among us, or alternatively, it would be met by assertions that all these claims are absurd. Paul has a valid point; the healing story cannot stop here.

In a sense, there are two Apostle Pauls. There is the more familiar Paul who talks about being saved by faith. This Paul is the Paul who is betraying his Jewish exclusivity and saying Jesus the Christ is for everybody, not only Jews. This is the missionary-Paul who went to the West, the Paul who went to the non-Semitic Greeks with their love of philosophy and thought outside of biblical understanding. This is the risking and suffering Paul who was often severely beaten with rods, put into jail, ridiculed, shipwrecked, stoned, tortured, forced to be sleepless, homeless, hungry… etc. But we can handle this more familiar Paul.

There is another Apostle Paul, who said, "It is not I but Christ who lives in me," meaning he actually became a Christ; he was not just talking about himself. Or perhaps it is more accurate to say this Paul no longer had a self. Did Paul take on the mind of Christ? Did Paul lose his personal ego and personal mind? Did Paul enter the Kingdom of God? Is this Apostle Paul a figure we would see as a Perfect Master like St. Frances of Assisi and Meister Eckhart, the two Perfect Masters of Christianity? We don't know the answers, but things change substantially in his message when one sees Paul in this way. And there are probably not many pulpits where this Paul could be preached about.

The first Paul is the **ex**oteric Paul, concerned about the movement, the message, the evangelist, the moralist, the starter of home churches. The second Paul is the **es**oteric Paul, wanting to stir up spiritual experiences that go beyond words, beyond our theories and doctrines, wanting to create connection and realization, wanting to awaken the sense of Kingdom and Christ within, or awaken the experience of "Self." However, that concept didn't exist in the first century.

The life of Apostle Paul in the Book of Acts began in a very different religious state: he was an orthodox Jew. He had a different name, Saul. He was identified as being from Tarsus, a city in south-central Turkey about 12 miles from the Mediterranean. Saul was educated by the esteemed Rabbi Gamaliel, President of the Sanhedrin in Jerusalem, and was known in the Mishnah as one of the greatest teachers in Judaism. There were two major Pharisaic schools in Jesus' day: the Hillel and the Shammai schools; the Shammai school was the more conservative and rigid when it came to Jewish traditions. Gamaliel was aligned more with the somewhat liberal Hillel school, named after his renowned grandfather, Rabbi Hillel, and he advocated a more lenient treatment of the Christian apostles. Nevertheless, apparently against his teacher's generosity, Saul took a militant, critical, and persecuting stance against the Christian movement.

The story of Saul's conversion is well known from the Book of Acts, where on the way to Damascus to round up followers of Jesus, he was confronted by the resurrected Christ, and he had what some today would call a psychotic experience, not unlike what some who have an enlightenment or God-realization experience, which for Paul resulted in temporary blindness and inability to function for quite some time. He did a "180 degree" turnaround, and, like Abraham's transformation, which changed his name from Abram to Abraham, Saul changed his name to Paul.

The term "apostle" was given to the male disciples who were physically with Jesus. Even though Paul was not physically with Jesus, he had a direct post-resurrection encounter with him. Despite his contentious relationship with the other apostles, he became the Apostle Paul. The story of Jesus and his message was not publicly told or, at least, written down as a gospel for well over a generation, but a decade or so after the crucifixion, Paul began to write. He didn't tell biographical stories of Jesus, but he told analyses of what Jesus had accomplished. Paul died in the mid-sixties before the canonical gospels were public. Seven of the thirteen letters attributed to Paul go under his name—Romans, 1 and 2 Corinthians, Galatians, Philippians, 1st Thessalonians, and Philemon. Three other letters, called Deutero-Pauline Epistles, were said to be Paul's, but weren't—2nd Thessalonians, Ephesians, and Colossians.

Previously, two distinct types of Jewish scripture were identified: Hebrew *halakha* and *Haggadah.* *Halakha* refers to the collective body of Jewish law—the written Torah and the oral Torah; it includes the biblical commandments (*mitzvot*) as well as the Talmudic and rabbinic laws, customs, and traditions. *Halakha* is often seen as Jewish law. The word *halakha* comes from the Hebrew verb "to walk," suggesting that following the commandments is a way of walking the path with spiritual mindfulness. The Apostle Paul was trained in *halakha,* and accordingly every word of his letters reflects his Thinking approach to religion and the Way of the Mind.

The Haggadah concerns experience, story, encounters, pilgrimages, births and deaths, family dynamics, and actions. The story of the Exodus, told at the Seder Passover, is the *haggadah.* The midrash, which were variant stories or reflections examined in the stories of Genesis, are largely *haggadah.* While Jesus often spoke to the one-sided Pharisaic fixation on the law, the accounts of Jesus's response were *haggadah,* which we more accurately see as about spiritual experience rather than intellectual knowing. In Judaism, there was never a fixed text of the *haggadah,* suggesting that spiritual reflection is situational, always arising from the specifics of the moment; there are no universal hard-and-fast rules. The way of *haggadah* is the Way of the Heart.

As we see the complementary aspects of Paul's Way of the Mind and Jesus' Way of the Heart, both are valid and important, but the mind is limited, the heart is without limit, and the ultimate way to God.

The Gospel of Truth Versus the Apostle Paul

I fed you with milk, not solid food.

The question is, what did the Apostle Paul *not* say? What did he keep hidden? Are we missing the deepest part of the Gospel, and being left with palliative and watered-down religious teachings? It is not enough to simply use the phrase "Christ crucified," or say "we are saved by faith," and not say more about what this means? In her 2018 book *Why Religion?*, Princeton biblical scholar Elaine Pagels suggests that the Gospel of Truth discovered at Nag Hammadi in 1945 may be the missing secret wisdom that Paul withheld from his letters. The Nag Hammadi manuscripts are 52 leather-bound books hidden in a jar not far from the Nile in Egypt in the fourth century, after Athanasius condemned the use of noncanonical books in 367 CE. In the early 1970s, Elaine Pagels was privileged to work with many of these manuscripts under Professor Krister Stendahl at Harvard, and she wrote the New York Times-acclaimed book, *The Gnostic Gospels*. While I had become familiar with the Gospel of Truth prior to Dr. Pagel's observation, I was stunned by her assertion that this Gospel of Truth may be "the true gospel to answer questions that Paul leaves dangling as the solid food beyond what he was preaching."[197]

How did the Apostle Paul's secret gospel end up in that cave? Again, it must be stated that, while the Gospel of Truth sounds like Paul, we can't be sure. The Gospel of Truth is believed to belong to the early church movement founded by Valentinus, a second-century Egyptian teacher and spiritual philosopher credited with founding the Roman and Alexandrian schools of esoteric knowledge known as "Gnosticism." His disciples claim that Theodas, a purported pupil of the Apostle Paul and a baptized Christian, had educated Valentinus. Valentinus moved to Rome in 136, where he was a candidate to be the Bishop of Rome. Many see the Gospel of Truth as having elements of Paul's mysticism.

Below is a rendition from the Gospel of Truth, with each section paired with a somewhat related passage from the Pauline epistles, and in cases, followed by a brief comment from my hand. The passages from the letters of Paul offer some of the esoteric, mystical aspects of Paul that possibly point to the solid food he was talking about. The Gospel of Truth has many passages that can be described as nondualistic (the oneness of everything), which is beyond our familiar way of thinking and beyond rational understanding. The passages from Paul's New Testament letters are translated by respected scholars, experts in dualistic understanding of scriptures, but they were never trained in the universal nondual wisdom of the Qabalistic and Universal Christ which affects their translation. With all humility, in places I have offered renderings of familiar passages that may reflect the nondual secret wisdom of the Apostle Paul.

---

[197] Elaine Pagels, *Why Religion: A Personal Story* (New York: HarperCollins, 2018), p. 196. Also Elaine Pagels, *Miracles and Wonder: The Historical Mystery of Jesus* (New York: Doubleday, 2025), p. 155 fff.

The Gospel of Truth[198] has 27 chapters, each with around 30 verses, all very dense with specialized terms that require clearer translation. Just to give an example of the complexity of the Gospel of Truth, the beginning verse reads, "*When the totality went about searching for the one from who they had come forth—and the totality was inside of him….*" What does this mean? We might say today the "totality" is what we might call Reality, or if we personalize it, totality would be God-the-Beyond-Beyond. I will attempt to summarize this Gospel with my own interpretive paraphrase, hoping that the Apostle Paul would agree. What makes this possible is that there is a vast body of nondual teachings from the great spiritual teachers in the tradition of the Ancient One that offers similar teachings, known as the Perennial Wisdom, and is taught by every Avatar-Christ.

1. Abstract—*We are born with the code of life; what we look for lies within each of us.*

> **Gospel of Truth:** All of reality, particularly as we human beings experience it, drives us to search for our Source, our beginnings. It takes a long time to realize that what we are looking for lies within each of us (17:3-10). We are born with the code of life, the truth of the universe. When people don't realize this, they focus on the material world, which makes them to suffer (17:14-20). Our true Self is beyond the material world. This Truth within is unchanging, but it is beyond our limited thought and understanding, so we are "cut off from the root" of our core being.

> **Apostle Paul**: We speak of mature wisdom, a wisdom that has been hidden, a wisdom that God destined for all before time began (1 Corinthians 2: 6-7).

---

[198] *The Gospel of Truth*, trans. Harold Attridge and George W. MacRae, *The Nag Hammadi Library*, ed by James M. Robinson (E.J. Brill: Leiden, 1978).

Apostle Paul: I would have you know that the gospel is not from a human source (Galatians 1:11-12).

Apostle Paul: But when he [God] who had called me forth [i.e., God showed me the Face of the Inner Self] before I was born… God was pleased to reveal the Christ in me,… I did not get this from any human being (Galatians 1:15-16, trans. the author).

Apostle Paul: God shows blessing on those He wills and is tough on whomever he wills [not because God is capricious, but because God gives people what they need.] Indeed, he says in Hosea, "Those who were not my people, I will call 'my people.' And the one who was not beloved I will call my beloved" (Romans 9:4, 8, 18, 25 slightly adapted, the author).

Comment: Paul alludes to a knowledge that is ancient. It is encoded in our genes. Sometimes it is said around the birth of babies, that as wonderful as they are, they don't come with an Operating Manual; but in truth, they do. We are all given knowledge that did not just come on the scene with the coming of Jesus Christ. Yet, the Christ lifted it up for all to see. This knowing of our true home, our origins, and our destiny is our birthright, and everyone has it. This ancient knowing isn't just for an elite few, not limited to a religious group, not really limited to just the followers of Jesus.

The verb at the end of the phrase, in Galatians 1, *aphorisas,* "set me apart before I was born," suggests "differentiation" and it also suggests "appointing" or "giving destiny to." We are all given this destiny (to become an Avatar-Christ, or to realize we are God).
The second phrase translated as "reveal Christ *to* me" in Galatians 1 and yet the preposition is "*en*" (in). Rather than meaning "having Jesus in my heart," the Perennial Wisdom would say the "Avatar is one's original and true nature, through and through, and nothing less. Meher Baba would say, "I am your Self."

"I did not get it from any human being…" Such realization can only come from one who has become divine.

2. Abstract—*God always sends us one who will help us with our ignorance.*

Gospel of Truth: We don't recognize that we are cut off from the Truth of our origins and cut off from our true Being, so God periodically sends one who will help us with our ignorance (18:12-15). When Jesus revealed the mysteries, the ignorant were upset, and they nailed him to a tree.

Apostle Paul: We preach Christ crucified, a stumbling block to Jews and folly to Gentiles, but to those who are called, both Jews and Greeks, Christ the power of God and the wisdom of God. And because of him you are in Christ Jesus, who became to us wisdom from God, righteousness and sanctification and redemption (1 Corinthians 1, 23, 30).

Comment: Christ shows us who we are, what is written in our hearts. The critical phrase here is "you are in Christ," which has the surface meaning of belonging to Christ. It can also mean "within" or "one with Christ." Christ-crucified means all who are in Christ are crucified with him, meaning they have crucified/annihilated their separate ego selves and have left all and come to Christ. This is what Jesus meant: "Leave all and come to me," ultimately meaning "leave yourself."

3. Abstract—*The Cross/Tree connects us to the Tree of Oneness in the Garden; the fruit returns us to Oneness.*

Gospel of Truth: But the tree [shifting from the Cross to the Tree of Life in the Garden of Eden] whose fruit, when eaten, made those realize that Jesus and his Truth was within them and they were within Jesus. And all was one (18:23-30). Jesus, the Father, and those who ate the fruit realized they were all one and the same [what is called nonduality]. These realized people then returned to the Source from which they originated (19:1-10).

Comment: The Gospel of Truth is radically changing the meaning of the cross, away from the idea that Jesus died for our sins. Instead, by going back to the Garden of Eden and the original nondual state of oneness, those who grasped the higher meaning of the cross and the death of illusions ate of the fruit of the tree, reversing what happened with Adam and Eve. Eating the fruit of the "tree" came to be similar to eating the bread and wine of communion: ultimately, one does not just (for some, symbolically) have Christ in them, but they become Christ. This was a move from dualism to nondualism, i.e., the true meaning of salvation. The Apostle Paul struggled with this move toward becoming one with Christ, for most of the time he moved only toward nondualism, a state that can be called "harmonious duality."[199]

Apostle Paul: Now you are Christ's body, and individually parts of it (1 Corinthians 12:27).

Apostle Paul: Now am hard pressed between the two. My desire is to depart and be with Christ, for that is far better. But to remain in the flesh is more necessary on your account (Philippians 1:23).

Apostle Paul: I don't have a righteousness of my own, but I have faith through Christ, righteousness comes from faith, that I may know him… and become like him.(Philippians 3:9-11).

4. Abstract—*The story of the Christ doesn't make rational sense. It seems foolish, but children are close to the Father and they get it.*

Gospel of Truth: To some people, Jesus was a teacher, but his wisdom put to shame those who considered themselves wise. But children [who have not been confused by ignorant worldly wisdom] know the Father, and they recognize Jesus. As we all do, the children had within them the original "book of Truth" from the beginning, the book of salvation, but they were closer to it (19:29-35).

---

[199] "Harmonious dualism" is a phrase coined by Neale Lundgren, Ph.D., to describe the state in between dualism and nondualism.

Apostle Paul: For the word of the cross is folly to those who are perishing, but to us who are being saved, it is the power of God. For it is written, "I will destroy the wisdom of the wise, and the discernment of the discerning I will thwart." Where is the one who is wise? Where is the scribe? Where is the debater of this age? Has not God made foolish the wisdom of the world? For since, in the wisdom of God, the world did not know God through wisdom (1 Corinthians 1:18-22).

Comment: When one sees the extended length Paul goes to address the wise and foolish, one must realize he is talking with a Greek audience as he is attempting to introduce the nonrational character of the atonement and the meaning of the incarnation and the cross. Paul goes back and forth, speaking about how sin is resolved at the cross, and on the other hand, that true redemption has to do with becoming a Christ, which doesn't have to do with sin. The belief that children are closer to the Father, as Jesus said, and that they bring an innocence that keeps them from getting tangled up in philosophical arguments, may connect them with the trust in the Source from which they came.

5. Abstract—*In the flesh, we are perishable; when we see the reality beyond the physical, we are eternal.*

Gospel of Truth: When one realizes who Jesus is, they have to die to "false self" [i.e., ignorance, attachment to personal identity, and false wisdom] in order to have the life beyond (20:1-14). Jesus himself is that "Book." He came as a perishable man, but he revealed his imperishability, i.e., his [and our own] divine nature (20:15-35).

Apostle Paul: I have been crucified with Christ; it is no longer I who live, but Christ who lives in me (Galatians 3:20).

Comment: God seeks to seduce us out of our physical and lesser preoccupations with worry, self-importance, and success. We ignore the higher implanted knowing we carry within [i.e., the Book]. And so we cling to what is lesser, hoping it will give us true life. W. H.

Auden said, "Life is the destiny you are bound to refuse until you have consented to die."[200]

Apostle Paul: Therefore, don't despair that the outer physical human being is decaying, for the inward [spiritual] being is developing day by day. We look not at the things that are seen [by our physical eyes] but at the things that are not seen, for the things that are seen are temporary, but the things that are not seen are eternal (2 Corinthians 4:16 and 18, rendering by the author).

Comment: The Hindus have a meditation called the "So Ham Meditation" that addresses the perishable and the imperishable:

I am not the body. I am not the emotions. I am not the thoughts. I am not even the mind. The mind is just a subtle instrument of the Soul. I am the Soul. I am a spiritual being of Divine Intelligence, Divine Love, and Divine Power. I am connected and one with my Higher Soul. I am that I am. I am one with the divine spark within me. I am a child of God. I am connected to God. I am one with God. I am one with All.

Christ also revealed our own imperishability: that we each are an eternal being beyond time and space, the core Self, which some think of as Soul. Every funeral reminds us that our body is temporary; our thoughts, feelings, experiences are temporary. All these things come and go. This teaching reminds us that we are not our body, our thoughts, our experiences; instead, we are the eternal soul behind all that we experience in this life. We are what lies beyond time and space, yet we have temporarily incarnated into this present life and experience in order that the soul may realize itself. This present life is not the sum-total of all that we are.

6. Abstract—*We end up where we began, with God, our original and true state.*

---

[200] W.H. Auden, "For the Time Being," quoted by Richard Rohr, *The Universal Christ* (New York: Convergent, 2019), p. 129.

Gospel of Truth: This is the Plan of Life for everyone. To return to the Source, the Father; to do so, one must be perfect, which is one's original state. We return to where we began; this is what Jesus the Christ said.[201] No one can be perfect on their own. But the Father who is perfection [and wholeness] gives perfection to everyone and to anyone who is ready (21:3-26). Still some remain ignorant, but Jesus enrolls them every one in advance to eventually awaken to the Truth within them (21:26-33).

Apostle Paul: Not that I have already obtained this or am already perfect, but I press on to make it my own, because Christ Jesus has made me his own. Brothers, I do not consider that I have made perfection my own. But one thing I do: forgetting what lies behind and straining forward to what lies ahead, I press on toward the goal for the prize of the upward call of God in Christ Jesus. Let those of us who are mature think this way, and if in anything you think otherwise, God will reveal that also to you (Philippians 3:12).

Apostle Paul: Who shall separate us from the love of Christ? Shall tribulation, or distress, or persecution, or famine, or nakedness, or danger, or sword? For I am sure that neither death nor life, nor angels nor rulers, nor things present nor things to come, nor powers, nor height nor depth, nor anything else in all creation, will be able to separate us from the love of God in Christ Jesus our Lord (Romans 8:35, 38-39).

Comment: Meher Baba said, "Nothing can separate you or all mankind from Me, because I am in all and God cannot be separated from Himself, can He? The goal still remains for you and all to attain perfection through duality."[202]

---

[201] Gospel of Thomas, Saying 18. http://www.gnosis.org/naghamm/gosthom.html

[202] From a letter Baba wrote to Delia DeLeon, in *The Ocean of Love* (Meher Baba Association, 1991), pp. 112-115.

Comment: In *The Universal Christ*, Richard Rohr said that humanity has never been separate from God except in our own imagination.[203] Perfection is to experience everything as one or as God. God is the only doer. Yet, a key idea in Baba's letter is, "The goal still remains for you and all to attain perfection through duality." Our work is to experience the real world of One by living in the world of "Two." We need the illusion of the perception of twoness, until we can see what it is. Baba says he (i.e., God) is fully in both worlds, the world of One and the World of Two. It is this very dynamic that the Christ helps us with. The way to wholeness and perfection is to remove or let go of what separates.

7. Abstract—We are God in human form; we imagine ourselves as separate and individual, but we are also inseparate and one with all.

Gospel of Truth: The person who has knowledge of the Truth within always knows where he/she has come from and where he/she is going (22:1-20). They know the truth of who they are [i.e., they are God-in-human-form]. While this person who has realized the Truth is in a body, they experience themselves as an individual. But they are at the same time a complete Book, a whole, a totality, a unity, and knowing this brings them into the Father and into Jesus in infinite sweetness (22:20–24:9).

Apostle Paul: Those of you who are mature be mindful of the upward call of Jesus Christ, and if you are otherwise minded, God will reveal that to you (Galatians 3:15).

Apostle Paul: Now you are Christ's body, and individually parts of it (1 Corinthians 12:27).

Comment: We need to be mindful that we are "the Book." Second Peter (1:3) says the Christ has given us the great promise that allows

---

[203] Rohr, p. 43. He quotes Colossians 3:11 (probably not written by the Apostle Paul): "There is only Christ. He is everything and he is in everything." Christianity has not seen the presence in the non-human world of plants and animals.

us to share in the divine nature. The Christian life is simply a matter of becoming who we already are. Richard Rohr says that "God must reveal himself in you, before God can reveal himself to you."[204] The story of the Apostle Paul's conversion is told as though it was an intervention from above and outside of him, but it happens first internally. We must go to that voice within ourselves that knows the truth of who we are.

8. Abstract—*When one can see beyond the forms (physical, emotional, mental), they can vanish into the unity of oneness.*

Gospel of Truth: The bosom of the Father is the Holy Spirit, who reveals what is hidden, and enables one to see beyond all the physical and mental forms [to the true reality that lies beyond]. When one sees beyond the forms, one vanishes into the unity of oneness. The former multiplicity becomes one, and all matter vanishes (24:10–25:35).

Apostle Paul: Even the mystery which hath been hid from ages and from generations, but now it is made manifest to his saints (Colossians 1:26).

Apostle Paul: By revelation he made known unto me the mystery… which in other ages was not made known unto the sons of men (Ephesians 3:3).

Apostle Paul: For us there is one God, the Father, from whom all things are and for whom we exist, and one Lord, Jesus Christ, through whom all things are and through whom we exist (1 Corinthians 8:6).

Apostle Paul: So that God will be all in all (1 Corinthians 15:28).

Comment: The translators understand that the Apostle Paul is speaking about monotheism—there is only one God—but that is a

---

[204] Rohr, p. 65.

dualistic, where the nondualism of the Jewish Shema speaks of God as one without number. The *Gospel of Truth, which* refers to the "unity of oneness," is nondualistic, meaning that the One is all there is, and the passage from 1 Corinthians 15:28 may reflect this perspective.

9. Abstract—*The Soul knows the truth. The truth is the Holy Spirit.*

Gospel of Truth: When the Word [which is itself a "form"] appears it becomes a body. The Word is in the heart. Ignorance has nothing to do with the Truth within [The Soul has no ignorance]. But when the Truth appears, everyone knows it. This Truth is the Holy Spirit, and it continues to reveal what is hidden, what hasn't taken form yet. The Holy Spirit allows Truth to take form and gives it a name (26:1–27:35).

Apostle Paul: And no one can say, "Jesus is Lord," except by the Holy Spirit (1 Corinthians 12:3).

Apostle Paul: But whoever is joined to the Lord becomes one spirit with him (1 Corinthians 12:3).

John: We are God's children now; what we shall be has not yet been revealed. We do know that when it is revealed we shall be like him, for we shall see him as he is (1 Jn. 3:1 NAB).

Comment: What makes us see the Truth is the Holy Spirit. The Holy Spirit monitors our inner "bullshit detectors" that tell us "No this isn't it!" And the Holy Spirit awakens the Soul to see the Truth. Truth is not something historical; it is not linked or bound by the past. Incarnation did not just happen two thousand years ago. It has been working throughout the entire arc of time and will continue.[205] The Holy Spirit is our effort to personify the intimate presence of God.

---

[205] Rohr, 52.

10. Abstract—*If one is not grounded in the Source, one is ignorant, and this leads to the shallow life.*

Gospel of Truth: One who does not know (i.e., one who is ignorant) has no root (i.e., no grounding in the Source). Those without roots live destructive lives. People without roots lead ephemeral lives, where living is like being asleep in a dream that is not real (30:2-3).

Apostle Paul: Do not be deceived: neither the sexually immoral, nor idolaters, nor adulterers, nor men who practice homosexuality, nor thieves, nor the greedy, nor drunkards, nor revilers, nor swindlers will inherit the kingdom of God (1 Corinthians 6:9–10).

Apostle Paul: See to it that no one takes you captive through philosophy and empty deception, which are based on human tradition and the spiritual forces of the world rather than on Christ (Colossians 2:8).

Comment: People who are unaware of the truth about themselves create an illusion about their life and what brings them true fulfillment. Not only are they vulnerable to schemes of making as much money as possible, hoping it will reduce their anxiety, but not knowing about their true selves creates idols of thought and belief in inadequate religious doctrines. They create scenarios of religious salvation, but also hold false beliefs that may initially seem good but ultimately block them from the peace and fulfillment they are seeking. When the Apostle Paul warned about the deception of elaborate philosophies (permeating the Greek world), he warned them against creating a belief system that could not lead them to God/the Christ. We risk doing the same thing with our creeds, doctrines, and theologies.

11. Abstract—*The Word from the Father awakens people and provides a way for people to come to him.*

Gospel of Truth: But when the Father speaks, he awakens people and gives birth to life. He gives thought and understanding, energy and salvation. He infuses into life the spirit from the infinite [everlasting, beyond time and space]. The word of the Father provides a "Way" for all to come to him (31:30).

The Word of the Father, like the shepherd looking for the lost sheep, is to support the fallen, to raise up those who wish to rise, to awaken those who sleep. Even those who are ignorant, the Father desires for them to bring them to Him. This is repentance (chaps 34 and 35).

Book of Acts: ...so that if he found any there who belonged to the Way, whether men or women... (Book of Acts 9:2).

Comment: The word "Christian" had not been created yet, and the early Jesus-movement was called "people of the Way." It is possible that the name of the movement may owe its origins to Psalm 5:9: "O LORD, lead me along Your righteous *path* because of my watchful foes; make Your way straight before me." It is interesting that the word "way" is linked to the Hebrew *hallak* having to do with "walking the way." It is also interesting that the idea of "people of the Way" does not mean "people of the belief," as many think Paul's approach became a way of belief.

Apostle Paul: Just as the testimony of Christ has been strengthened among you—so that you are not lacking in any spiritual gift as you wait for the revealing of our Lord Jesus Christ. He will also strengthen you to the end, so that you may be blameless on the day of our Lord Jesus Christ. God is faithful; by him you were called into the fellowship of his Son, Jesus Christ (Corinthians 1:4-9).

Comment: The Gospel of Truth states that God will bring seekers to Him. God is the doer. Paul says the preaching about Christ will strengthen people, encouraging them to become perfect. But the way of Paul is that we must do hard work, practice the spiritual disciplines, have true beliefs, and put in high effort to reach God. We believe we will come to God when we have enough faith, which sounds like we have to earn grace through our belief. But the Gospel of Truth says we will come to God only when God allows it.

Everything that we experience, everything we think, every action, every moment impacts our living toward God, not just our religious effort. But more importantly, rather than creating our salvation, we are given everything we need to know God.

Apostle Paul: Inasmuch as they could not *see* God (*lit.*, they had nothing worth holding on to), (since what they did value blocked them from high Knowledge), God piled on even more of their worthless understandings and their doings that were utterly ineffective, that they might wake up to these understandings/forms (Greek, *vous*) that were blocking them (Romans 1:28, rendering and paraphrase, the author).

Comment—The familiar translation of this passage from the book of Romans is, "*And since they did not see fit to acknowledge God, God gave them up to a base mind and to improper conduct*" (RSV). The meaning is usually interpreted as a story of punishment. What this means is that sometimes we get into habits and behaviors that are not helping, even if we think they are. God may put us further into that unhelpful behavior increasingly until we "get it."[206]

---

[206] Meher Baba tells the following story about a Hindu Perfect Master: A Sadguru once set out with his disciples for begging. He approached a rich merchant who, instead of giving alms, shouted abuses and obscenities. Nevertheless, the Master blessed him saying, "Your profits will double." The Sadguru then approached another wealthier merchant who mistreated him even more. He, however, blessed this man, saying, "Your profits will quadruple!" Then the Sadguru, with his disciples, approached the shop of a poor, old man who received them with reverence and offered whatever he could provide from his meager store. The old shopkeeper had only one son whom he loved dearly. Before leaving, the Sadguru cursed him! "By the power of God, I pray that your son dies soon!" The next day, the son was found dead. When the Sadguru's disciples found this out, they were bewildered by their Master's behavior. The only man who had received them with humble reverence had been cursed, not blessed. Afterward, the Sadguru explained: "Both merchants were immersed in the mire of worldliness and did not want to be extricated. For that reason, I had to submerge them even more in the mire of the world by my blessings, so that one day they will cry to be pulled out. The poor shopkeeper was spiritually inclined, however, his love for his son was much too binding. It was an obstruction to the old man's progress on the path. The son was, unknowingly, a thorn in his father's side,

***12. Abstract**—The knowledge of the truth always keeps people fulfilled and satisfied.*

Gospel of Truth: People who are unknowing are not bad. They just live a diminished life and don't know it. Once you know the Truth, whatever you lack is filled up again (36:1-35). When we become filled up, it is then that we receive grace. That is why we speak of Christ to those who are deficient.

Apostle Paul: Those who think they know something do not yet know as they ought to know (1 Corinthians 8:2).

Apostle Paul: And be not conformed to this world: but be ye transformed by the renewing of your mind, that ye may prove what is that good, and acceptable, and perfect, will of God (Romans 12:2).

Comment—Becoming a learned scholar enriches life and provides deeper meaning. But philosophy and theology also inflates the spiritual ego and creates a false sense of spiritual advancement. The more learned one is, the more they have to unlearn as one moves closer to the goal of coming to God.

Comment—"Be transformed by the renewing of your mind" is a major idea of the Apostle Paul. What does this mean? What is thought of as spiritual enlightenment is the inherently complete and pure mind, in which there is no false discrimination, and body and mind are fundamentally pure, unborn and undying. The mind is covered up by the clouds of obsession with objects, arbitrary thoughts, psychological afflictions, views, and opinions. The true mind is natural and does not come from outside. The renewed mind is not about having pure and good thoughts. For one thing, the renewal of the mind is to see the mind for what it is. Mind is

---

and so I opened the door to the path by removing his son. Now, you tell me who was blessed and who was cursed. *Lord Meher*, p. 362.

consciousness which has put on limitations. Everyone is originally unlimited and perfect.

The true Self lies beyond the mind, beyond time and space, and is also beyond birth and death. So we must ask why study and try to transform the illusory mind instead of letting go to realize the true Mind behind the mind? **A growing awareness of the limits of mind eventually opens the door to transcending the mind.** By grasping forms given to us by our everyday interpretation, the mind becomes deluded, not true to reality. All philosophies in the world are mental fabrications; there has never been a single doctrine by which one could enter the true essence of things.

Jews and Buddhists also distinguish between Knowledge and Wisdom. Knowledge arises out of the highest thought-forms the mind can offer. Wisdom transcends the mind with its finite limitation and wisdom arises out of true appearance/direct experience of ultimate Reality. It seems that Christians are not very interested in the nature of mind, but rather in having belief. Belief is a "contrivance of the mind."

13. Abstract—*Nothing happens without the will of the Father, but the Will is beyond our knowing. What God wills is knowledge of the beginning and the end and the love of the Father.*

Gospel of Truth: Nothing happens without the will of the Father, but the working of the Father cannot be understood (37:20). What God wills is the knowledge of the beginning and the end, and the knowing of the One who is hidden, this being the Father.

Ephesians: Acting not by the way of doing works to be seen by others, as people-pleasers, but as bondservants of Christ, doing the will of God from the heart, rendering service with a good will as to the Lord and not to man, knowing that whatever good anyone does, this he will receive back from the Lord (Ephesians 6:6).

Letter of Peter: Wherefore let them that suffer according to the will of God commit the keeping of their souls to Him in well doing, as unto a faithful Creator (1Peter 4:19).

Comment—The passage from Peter suggests that if one doesn't understand the will of God, then God will hold their souls in His keeping until they understand. The key phrase in the non-Pauline Ephesians passage is "doing the will of God from the heart." The Gospel of Truth says the will of God cannot always be understood, and often with the Apostle Paul, it seems that discerning the will of God is a mental activity. Nevertheless, in 1 Corinthians 13, Paul cites the virtues of faith, hope, and love (and no mention of mind), as the trinity of being in the will of God, with the greatest being love. One can't grasp the Kingdom with the Mind. Only the Heart can.

This struggle between head and heart seems to often come up for the Apostle Paul. The matter turns on the oneness of all reality, and the divine will is to enter into this oneness. Richard Rohr says, "God loves you by becoming you."[207]

14. Abstract—The name of the Father is unknowable, meaning the state of the Divine and our core Self is beyond the reach of belief and the mind.

Gospel of Truth: Everyone returns to the beginning, to the "one" (38). The name of the Father is the Son. The Son is God himself; God (the One without a Name) begot himself a name in the Son. His is the name given to all that exists. But the true divine name is unknowable. The Father's name is not spoken, but He is apparent through the Son (38:9). It is possible for the Son to be seen. The Father alone is the "One" (38:34). The Father gave the name alone to the Son, for the Son alone can see the Father (39:9). The Son alone can give a name to the Father who existed before him. The offspring does not receive a name from those who begot them (40:1). Others receive a name on loan, but the name of the Son was not on loan. The Son alone has the power to speak his name and see it (40:20).

Apostle Paul: God has highly exalted Him and given him a name above every name… that every tongue confess that Jesus Christ is Lord to the glory of the Father (Philippians 2:9-11).

---

[207] Rohr, p. 79 and "God loves things by becoming them," Rohr, p. 113.

Comment: Ahhh, the problem of names. Names establish a conscious relationship, but they are not the true Reality. One thinks of the naming of the animals by Adam and Eve, an exercise in consciousness and differentiation. But names create definition and separation, a fiction in the mind. The Ultimate God has no name, not even "God." That being said, God wanted to be known, and so God entered into consciousness as the Son. But only the Son knows the Father beyond all names. This is a mystery for us as we try to understand ultimate Reality and the One beyond all number and name. Such mystery takes us beyond ourselves.

15. Abstract—*Every aspect of the material and immaterial universe is from the Father (and is God-in-form and God-not-in-form), and every aspect is perfect and has the glory of the Divine.*

Gospel of Truth: The Name of the Son is given to the universe and all levels of reality, for every level of Reality comes from the Father. The root of all the emanations of the universe is the Father (41:15-29). Every aspect of the universe blesses the root in the Father, but none of them are exalted or have more glory than any of the others. Nothing that comes from the Father is small, harsh, wrathful, evil, or negative.

Apostle Paul: Therefore, as to the eating of food offered to idols, we know that "an idol has no real existence," and that "there is no God but one." For although there may be so-called gods in heaven or on earth—as indeed there are many "gods" and many "lords"—yet for us there is one God, the Father, from whom are all things and for whom we exist, and one Lord, Jesus Christ, through whom are all things and through whom we exist (1 Corinthians 8:4-6).

Comment: Again, the message is that all is One, but this is beyond the differentiating brain to comprehend because all separations and levels of thinking have to be dissolved. We think we are observing the world around us, but quantum physicists say "consciousness not only reveals what we observe, but it creates the reality we see. Life creates the universe. Our individual separateness is an illusion."[208] A century ago, the universe seemed like a self-operating machine; now we realize that matter is derivative from consciousness (Max Planck) and that we are involved with everything.[209] To realize this is a short step to the Gospel of Truth which says all emanations of Reality come from the Father (i.e., the One).

16. Abstract—*We ourselves are the Truth, being continually refreshed by the Spirit and in our essence we are perfect and worthy of His Name.*

Gospel of Truth: All have come into existence and none has need to be instructed (42:10). They are all the one. They themselves are the truth. The Father is within them and they are continually refreshed by the Spirit. They heed their root and suffer from no loss of soul (42-43). The Father is poured out into all existence, and everything is perfect and is filled with the seed of the Father in which His heart rejoices. And his children are perfect and worthy of his name (43:20).

Apostle Paul: If anyone is in Christ, he is a new creation. The old has passed away; behold, the new has come (2 Cor. 5:17 ESV).

Comment: I am not sure whether Paul's announcement here that a follower of Christ is a "new creation" matches the Gospel of Truth's assertion that we have reached perfection. Maybe the phrase "in essence a new creation" works because it points to the Self within each of us, which is the same as the Soul, the Christ, and God; and listening to the physicists, the Universe is yet another synonym of the Self (meaning we are everything). St. Hildegard of Bingen in the twelfth century said, "We don't have a Self, it has us." It should be said at this point that there is only one Self and one Soul which we all are, so there are not seven billion Selves wandering around. The Christ comes to introduce each of us to the Self, and once accomplished,

---

[208] Lanza and Pavsic, p. 17, 21, 71.
[209] Lanza and Pavsic, p. 78.

the work is done. The inner universal Self is also the Holy Spirit, which refreshes all of life, even the universe.

*17. **Abstract**—Every form points to the Father.*

Gospel of Truth: Every form has destiny. The form itself is not to be exalted, but every form points to the Father. God is in everything and everything is in God. Reality is one, it is undivided (42:29). Everything needs to heed its root (43).

Apostle Paul: There is one God, the Father, from whom are all things and for whom we exist, and one Lord, Jesus Christ, through whom are all things and through whom we exist (1 Corinthians 8:6).

Comment: Christ is a good and simple metaphor for absolute wholeness, complete incarnation, and the integrity of creation. The *Gospel of Truth* ends on the same note where it began, with Jesus Christ the Alpha and Omega. There is no mention of heaven or hell, for those concepts belong to dualistic thinking. We begin with God, and we end up with God; there are no other possibilities. This the truth of the Shema, all is one. Nothing but one.

Paul and Three States of Consciousness

The Gospel of Truth and the related links from the writings of the Apostle Paul make a case for oneness and a nondual spirituality. But there are a number of issues that are not addressed, including the crucifixion, suffering, the atonement, and being saved by faith. Much more could be said on each topic, but in this approach to the Apostle Paul, we are considering the theme that runs throughout the Bible: how healing comes from experiencing a wholeness that results from becoming one with God.

The story of the Garden of Eden may be the greatest mythic story ever told. It is repeated in many traditions with different details. On the surface, it sounds simple and naïve, but it establishes the story of spiritual evolution from beginning to end. It starts with creation without defined form, just a primordial soup with latent forms within the Garden. "In the beginning God…" and all else flowed from that. There was no consciousness whatsoever because consciousness requires separation and distinctiveness. Everything was a part of everything. We use a weighty philosophical word to describe this original state—"nondualism." It means "one," not "two." It was a state of infinite bliss, even though there was no consciousness to experience oneness.

We know the story that followed. Words came to be formed. Language. Experience was described when one could be separate enough to see it. Meaning became possible. God and human beings emerged out of the mists. Pain, betrayal, shame, hurt, brokenness, good and bad all came into being. High creativity and novelty was born, which made living interesting. And all this gave rise to an experience called "spirituality." Spirituality belongs to dualism. This was no longer a state of oneness—it became twoness which became many-ness. This was given another name, which was "dualism." Dualism and consciousness are close friends and teamed up to create an evolutionary story.

Eventually, the original state of oneness in the Garden was given a new name, "Paradise." It was imagined that the greatest possible outcome for the story was to return to the original state of God, but this time it meant bringing back home consciousness of the evolutionary story. When Jesus was asked what the outcome of the whole spiritual enterprise was, and where we end up, he said, "You end up where you began."[210] He didn't say, "You end up on heavenly clouds listening to harp music."

When the Christ knocked out Saul on the road, he wiped out the scholar's goals, his religious agenda, his fixation on righteous *mitzvot*, and his former plan to live a righteous life for God. The change for Paul was nearly impossible to put into words. How does one tell others that they have to let go of all religion, all meaningful thoughts, to leave everything and fall into the original state of oneness?

---

[210] Gospel of Thomas, Saying 18. http://www.gnosis.org/naghamm/gosthom.html.

So Paul struggled with three states of essential consciousness. The first state of duality (the holding of opposites) would carry the message to keep living in the world. In this consciousness, one would practice acts of kindness and righteousness, discern what is good and bad, and pay attention to the nature of sin. Dualistic people develop a belief system around Jesus Christ; they would like the passage, "For if you confess with your mouth the Lord Jesus, and if you believe in your heart that God has raised him up from the dead, you shall be saved."[211] Dualistic people worry. They worry about success and security. They fend against evil. They believe in Heaven and Hell. They struggle with death. They create organized religion and seminary schools to promote orthodox belief. This is the level of religious ideas that we know with familiarity. This is ordinary dualistic consciousness that arises out of an infinite pairing of opposites.

The next state of consciousness can be called "duality with union,"[212] a state that comes closer to oneness with God and entering the Kingdom, but not quite there. It is an intermediate state of spirituality, between dualism and nondualism, with an awareness of how thoughts, language, beliefs, and the identities of the gross world still inform one, but stand between the oneness of the nondual consciousness. A familiar New Testament metaphor for this state is the marriage of bride and bridegroom, and the experiences of soul-love/soul-mate/twin-souls, deep connection, lover-beloved. In this duality-with-union, one is no longer dominated by the personal ego and exists within the Mind of God and the Heart of God.

In this state of duality with union, they recognize the false self and the illusion of the material world, and they can see beyond forms but also enter into forms at will. They experience themselves as separate and not-separate. They can realize in their core that they are God, but there remains the "I" who is doing the realizing. It is the Apostle Paul who in this state says, "My desire is to depart the physical world and be with Christ" (Philippians 1:23), and it is this state where Paul speaks about

---

[211] Romans 10:9

[212] These three states of consciousness (oppositional dualism, harmonious dualism, and nondualism) were coined by Dr. Neale Lundgren, Ph.D., a scholar in the Perennial Wisdom and related to me in personal friendship.

revealing the Christ **to** me versus revealing the Christ **in** me" (Galatians 1:16). It is this level of consciousness where one can hear both Jesus the Christ and Avatar Meher Baba say, "I am your Self."

The ultimate spiritual state is called "nondualism," not two but one, and "one" is not a number but the only true and absolute state of Being. It is the "I am God" state, only there is no separate identity in "I am." Here one is "home." There is no such thing as time and space, which is the deeper meaning of eternity. There is consciousness of everything and consciousness of nothing. Words and meaning do not really touch this state. The Apostle Paul did not say a lot about this state. "It is not I who live, but Christ who lives in me." He hints at it in First Corinthians, "There is one God, one Lord through whom all things exist" (15:28) and "Whomever is joined to the Lord is one with Him" (12:3).

In our time, effort is made to define "happiness," but it is difficult to move beyond the shallow. Many feel the word "joy" goes beyond happiness, pointing to a higher state of being, contentment, acceptance, and beauty. Another word, "bliss," has been co-opted to express the ultimate state of experience, but from what we can discern, the bliss at the highest level is infinitely beyond anything one can possibly imagine, and of course, it is beyond all experience and senses as we know them. It is very difficult for anyone who has experienced the bliss of being God to "empty' themselves and enter into human form.[213]

In saying he was giving his listeners milk and not solid food, the Apostle Paul was trying to navigate these levels of experience, dualism (holding the opposites), dualism-with-unity, and nondualism. It was daunting and really impossible to explain a way that took one beyond the limits of words and conscious understanding. Many who follow the Apostle Paul say, "We are saved by faith," but that is vastly more than belief and what the mind can grasp. The fact that the way of the Christ is beyond all belief and human understanding legitimizes it as a spiritual experience that can take us beyond ourselves. Any religion that doesn't do that is a false religion.

---

[213] Philippians 2:7-8. [Christ] emptied [Greek: *kenosis*] himself, by taking the form of a servant, being born in the likeness of men. And being found in human form, he humbled himself by becoming obedient to the point of death, even death on a cross.

A New View of Atonement

The Apostle Paul had a message: "We preach Christ crucified." What does this mean? Usually, it brings up the assertion that Jesus "died for our sins," which can mean we killed Jesus with our sins, or it can mean that Jesus bore our sins on the cross, relieving us from the consequences of our sins. In this interpretation, it is often said, "We are saved by the cross."

Before we turn to how Jesus saves, which is called the "doctrine of the atonement," let's revisit the nature of the sacrifice of our Lord. We go back to Abraham's sacrifice of his son to clarify the meaning of this archetype, for that event is the foundational event of the Jewish Bible (Old Testament) just as the Crucifixion-Resurrection is the foundational event in the New Testament.

In both Testaments, God is asking us to look at our attachments and what binds us, for these are blocks in coming to God. "But we are talking about love, and isn't love what takes us to God?" we say. "Love both frees and binds," God says. To Abraham, God says, "Take the one you love most and sacrifice him to me." "If you are attached to a child, a spouse, a parent, an identity, a good work, a mission… these are good things, but they are binding as well. They bind your ego." It is difficult to see Abraham's dilemma from this perspective, and just as hard to see what Jesus was doing.

I wonder whether every Avatar asked such a sacrifice. In personal conversation, Bill LePage said the Meher Baba once asked him whether he was willing to drown his three children in the ocean. Bill said, "Yes, Baba," but he added, "Both Baba and I knew he would never ask that." But every one of us sooner or later is ultimately tested in our love for God.

What if Jesus were able to talk Pilate out of capital punishment, allowing him (Jesus) to do divine deeds for another forty years? His message was "See beyond your attachments and commitments and what you think is important, go beyond that, let yourself die to all that, and then you will be free for God. I will have to show you." Crucifixion (not necessarily literal crucifixion) is the cost of entering the Kingdom.

Here in the South (of the United States), one often sees along the country roads the words painted on rocks, "Jesus saves." How? We saw in the midrash reflections on the Garden of Eden that the struggle was how to make things right with God. Forgiveness may be one of the most difficult human transactions. Does it simply mean amnesty? Does one forget the action or thought that caused hurt? What is involved in letting go?

Much of the Jewish Bible struggles with this. We reviewed in the story of Moses that the Book of Leviticus is concerned with building a house (tabernacle) for God to make up for the transgression of building a Golden Calf, i.e., going back to the good ole religion of Egyptian days. Did that work? How does one atone or compensate for wrongdoing?

The first religious institution to atone for sins was to make a sacrifice of a choice animal or agricultural product, dedicating it to God. The prophet Micah asks, "Shall I come before him with burnt offerings, with calves a year old? Will the LORD be pleased with thousands of rams, with ten thousands of rivers of oil? Shall I give my firstborn for my transgression, the fruit of my body for the sin of my soul? He has told you, O man, what is good; and what the LORD requires of you...."[214] Giving of "first fruits" and tithing goes back to this practice. The practice of cultic sacrifice has significant parallels in all the religions of the Ancient Near East. The thinking was that disobeying God and sinning made God angry, and the sacrifice of one's best would appease God's anger. Gradually, institutional temple religion expanded this into a profitable business, with elaborate rituals and prayers, ovens, animals for purchase, professional "clergy" who did the work for the people, with the ritual's purpose to absolve guilt.

A second major innovation in atonement evolved as seen in Leviticus 16, and formed the essence of the modern Jewish Day of Atonement. Two goats were involved, the first sacrificed in the temple in classical fashion, often along with a bullock. The second goat had all the sins of the people placed on its head and it was led into the wilderness and left where it would die and all the sins died with it. This has been called

---

[214] Micah 6:6-8

the "scapegoat," and Jesus was likened to the sacrificial "Lamb of God." This is substitutionary atonement.

Figure 15: Models of Atonement

From these Jewish images of atonement, with the idea of sacrifice, of appeasing God, coupled with the hope for the purification and cleansing of sin, the explanations of the Crucifixion took on a similar meaning, familiar to a Jewish audience. Just as physical Israel depended on the high priest to make atonement for his nation on Yom Kippur, many came to see Jesus as high priest helping everyone to atone for their sins by appeasing Satan and establishing Christ's kingdom on earth.

For some reason, the theme of money played a prominent role in the Christian effort to be absolved of sin: one has to "pay" for sin, and it was Christ who paid the penalty; on the cross, he paid the ransom to remove sins. His death on the cross "redeemed" the sinfulness of everyone. The way the church expressed it, God's expiation (making reparations for wrong) was displayed publicly as a propitiation (sacrifice of atonement) in His blood through faith. The letter of First John says, "The blood of Jesus his Son cleanses us from all sin. If we confess our sins, he is faithful and just to forgive us our sins and to cleanse us from all unrighteousness."[215]

---

[215] 1 John 1:7, 9

The Book of Hebrews is more blunt: "Without the shedding of blood there is no forgiveness of sins.[216] One prominent theological perspective on atonement is the doctrine of substitutionary atonement, which states that through his sacrificial death on the cross, Jesus served as a substitute for humanity, bearing the consequences of sin and reconciling humanity with God, satisfying the demands of justice while extending divine grace to humanity.

For many, this view of the cross and the saving work of Jesus through his blood doesn't make a lot of sense. But this view has dominated the entire life of the church for two millennia, and it has shaped how the Apostle Paul has been understood.

Figure 15 above offers an entirely different view of how we handle the problem of sin and forgiveness, and make things right with God. As one tracks the progression from dualistic conscious (holding the opposites together (which the doctrine of atonement attempts to do), what the Apostle Paul attempted to say was if we totally surrender our life, messy as it is, to the Christ, in an instant the Christ will wipe out all sin and remove all obstacles so that we will become one with God. There is no ritual, no sacrifice, no purification, no conditions except to love God, and God will take care of the rest. This is what is meant by "grace." Bam!

For many, this new step of atonement sounds too simple, too easy. One could hear theologian Dietrich Bonhoeffer's caution about "cheap grace." However, surrendering one's life to Christ is about as easy as jumping off a cliff. In this process of coming to God, it is not only our sins that block us, but our monkey-brains, our distractions, our illusions, our lesser minds, selfishness, our clinging to false beliefs, and our efforts to literalize and physicalize the divine.

Since the 1960s, concepts from the Hindu Vedas have crept into Western ideas of atoning reconciliation. It is commonplace to talk about the Sanskrit word "karma." Karma simply means consequences. Everything, every thought, every action has consequences. The Bible says of karma, "As you sow, so shall you reap."[217] In a sense, karma is the order of the universe, and everything, even God, is subject to consequences. In a deeper sense, there is no such thing as bad karma. We deserve to

---

[216] Hebrews 9:22
[217] Galatians 6:7-9

experience the results we create. Regarding the question of free will, teacher Maharishi Mahesh Yogi said, "You are free to do anything, you are just not free from the consequences."[218]

Many believe we carry the karmic effects of history and culture, and we carry the karma of past lives; we also carry the effects of the past life we just lived prior to this one; furthermore, we are creating karma every day that affects our journey, and then there is future karma that we are partially creating. All this karma is between God and us. We are not free from this karma, and the question of being one with God confronts us: how do we get rid of this karma?

There is another related effect that impacts us as we seek to *leave all* and come to Christ. This is given the Sanskrit word "*sanskaras.*" Meher Baba talked a lot about sanskaras, and he said that Jesus also taught about sanskaras, using a different word. Sanskaras are mental impressions that we use to create our world—our beliefs, our values, the way we see and think. If I think I don't like our President, I create binding sanskaras of judgment and bias that function almost like a sin. If I think about God, I create binding sanskaras. Our worship is loaded with sanskara-impressions. Our actions, our relationships, our prayers, our love constantly create sanskaras, which accumulate to an unthinkable degree, and every sanskara stands between us and God. What can we do?

Sanskaras rivet our consciousness to the phenomenal material world. They are what create the illusions of our living. Sanskaras are the 4th of Buddha's 10 Skandas (10 kinds of form). Separation and duality is illusion sustained by sanskaras. Jesus said, "I came to set free those who are bound." In a sense, we could understand that this is possibly what he meant when he said, "I came with a sword," to cut what binds people. The sum total of sanskaras makes up the personal ego.

At times, a positive sanskara can cancel a negative sanskara, and so to a very limited extent we can clean up our act, a very mild form of atonement. Forgiveness, acts of kindness, and love help. But we create new sanskaras in trying to get rid of old sanskaras. We can't clean up the

---

[218] From Thomas J. Hickey, Ph.D., the author's teacher. Tom Hickey was the Dean of Students at Maharishi International University for 20 years, and daily interacted with Maharishi Mahesh Yogi.

mess, especially when most of it is unconscious. Meister Eckhart, a thirteenth-century Christian Perfect Master said:

> If this work [of realizing God] is to be done, God alone must do it, and you must just suffer it to be. Where you truly go out from your will and your knowledge, God with His knowledge surely and willingly goes in and shines there clearly. Where God will thus know Himself, there your knowledge cannot subsist and is of no avail. Do not imagine that your reason can grow to the knowledge of God.

> If God is to shine divinely in you, your natural light cannot help toward this end. Instead, it must become pure nothing and go out of itself altogether, and then God can shine in with His light, and He will bring back in with Him all that you forsook and a thousand times more, together with a new form to contain it all.[219]

In other words, we can't get rid of our karma and our sanskaras. Only God does that. But if we come to the Christ, and surrender all to him in a superior love, everything that has hitherto stood between God and us will be erased in less than a millionth of a second. We will no longer be ourselves. How's that for atonement!

All this exists in prototype as a new form of atonement introduced by the Apostle Paul. It is a major innovation in the evolution of religion.

Beyond Belief: From Head to Heart

But when God called me forth [i.e., God showed me the Face of the core Self within] before I was born… God was pleased to reveal the Christ in me,… I did not get this from any human being.
— *Apostle Paul, Galatians 1:15-16 (rendering by the author)*

---

[219] Meister Eckhart, *The Complete Mystical Works Of Meister Eckhart*, Sermon 4, Translated and Edited by Maurice O'C. Walshe, revised with a foreword by Bernard McGinn (NY: Herder & Herder Crossroad, 2009), p. 56.

"For it is by grace that you are saved by faith" (Ephesians 2:8). This is a teaching from the Gospel of John and throughout the rest of the New Testament. Every child is taught in Sunday School John 3:16, "For God so loved the world that whomever believeth in him should have eternal life." Is being a Christian a "belief" experience, a knowing that we call faith? We have just learned that belief and knowing are created by sanskaras that connect to the physical world of subjectivity. We make up our beliefs based on the sanskaras our community has taught us and the sanskaras of the way we see the world.

We are exploring whether the Apostle Paul was trying to take us to an experience of Christ beyond our limited belief. We want to say that we are saved by faith, and faith means trust. Richard Rohr asks, can we live with a trust that it all means something? Can we allow a trust in the universal Christ that there is an inner coherence that is going somewhere good?[220] That is a big bite to take.

It is a call for a spiritual faith to move beyond its doctrines, creeds, and beliefs and move from the head to the heart. Jesus put healed people back on themselves, never creating any kind of dependency or codependency on him... to trust their own inner Christ.[221] Beyond following the glorious forms of worship and praise held in the arms of institutional religion, Richard Rohr says we are given permission to become intimate with our experiences, to learn from them, and to descend to the depth of things, even our mistakes, for God hides in the depths.[222]

This book began with a quote from Jewish sage Elie Wiesel, "God made man because he loved stories." And that is what we do. We keep making up new stories, adding to the old ones we tell over and over. I don't think God laments, shaking his head from side to side, as he hears the stories, each time with new understanding. I imagine God laughs, knowing we are working hard to understand the truth and illusion of our stories, all because where the stories lead is beyond our imagination.

---

[220] Rohr, p. 66.
[221] Rohr p. 76.
[222] Rohr, p. 111.

I wonder whether there will emerge a New-New Testament, taking us into an emerging story yet to be told. To be sure, the Real Christ is yet to be revealed, and that is exciting. It is not that the Bible is "Religion for Dummies," but we are caught in new insights into Soul and Self. We have been in the process of evolution through innumerable forms, but now that we like thinking about Soul and Self, we are in a process of involution, a process that takes us back to God, back to where we began. It will never end. We will never end.

Is this the sacred healing story?

As a mental health practitioner and as a member of the clergy, there are two approaches to healing. There is the view that people suffer from pathology, that something within them is damaged and needs to be fixed. There is a vast catalogue of physical, emotional, and mental disorders called the DSM-5-TR Diagnostic Criteria, and everything that happens in the therapeutic office, rehab facility, or hospital is assigned a number, and insurance companies qualify and determine payment. This approach to healing rests on a definition of pathology and what is needed to restore one to "normal functionality." Some of the biblical stories tell of sinful acts and genocidal acts that relate to moral and spiritual pathology.

Another approach is called Humanistic Psychology, or Self Psychology. This view sees physical and emotional symptoms as the psyche's effort to get well. A fever is not a pathology, but an indication of, say, an infection, and this is an alarm system driving the person to take steps to reduce the fever. It isn't that we ignore the usefulness of medical and pharmaceutical interventions, but there are times when we recognize that sometimes illness is necessary. This approach is not to judge and correct what is wrong, but to look at what is needed to live more fully, communicate better, be healthier, bring life into more balance, be available to the transcendent opportunities that come our way, and to be aware that our true Self (our Highest Being) lies within far beyond the ego self, and this is the Kingdom or the Christ within.

This book questions what was healing about the stories in the Bible, from Genesis through the Apostle Paul. This question requires us to look beyond the wounds of disobedience and sin, the wounds of ignoring God, the wounds of hubris, the wounds of betrayal, and the wounds of enslavement. These wounds also ask for healing, but in a significant way, the healing comes from a higher connection to our source and our journey.

In surveying the biblical stories, one might wonder whether there is an evolution into ever higher healing. Is the healing within the story of the Christ a higher healing than the stories of Abraham and Moses? I think the answer is probably, "not really." The intent of Chapter 6, titled "Eight Ways of Finding Salvation," says that there are unnumbered ways to God, and every path gets us there. Some may take longer than others. The Apostle Paul may be the "express train," but we are still hammering out the details of how this works.

In many of the healing stories considered here, we departed from the canonical text to consider midrash and other variant interpretations, because these stories get in between the lines of the stories in the Bible—they get into the psyche and imagination and almost the dream life of the stories—and it is at this level where true healing happens.

Interestingly, the holy scriptures take us beyond the factual events of Israel's and the early church's experience. We are often taken into the liminal areas of the psyche, areas that go beyond our knowledge, beyond our history, beyond our theologies, beyond our beliefs. It is as though the scriptures say that to get to the truth, you have to go beyond everything you know. It is the Universal Christ who waits for you there. It is Father Abraham and Master Moses who wait there. It is Lord Buddha and God's Servant Mohammed who wait there. It is Meher Baba, also the Avatar Christ, who waits for each of us every day.

Five-year-old Georgina Papakarageorgis handed me a piece of bread in that thirteenth-century Greek Orthodox church in the village of Dali, Cyprus, and she said in the few English words she knew, "It is Jesu. Take him home and eat him." She taught me to go beyond everything I knew and would ever know. Her healing words liberated me from a cognitive seriousness, enabling me to become a lover. Many times since that day, I have been asked, "What do I need to do to go to God?" "Just live your life!" I say. "God gives you every day exactly what you need. Just live your life!"

9 781957 176383